Beyond Little Rock

Beyond Little Rock

*The Origins and Legacies
of the Central High Crisis*

John A. Kirk

The University of Arkansas Press
Fayetteville • 2007

ISBN-10 (cloth) 1-55728-850-X
ISBN-13 (cloth) 978-1-55728-850-9

ISBN-10 (paper) 1-55728-851-8
ISBN-13 (paper) 978-1-55728-851-6

11   10   09   08   07   5   4   3   2   1

Text design by Ellen Beeler

⊗ The paper used in this publication meets the minimum requirements of the
American National Standard for Permanence of Paper for Printed Library
Materials Z39.48-1984.

Library of Congress Cataloging-in-Publication Data

Kirk, John A., 1970-
  Beyond Little Rock : the origins and legacies of the Central High crisis /
John A. Kirk.
    p. cm.
  Includes bibliographical references and index.
  ISBN-13: 978-1-55728-850-9 (hardcover : alk. paper)
  SBN-10: 1-55728-850-X (hardcover : alk. paper)
  ISBN-13: 978-1-55728-851-6 (pbk. : alk. paper)
  SBN-10: 1-55728-851-8 (pbk. : alk. paper)
  1. African Americans—Civil rights—Arkansas—History—20th century.
2. African Americans—Civil rights—Arkansas—Little Rock—History—20th
century. 3. Civil rights movements—Arkansas—History—20th century.
4. Civil rights movements—Arkansas—Little Rock—History—20th century.
5. African American civil rights workers—Arkansas—Biography. 6. School
integration—Arkansas—Little Rock—History—20th century. 7. African
Americans—Education—Arkansas—Little Rock—History—20th century.
8. Arkansas—Race relations—History—20th century. 9. Little Rock (Ark.)—
Race relations—History—20th century. I. Title.
  E185.93.A8K57 2007
  323.1'19607307677309045—dc22

                                                            2007015444

For Edith and Frank

Contents

Foreword

Half a century has passed since the disturbing scenes of white opposition to school desegregation in Little Rock, Arkansas. The entire world watched spellbound as events unfolded in America, the land of freedom and justice for all.

Was Little Rock somehow an aberration? Did this race hatred spring up as mushrooms in a field, invisible only hours before? What sparked the nine African American children who attempted to enter Central High School to risk life and sanity for education? Did that crisis change the way things were, or did it somehow forecast the persistence of segregation today?

Forget for now the déclassé mobs and the ambitious governor who blocked Central High School's doors with state militia and subsequently closed the city's schools to prevent integration. Instead, level your gaze at the ideological framework of race hierarchy that has supported economic and social inequality over centuries. Segregation is embedded in all social relations in the entire county.

Black struggles for freedom and equality have often focused on education as one of the best means of dismantling Jim Crow. However, the constraints of a segregationist past still persist beyond the schoolroom. Attention now needs to shift toward the interrogation of municipal bylaws, tax structures, school funding formulas, and court decisions that continue to maintain the legacy of segregation. Segregation is the state of the national mind. Many blacks, demoralized by the persistence of segregation, have given up on the possibility of integration. Young people live comfortably in separate ethnic enclaves, believing that this is the natural order rather than a consequence of conscious decisions and policies that were made to achieve those ends. We are all the victims of skewed social memories that support separation and domination.

The debate is stifled. Racism is a taboo subject. We too often hear the view expressed: "That was then and this is now, forget about the past." We are too easily distracted by the desire to spread democracy to the world while it languishes here.

An authentic discussion must take place in order to challenge our miseducation and denial of the historical forces that helped to shape the present. John Kirk provides a record of activism that may catalyze the dialogue on the causes and cures of segregation.

Kirk's research chronicles civil rights activism in Arkansas. He is based outside of the United States, and this provides a view of race in America from a different perspective. Often we fail to see our own belief systems with clarity because our society has difficulty seeing itself. John Kirk presents the marginalized emancipatory histories that serve to interrupt the dominant exclusionary narrative. His research helps to expand the discussion about both black (and white) efforts to resist segregation and white efforts to oppose integration.

Minnijean Brown Trickey
member of the Little Rock Nine

Preface

The dominant theme of my research on the civil rights struggle in Arkansas has been the need to understand the events of the 1957 Little Rock crisis within the context of an unfolding struggle for African American freedom and equality, and a constantly changing set of race relations, in both Little Rock and Arkansas, over the course of the twentieth century. The fiftieth anniversary of the crisis provides a timely moment to reemphasize and to reexamine that theme. Before, during, and after the publication of my first book, *Redefining the Color Line: Black Activism in Little Rock, Arkansas, 1940–1970* (Gainesville: University Press of Florida, 2002), I was handed a number of opportunities, in book chapters, articles, essays, and conference papers, to expand upon my research and to explore new material, new ideas, and new interpretations that extended beyond the scope of my first book's primary purpose of presenting a tight-knit and cohesive narrative-driven thesis about the development of black activism in the city and state between 1940 and 1970.

A number of these pieces of written work, along with some new, previously unpublished essays, are presented in this book. Whereas my earlier book was grounded in telling the story of developments in black activism in Little Rock and Arkansas within the context of evolving civil rights historiography, this book is grounded in exploring issues in evolving civil rights historiography within the context of developments in black (and white) activism in Arkansas. Each chapter concentrates on a specific research question and constitutes a distinct meditation in its own right, although of course each essay is ultimately linked to and overlaps with the others in emanating from the same focus on black activism and race relations in Arkansas.

The chapters variously seek to address the following questions: How has the historiography of the Little Rock crisis developed in the past fifty years and where does it stand today? What impact did the New Deal have on the civil rights struggle? In what ways did early black political activism in the 1920s, 1930s, 1940s, and 1950s pave the way for later civil rights protests? How did black activists begin the task of mobilizing the black masses for change? What role did gender play in the civil rights struggle? In what ways did whites seek to oppose racial change? How and why did some whites support it? What larger structural issues, such as city planning, have impacted upon the position of blacks in American politics, society, and the economy? The title *Beyond Little Rock* thus reflects not only the wider body of research and themes covered in this volume, but also the wider significance of the 1957 Little Rock crisis and the civil rights struggle in Arkansas, and their relevance as touchstones for the wider experiences and developments in black activism and race relations in the South and in the United States.

Even the most self-indulgent acknowledgements essay (which I will forgo here) could not begin to express the thanks due to so many people both in the United States and United Kingdom who have contributed vital help and assistance to my research in so many different ways. It would take another book at least to do that. All I can do here is to point a nod in the right direction to express my thanks, and profusely apologize to those people who I will inevitably and unjustly forget in the process: John Adams, Karen Anderson, the Arkansas Historical Association, the *Arkansas Historical Quarterly,* Raymond Arsenault, , Tony Badger, Bruce Baker, T. Harri Baker, Numan V. Bartley, Jonathan Bell, the British Academy, the British Association of American Studies, Minnijean Brown Trickey, Andrea Cantrell, William H. Chafe, Justin Champion, David L. Chappell, Jean Clancy, Walter Clancy, David Colburn, Jan Cottingham, Michael Dabrishus, Jane Dailey, Robin Giles Devan, Willie Dillahunty, Tom Dillard, Elizabeth Eckford, Sylvia Ellis, the Encyclopedia of Arkansas History and Culture (http://encyclope-diaofarkansas.net/), Adam Fairclough, Stephanie Flowers, Zeerie Flowers, Tony Freyer, David Garrow, Willard B. Gatewood, Fon Gordon, John William Graves, Adam Green, Omar Greene, Simon Hall, Jane Hooker, John Howard, Joel Isaac, Elizabeth Jacoway, Ben F. Johnson III, Mara Keire, Judith Kilpatrick, Richard H. King, Michael J. Klarman, Kevin Kruse, Sharon La Cruise, Steven Lawson, George Lewis, Todd Lewis, Peter Ling, Berna Love, Robert McCord, Vivien Miller, Tim Minchin, Sharon Montieth, G. Gordon Morgan, Iwan Morgan, the Mosaic Templars Building Preservation Society (http://www.mosaictemplarspreservation.org/), Thelma Mothershed-Wair, Timothy G. Nutt, Kendrick Oliver, James T. Patterson, Elizabeth Payne, William Penix, Michael Pierce, Dale Lya Pierson, Terry Pierson, Linda Pine, the Pryor Center for Arkansas Oral and Visual History (http://libinfo.uark.edu/SpecialCollections/pryorcenter/), the Pulaski County

Historical Association, Steven Recken, Keith Robbins, Linda Schilscher, Marvin Schwartz, Adam Smith, Doug Smith, Morton Sosna, Ian Steinberg, Randall Stephens, Griff Stockley, Melvyn Stokes, Brock Thompson, Stephen Tuck, Timothy B. Tyson, Kevern Verney, Steven Walsh, Brian Ward, Jenny Ward, Jonathan Watson, Clive Webb, Emily West, Jeannie Whayne, C. Fred Williams, LeRoy T. Williams, Mamie Ruth Williams, Patrick G. Williams, Blake Wintory, and Nan Elizabeth Woodruff.

Integral to my research are a number of oral histories that have helped to illuminate the written record. All of the tapes of the interviews are deposited at the Pryor Center for Arkansas Oral and Visual History, Special Collections, University of Arkansas Libraries, Fayetteville. As I write, they are in the process of being transcribed so that they can be accessed more easily by other scholars. As well as thanking the Pryor Center for its efforts, I should also like to thank and acknowledge the help of the following people who agreed to be interviewed: Daisy Bates, Bobby Brown, Robert Brown, Leroy Brownlee, Charles Bussey, Elijah Coleman, Edwin E. Dunaway, Orval E. Faubus, Jeffery Hawkins, Perlesta A. Hollingsworth, George Howard Jr., Dr. Maurice A. Jackson, Dr. Jerry Jewell, Henry Jones, Jacquelyn Jones-Gibson, Frank Lambright, Worth Long, Howard Love, Mrs. I. S. McClinton, Sidney S. McMath, Christopher C. Mercer, Sue Cowan Williams, Sara Alderman Murphy, William Nash, Hugh Patterson, Albert J. Porter, Victor and Ruth Ray, Roy Reed, Rev. William H. Robinson, Irene Samuel, Ozell Sutton, Dr. William H. Townsend, B. Finely Vinson, William "Sonny" Walker, John Ward, E. Grainger Williams, Howard Woods, and Rev. Rufus King Young.

The team at the University of Arkansas Press, headed by Larry Malley, and including Julie Watkins, Tom Lavoie, Brian King, and Sarah White, have been great publishers and great friends.

As always, special thanks are reserved for my family: my wife Charlene and baby daughter Sadie; my mother and father, Anne and William; my brother and his family, Alan and Louise, and my niece Annabelle; and my Arkansas in-laws, Bud and Linda, and the extended Coker and Heaps families. This particular book is dedicated to my aunt and uncle, Edith and Frank Powers, who have been among the most reliable and ardent supporters of me and my work over the years.

Acknowledgments

The author thanks the editors of publications in which some of these essays previously appeared.

"The 1957 Little Rock Crisis: A Fiftieth Anniversary Retrospective," by John A. Kirk from the *Arkansas Historical Quarterly*. By permission of the *Arkansas Historical Quarterly*.

"Dr. J. M. Robinson, the Arkansas Negro Democratic Association and Black Politics in Little Rock, Arkansas, 1928–1952," by John A. Kirk pages 2–16 from the *Pulaski County Historical Review* (Spring 1993) 41:1 and pages 39–47 from the *Pulaski County Historical Review* (Summer 1993) 41:2. By permission of the *Pulaski County Historical Review*.

"'He Founded a Movement': W. H. Flowers, the Committee on Negro Organizations and Black Activism in Arkansas, 1940–1957," by John A. Kirk pages 29–44 from *The Making of Martin Luther King and the Civil Rights Movement in America*, edited by Brian Ward and Tony Badger (London: Macmillan, 1996). By permission of Palgrave Macmillan Publishers.

"Daisy Bates, the National Association for the Advancement of Colored People, and the Little Rock School Crisis: A Gendered Perspective," by John A. Kirk pages 17–40 from *Gender and the Civil Rights Movement*, edited by Peter Ling and Sharon Montieth (New York: Garland Publishing, 1999; reprinted New Brunswick, NJ: Rutgers University Press, 2004). By permission of Rutgers University Press.

"Massive Resistance and Minimum Compliance: The Origins of the 1957 Little Rock School Crisis and the Failure of School Desegregation in the South" by John A. Kirk pages 76–98 from *Massive Resistance: Southern Opposition to the Second Reconstruction*, edited by Clive Webb (2005). By permission of Oxford University Press.

"A Study in Second-Class Citizenship": Race, Urban Development, and Little Rock's Gillam Park, 1934–2004 by John A. Kirk pages 282–286 from the *Arkansas Historical Quarterly* 64:3 (Autumn 2005). By permission of the *Arkansas Historical Quarterly.*

"Housing, Urban Development, and the Persistence of Racial Inequality in the Post-Civil Rights South," by John A. Kirk pages 47–60 from *Souls: A Critical Journal of Black Politics, Society and Culture* 8:1 (Winter 2006). By permission of *Souls: A Critical Journal of Black Politics, Society and Culture.*

1

The 1957 Little Rock Crisis

A Fiftieth Anniversary Retrospective

The 1957 Little Rock crisis has generated a large body of monographs, essays, articles, theses, radio broadcasts, music, and films over the past fifty years. The purpose of this chapter is twofold: first, to provide a very brief summary of the events of the crisis, and second, to provide an outline and a guide to the work that it has inspired.

On September 2, 1957, Gov. Orval E. Faubus drew national and international attention to Little Rock, Arkansas, when, in the name of preventing disorder, he called out the National Guard to prevent the implementation of a court-ordered desegregation plan at Central High School. In defying the local courts and, ultimately, the U.S. Supreme Court's 1954 *Brown v. Board of Education* school desegregation decision, Faubus directly challenged the authority of the federal government as no other elected southern politician had since the Civil War. Over the following weeks, frantic negotiations took place between the White House and the governor's mansion that finally led to the withdrawal of National Guard troops. However, when nine African American students—Minnijean Brown, Elizabeth Eckford, Ernest Green, Thelma Mothershed, Melba Pattillo, Gloria Ray, Terrence Roberts, Jefferson Thomas, and Carlotta Walls—attempted to attend classes on September 23, an unruly white mob caused so much disruption that school officials withdrew them from Central High for their own safety. The scenes of violence finally prompted Pres. Dwight D. Eisenhower to intervene in the crisis by sending federal troops to secure the students' safe passage. On September 25, the nine finally completed their first day of classes under armed guard.

Although the admission of the students to the school resolved the immediate constitutional crisis, and the media spotlight quickly moved elsewhere, that was not the end of the story. The nine students endured a campaign of harassment by white segregationist students inside the high school. On February 6, 1958, Minnijean Brown was expelled for reacting to provocation by white students, although none of the white intimidators of the nine was ever similarly dealt with. On May 25, 1958, Ernest Green, the only senior among the nine, became the first African American student to graduate from Central High.

As the academic year ended, and soldiers were withdrawn from Central, the battle over school desegregation continued. On February 20, 1958, the Little Rock school board had requested a two-and-a-half-year delay in its desegregation plan. On June 21, federal district court judge Harry J. Lemley granted the delay. But on August 18, National Association for the Advancement of Colored People attorney Wiley Branton successfully overturned the delay on appeal. The school board then appealed to the U.S. Supreme Court, which, on September 12, ordered school desegregation to continue.

In the meantime, Governor Faubus had convened a special session of the Arkansas General Assembly and pushed through six new state laws that provided him with sweeping powers to uphold segregation. One of the laws enabled Faubus to close any school integrated by federal order. Voters in the school district could then decide if the school should reopen on an integrated basis. On the day the U.S. Supreme Court ordered integration to proceed in Little Rock, Faubus closed all of city's high schools. In the referendum held on September 27, 1958, the governor stacked the cards in his favor by providing a stark choice between keeping the schools closed or accepting "complete and total integration." By a margin of 19,470 to 7,561 voters decided to keep the schools closed.

After a brief and failed attempt to run the public high schools as segregated, private institutions, African American and white students were forced to make alternative arrangements for their education while their teachers sat in empty classrooms. In the November 1958 election, Faubus became only the second governor in Arkansas history to win a third consecutive term in office. In exasperation, the existing members of the school board resigned, with the exception of segregationist Dale Alford, who soon after left his post to take up a new role as U.S. congressman.

The election of a new school board proved a watershed event. The city's business and professional elite, who had stood on the sidelines since September 1957, were finally spurred into action. Closed schools and the drying up of outside economic investment convinced them that they had to take a stand to prevent community collapse. Another important factor in their decision to act was the formation of the Women's Emergency Committee to Open Our Schools, which was composed of the spouses of many of the male elite. The committee was initially formed to campaign for keeping the city's schools open at the September 27 referendum. Although unsuccessful on that occasion, Adolphine Fletcher Terry, the wife of former Arkansas U.S. congressman David D. Terry, persuaded five business candidates to stand against segregationist candidates in the school board election on December 6, 1958. In a close contest, three business candidates and three segregationists won positions on the school board.

A showdown between the businessmen and the segregationists came in May 1959, when segregationists attempted to remove anyone unsympathetic to their cause from the public school system. Blocking each of the measures in turn, the business candidates then withdrew from the meeting so that there would be no quorum to make any further decisions. However, after they left, Ed McKinley, the segregationist president of the school board, ruled that the meeting could continue as normal. Segregationists proceeded to make a series of arbitrary decisions about the running of the school system. Most dramatic of all was the decision not to renew the contracts of forty-four public school employees, including seven principals, thirty-four teachers, and three secretaries.

On May 8, a group of business and civic leaders met to form Stop This Outrageous Purge, with the goal of ousting the board's segregationists in a recall election. On May 15, segregationists, similarly intent on recalling business representatives on the school board, joined forces in a Committee to Retain Our Segregated Schools. On May 25, the day of the recall election, the vote narrowly went the businessmen's way, with all of the business representatives reinstated and all of the segregationists ousted in favor of additional business-backed candidates. The new board prepared to reopen the schools. On June 18, the U.S. District Court upheld the NAACP's contention that Faubus's school closing laws were unconstitutional. In a surprise move designed to limit Faubus's options for further opposition, the new school board announced in July that the next school term would begin a month early, on August 12. The schools successfully opened on a token integrated basis without trouble.[1]

For those interested in archival materials on the crisis, the best starting point is Michael Dabrishus's essay on the subject.[2] There are, in addition, a number of published primary sources that serve as a good introduction to events. One of the earliest and most accomplished of these is *Little Rock, U.S.A.* complied by a husband and wife team, Wilson Record and June Cassells Record, in 1960. Its first section contains an impressive collection of press accounts, while a second section consists of opinion pieces, some of which were specially commissioned for the project. The superlative *Eyes on the Prize* documentary series on the civil rights movement, which has now received a much welcomed rerelease, devotes half of one episode to the Little Rock crisis. A collection of oral histories and a document collection that accompany the series are also useful. Well worth a listen (and a look on the website) is a radio documentary made by the Southern Regional Council, *Will the Circle Be Unbroken?*, which includes five programs on Little Rock before, during, and after the crisis.[3]

One of the most striking things about the specialist secondary literature on the Little Rock crisis is the panoramic view it provides of a white southern community in the mid-1950s. Several historians, most notably David Chappell, C. Fred Williams, Pete Daniel, and Karen Anderson, have examined the competing tensions and factions that existed among whites.[4]

From a local perspective, Governor Faubus has garnered the most attention as a key figure in events. Early accounts presented him as a demagogue who either contrived or manufactured the crisis for his own political gain.[5] Later analyses, notably the work of Roy Reed, provide a more nuanced picture of a politician who was the son of a socialist and who entered Arkansas politics by way of the progressive 1948 administration of Gov. Sidney S. McMath. These studies argue that a set of concerns more complex than simply naked political ambition weighed on Faubus's decision to call out the National Guard.[6]

Faubus's own reflections on the crisis were often guarded and evasive. His first book ignored the events altogether and instead recounted his wartime army service overseas. Two subsequent volumes, *Down from the Hills*, and *Down from the Hills II*, were merely press collages from his time as governor. A further book, on the various dogs and menagerie of other pets that Faubus owned as governor, is willfully obscure. Faubus did, however, late in life produce a short self-published booklet that came closest to a written account and explanation of his actions. In addition, he offered candid accounts to historians when he was interviewed. Yet to his death in 1994, Faubus remained unwilling to accept that he had any politically viable alternatives to the course of action he took.[7]

If Faubus dictated political developments in Little Rock, the chief architect of public school policy was the city's superintendent of schools, Vigil T. Blossom. In 1955, Blossom drew up a plan for school desegregation that provided for some, albeit very closely guarded and controlled, integration in city schools. The merits and demerits of the so-called "Blossom Plan" have met with varying interpretations. Elizabeth Jacoway has been Blossom's and the school board's leading defender, claiming that, in taking a gradualist approach to the problem of school desegregation, they did the best job they could under pressure from segregationists and widespread community opposition (echoing the argument Blossom himself made in his memoir). Numan V. Bartley flagged the many inherent flaws of the Blossom Plan in one of the earliest scholarly studies of the crisis. Yet Bartley still attributed the plan's eventual downfall to "an accumulation of failures by well-meaning leaders." My work has been the most critical of Blossom's intentions, arguing that his call for "minimum compliance" with the *Brown* decision was in fact just another, if more subtle, form of resistance to school desegregation.[8]

Despite the fact that Little Rock became a focal point for massive resistance, prior to the events of September 1957 it was regarded as a moderate upper-South city in a progressive upper-South state. Contributing to this image was congressman L. Brooks Hays. Hays's story is a case study of the dilemmas faced by southern moderates in the post-*Brown* political landscape. Before the crisis, Hays had a distinguished record of service, which included holding Arkansas's Fifth Congressional District seat in the U.S. House of Representatives since 1942. In September 1957, Hays attempted to conciliate between Faubus and Eisenhower through his friend Sherman Adams, Eisenhower's chief of staff. But Hays's efforts to help proved his undoing. Running for reelection in 1958, he found himself facing a "write-in" campaign from Little Rock optometrist, school board member, and segregationist candidate Dale Alford. Alford pulled off a shock election victory that ended Hays's career as an elected politician. Hays's defeat only added to the clamor of other southern politicians to take the most extreme segregationist position possible in political contests.[9]

One of the ironies of Hays's defeat was that he, like all of Arkansas's congressional delegation, signed the "Southern Manifesto" in 1956, which condemned the U.S. Supreme Court for handing down the *Brown* decision. The fact that U.S. Senator John McClellan, or U.S. House of Representatives members Oren Harris, E. C. Gathings, W. F. Norrell, and Wilbur D. Mills all signed the manifesto was not surprising given their previous staunch support for the preservation of segregation. However, U.S. Senator J. William Fulbright and Representative James W. Trimble, along with Hays, were all considered moderates on the race issue who, although often ambivalent about the prospect of racial change, did not look to actively oppose it. Fulbright, the most eminent of Arkansas's political moderates, has received the most criticism for bowing to segregationist pressure. Trimble had a more plausible defense for signing: he was badgered in his hospital bed for three hours by Orval Faubus, accompanied by Oren Harris and Brooks Hays, before finally doing so. Tony Badger argues that the signatures of political moderates on the Southern Manifesto, in Arkansas and elsewhere, helped to undermine calls for compliance with *Brown,* and gave the upper hand to the segregationists in the battle over school desegregation.[10]

It was not just Brooks Hays's political background but also his religious beliefs that marked him out as a moderate. Hays served as president of the Southern Baptist Convention from 1957–58. Although by no means uniform in sentiment, as Mark Newman has observed, there were members of the Southern Baptist Convention and the Arkansas Baptist Convention who were prepared to speak out for accepting school desegregation. As sociologists Ernest Q. Campbell and Thomas F. Pettigrew noted, this muted support for desegregation was reflected in other denominations and, as Carolyn Gray LeMaster points out, in other faiths as well.[11] David Chappell argues that such divisions reflect the wider reality that organized religious opposition to *Brown* was weak across the South, although Jane Dailey has questioned that conclusion, maintaining that if religion was not always an overt part of resistance to segregation, it was often integral to it.[12]

Another source of moderation was Little Rock's business and professional elite, which had successfully steered the community toward economic, political, and social progress in the postwar period. That elite had helped to create an industrial zone on the outskirts of the city to lure northern investment, secured the location of a federal air base nearby, and just a year before the crisis organized a Good Government Committee in a successful bid to reform the way that city government was run. But when it came to school desegregation, the elite proved flat-footed in dealing with an issue that would strike at the very heart of the city's progress. The reasons for this have been a matter of debate. Elizabeth Jacoway argues that the city's elite was "taken by surprise" by events that quickly escalated beyond their control, although she contends that the crisis did ultimately lead to them to realize that racial progress was necessary for economic progress, which in turn forced a reordering of their priorities. By contrast, Tony Badger finds striking, in Little Rock and elsewhere, the "persistent determination of businessmen that economic change should not lead to racial change."[13]

The most visible advocate of moderation in Little Rock during the crisis was the city's leading newspaper, the *Arkansas Gazette,* whose opinions reflected those of its executive editor, Harry S. Ashmore. A seasoned journalist and a war veteran, Ashmore was a supporter of southern political, social, economic, and racial progress. He continually criticized the reckless actions of Governor Faubus and called for a more enlightened approach to school desegregation. In 1958, he won a Pulitzer Prize for his editorials, but he was forced to leave the city a year later because of segregationist harassment. Ashmore published several books on race in the South and the United States, and there are a number of collections of *Gazette*-related materials. For the pro-segregation position of the *Gazette*'s rival city newspaper, the *Arkansas Democrat,* see the collection of articles published by columnist Karr Shannon.[14]

To those who see the failure of the moderates in Little Rock, whether politicians, public policy-makers, or businessmen, as pivotal to the crisis that befell the city, the apparent weakness of the opposition they faced is grist to their mill. In Little Rock, and in Arkansas, the most active segregationists were not respected figures of great social standing, as they were in many other southern states, but were instead the socially, economically, and politically marginalized who found in the segregation issue a way to transform, if only temporarily, their circumstances. Several articles by Graeme Cope have profiled segregationists in Little Rock, and Neil McMillen has examined the activities of the White

Citizens' Councils in the state. McMillen notes that the Citizens' Council membership in Arkansas was just one-tenth that of neighboring Mississippi.[15]

Segregationists in Little Rock were, however, bolstered by the regionwide movement of massive resistance, which also, as Jeff Woods and George Lewis have noted, rode the tide of post-McCarthy era anticommunism.[16] In Arkansas, attorney general Bruce Bennett attempted to cash in politically on that bandwagon, but without much success. He did nevertheless push a number of harassing measures through the Arkansas General Assembly, including Act 10, which required state employees to list their political affiliations, and Act 115, which outlawed public employment of NAACP members.[17]

Beyond the state borders, Joseph P. Kamp wrote *The Lowdown on Little Rock and the Plot to Sovietize the South,* which began by comparing Eisenhower's decision to send troops into the city to Hitler's use of storm troopers, before going on to assert that in fact Eisenhower was less justified in his actions. On the opposite end of the political spectrum, James Jackson's conclusion that Little Rock represented an "opening wide of the doors to great new initiatives of struggle to advance, under the leadership of the working-class, along the whole social frontier" sounded almost as misdirected given the composition of those opposing school desegregation in Little Rock.[18]

Little has been written about the ongoing military operation at Central High School after September 1957. Federal soldiers remained on patrol inside the school for only a short time before being replaced by federalized National Guard troops. Robert W. Coakley's fairly plaintive military overview of the operation provides some useful information about how the mission was run, but it is Elizabeth Huckaby, a white vice principal at Central, who provides the most vivid insider account of events at the school. Huckaby's book provided the basis for the first cinematic dramatization of events in *Crisis at Central High.* Phoebe Godfrey's work has touched upon what was happening inside the school by looking at Faubus's attempts to discredit federal soldiers by claiming that they were loitering around the girls' locker rooms. She also examines the prominence of discourses of race, gender, and sexuality, focusing on miscegenation in Little Rock segregationists' rhetoric.[19]

The following, so-called "Lost Year" of 1958–59, when Little Rock's high schools were closed, has been the subject of much recent attention. Beth Roy has conducted a study based on a number of interviews with white students, and Sondra Gordy has written about the experiences of teachers. Much of this work is imbued with a sense of loss, regret, and more than a tinge of nostalgia. As important as it is to recognize that all of the city's teachers and students were the victims of closed high schools, it must also be remembered that it was the predominantly white electorate that voted to keep the schools closed rather than to integrate them. That electorate presumably included the parents of many of the white children who were left without an education. In that sense, the year was less lost than tossed—given away.[20]

Alongside the detrimental effects of closing the schools, it was the drying up of outside economic investment that finally prompted the city's elite to mobilize against the segregationists. The economic impact of the crisis on the city is documented by Gary Fullerton in a 1959 article in the *Nashville Tennessean,* and it is the subject of studies by James C. Cobb and Michael Joseph Bercik.[21]

A good deal has been written on the campaign to reopen Little Rock's schools, with the preponderance of work examining the efforts of the Women's Emergency Committee to Open Our Schools. There are a number of scholarly works on the committee and its members, as well as one short documentary film on the subject, and two first-hand participant accounts by Sara Murphy and Vivion Brewer.[22] Irving Spitzberg's study provides a good overview of the formation of Stop This Outrageous Purge, and Henry M. Alexander provides a useful account of the recall election that led to the removal of segregationist members from the school board and the installation of business candidates.[23]

There is a long list of other white characters in the Little Rock crisis whose actions have been touched upon by scholars or chronicled in memoirs. Mayor Woodrow Mann, who was left a lame duck official by the reforms to city government enacted in 1956, urged Eisenhower to intervene to quell the growing disorder in the city. Chief of Police Eugene E. Smith valiantly tried to uphold law and order at Central High in the period between Faubus abdicating responsibility for events and Eisenhower sending the soldiers in. Nat Griswold, executive director of the Arkansas Council on Human Relations, an affiliate of the Atlanta-based Southern Regional Council, attempted to keep lines of racial communication open in the city. Another member of the council, Prof. Georg Iggers, a German, Jewish immigrant to the United

States, taught at Little Rock's African-American Philander Smith College and was one of a handful of white members of the city's NAACP branch. Osro Cobb, U.S. attorney for the Eastern District of Arkansas, was the federal government's all too anonymous chief law enforcement officer in the city, who was responsible for liaison with the Justice Department. Gov. LeRoy Collins of Florida publicly criticized Faubus for his actions as the crisis unfolded and urged a more moderate approach to school desegregation by state officials.[24]

In contrast to the rich and detailed portrait of the white community, Little Rock's African American community has been relatively poorly served in the historiography of the crisis. Most attention has focused on Daisy Bates, the president of the state NAACP conference of branches and, along with her husband, Lucious Christopher (L. C.) Bates, owner of the city's and state's leading African American newspaper, the *Arkansas State Press.* As an important study written by two African American sociologists, Tillman Cothran and William Phillips Jr., points out, Daisy Bates was unquestionably the key local African American figure during the crisis years. Bates's account of events, *The Long Shadow of Little Rock,* first published in 1962, for a long time remained the sole voice of the African American community on the crisis. Several articles have touched upon Bates's life and career since, but only recently have fully fledged biographies begun to appear, with the most accomplished to date being Grif Stockley's account.[25] Stockley makes the case for giving due credit to Daisy's husband, L. C. Bates, for his leadership role in the crisis, which has remained neglected.[26]

There is surprisingly little substantive literature on the Little Rock Nine, the African American students who were at the very heart of the events. One of them, Melba Pattillo Beals, has written two autobiographical accounts, but beyond personal detail, neither work really moves the story of the crisis much beyond Bates's book. Ernest Green's story has received the Disney treatment on film, and Minnijean Brown has spoken about events in a published oral history. Several profiles of the nine have appeared over the years, the best being the series of articles by African American journalist Ted Poston published in the *New York Post* in October 1957. Although a number of scattered oral histories and interviews exist, the history of the crisis still cries out for a uniform collection of stories of the nine, both as individuals and as a collective group of ordinary people thrust into extraordinary circumstances.[27]

My own work on African American history in Arkansas has sought to contextualize the experiences of Bates and the Little Rock Nine within the unfolding struggle for African American freedom and equality in the state. The interaction between local, state, regional and national activists and organizations played a prominent role in that history.[28] In the Little Rock crisis, they were bound together in the *Aaron v. Cooper* (1956) lawsuit, which was launched by the local NAACP branch, before being taken over by the national NAACP's Legal Defense and Educational Fund, Inc., lawyers. Under the title of *Cooper v. Aaron* in 1958, it became a landmark case in the civil rights struggle when the U.S. Supreme Court ruled that violence and disorder could not be used as excuses for delaying school desegregation, and a number of works have assessed its significance.[29] Several excellent studies frame the lawsuit and the Little Rock crisis within wider developments in the courts.[30]

Did the Little Rock crisis represent a victory for the NAACP or for massive resistance? From a regional perspective, this has proved a key question. Adam Fairclough succinctly sums up the arguments in his short opinion piece for a special issue of the *Arkansas Historical Quarterly* commemorating the fortieth anniversary of the crisis. Those pointing toward a victory for massive resistance can plausibly contend that Eisenhower only sent in troops to the city as an ad hoc response to events, and that his actions did not immediately pave the way for further strong executive action in defense of civil rights. Neither did it prevent Faubus from closing the city's high schools the following year. If *Cooper v. Aaron* represented a triumph for the NAACP, another court decision the same year, *Shuttlesworth v. Birmingham Board of Education* (1958), upheld the use of pupil placement laws that significantly slowed school desegregation. These laws permitted school boards to assign school places to students on a number of criteria other than race, but in practice they were often used simply to perpetuate segregation. The NAACP proved vulnerable to attack and its branches in Arkansas and across the South were decimated by the late 1950s. Thus, scholars such as Michael Klarman have argued that *Brown* actually helped to strengthen white resistance more than it aided the cause of African American advancement.[31]

Nevertheless, Fairclough argues, Little Rock was ultimately a triumph for the NAACP. It forced the issue of school desegregation and moved both the president and the Supreme Court, however reluctantly, to act. Segregationists viewed the episode as a defeat, yet still failed to unite in a common strategy of opposition. The enduring lessons of Little Rock, Fairclough asserts, were the futility of directly defying court orders, the folly of closing schools, and the social and economic costs of racial turmoil. Few other governors tried to emulate Faubus's stand and few other business communities wanted to risk the cost of racial conflict. *Brown* may not have delivered all that many hoped it would, but it did expose a legal Achilles heel for segregation that paved the way for successfully challenging other aspects of Jim Crow. In demonstrating the futility of violent resistance, the Little Rock crisis encouraged segregationists to take to state legislatures and the courts rather than to the streets, thereby reducing the potential casualties of change. It also brought international pressure to bear on the United States to tackle the problem of racial inequality.

From a national perspective, Pres. Dwight D. Eisenhower's response to the *Brown* decision has been viewed as one of the major blights on his otherwise popular presidency. Eisenhower was reluctant to voice support for *Brown* in public and he was disparaging of the Supreme Court's decision in private. It was with much reluctance that he eventually sent federal troops into Little Rock, and then only when Governor Faubus issued such a direct challenge to his executive authority.[32] But there were more enlightened and progressive figures in Eisenhower's presidential administration who sought to take a stronger stand for civil rights, foremost among them Attorney General Herbert Brownell and Arthur B. Caldwell, the latter a native Arkansan and assistant to the assistant attorney general for the Civil Rights Division of the Department of Justice, which was established in 1957.[33]

The images of the Little Rock crisis that flashed around the world were some of the earliest and most dramatic of the unfolding civil rights struggle. Despite being one of its first major televised events, some of the most memorable visual images of the crisis came from photographs. *Arkansas Democrat* photographer I. Wilmer Counts's published collection is an excellent starting point for these, and it includes the famous photograph of white student Hazel Massery hurling abuse at Elizabeth Eckford, an image that has become one of the most enduring emblems of the crisis.[34]

So iconic were events in Little Rock that they instantaneously became a reference point for popular culture, with an influence that stretched into theater, poetry, music, and intellectual debate. In Sep-

tember 1957, in a New York City suburb, a young actress found herself playing a role with an unfortunate-sounding name from a woe
betide place in the musical *South Pacific*—Nellie Forbush from Little
Rock, Arkansas—that brought a halt to the performance because of
the ferocity of the jeers that it prompted. African American poet
Gwendolyn Brooks wrote "The *Chicago Defender* Sends a Man to
Little Rock," included in her 1960 collection of poems *The Bean
Eaters,* which vividly portrayed the violence and hatred displayed by
the white mob in the city. Her muse was African American newspaper
reporter L. Alex Wilson, who the mob turned upon and beat during
the first day of integrated classes at Central High. Wilson was the editor and general manager of the Memphis-based *Tri-State Defender,* the
Chicago Defender's southern affiliate. German-American political
theorist Hannah Arendt stoked controversy with her essay "Reflections on Little Rock," which questioned whether schools were in fact
the best place to begin the process of desegregation.[35]

African American jazz musician Charles Mingus composed music
for and penned lyrics to a song called "Fables of Faubus," which lambasted the Arkansas governor, labeling him, among other things, a
"Nazi Fascist supremist." Columbia Records felt the lyrics too contro-
versial and would only release the track as an instrumental on Mingus's
1959 album *Mingus Ah Um.* The following year, Mingus recorded the
song with a different label, this time with lyrics, as "Original Faubus
Fables," for his album *Charles Mingus Presents Charles Mingus.* The
song proved a popular favorite with Mingus and his audiences over
the years, and in 1973, in the midst of the Watergate scandal, it was
transformed into "Fables of Nixon." It has been covered by a number
of other artists since, the most recent being the Normand Guilbeault
Ensemble version "Fable of (George Dubya) Faubus," released in
2005.[36]

Another jazz great, Louis Armstrong, abandoned a planned
government-sponsored trip to Moscow because of events in Little
Rock. Described by the U.S. State Department as "perhaps the most
effective un-official goodwill ambassador this country ever had,"
Armstrong told the press that "the way they are treating my people in
the South, the government can go to hell." He called Faubus "an une-
ducated plow-boy," and insisted that if he had to choose, he would
rather play in Moscow than in Arkansas, because Faubus "might hear
a couple of notes—and he doesn't deserve that."[37]

As the Armstrong incident illustrates, from an international perspective, the Little Rock crisis was a public relations disaster for a country engaged in an effort to win hearts and minds in the Cold War. Several historians have written about Little Rock's global impact in recent years, with the crisis featuring most prominently in the work of Azza Salama Layton and Mary Dudziak. Dudziak labels Little Rock "a crisis of such magnitude for worldwide perceptions of race and American democracy that it would become a reference point for the future." Newspapers around the world reported events in Little Rock, critics of the United States pointed to the crisis as evidence of the country's disregard for human rights, and federal officials wrung their hands over the damage done. In later years, the U.S. Information Agency tried to reclaim Little Rock as a victory by holding it up as a triumph for presidential action in support of civil rights.[38]

The Little Rock crisis has continued to linger indelibly in historical memory. Several studies by first-hand participants in events have updated the ongoing story of school desegregation and the accompanying court litigation since 1957. Each gives a snapshot of the different stages of that process over the years.[39] In addition to the contemporary impact of the crisis, commentators' reflections on the actual events of 1957–59 and their wider significance for the city and the South have continued to be published, clustering around landmark anniversaries.[40] Indeed, those reflections and memories have become subjects of study in their own right.[41] With the opening of the Central High Museum and Visitors Center in 1997, the Little Rock crisis has become part of a growing heritage industry in the South devoted to the civil rights movement.[42]

The Little Rock crisis has provided an inspiration for many writers, poets, musicians, and filmmakers over the past fifty years. Such has been its grip on the scholarly, artistic, popular, and public imagination that it will surely continue to fascinate and to attract attention for many more years to come. There are a number of works whose publication has been scheduled to coincide with the fiftieth anniversary of the crisis.[43] All the indications are that the anniversary will itself become one more landmark in the crisis's still unfolding legacy.

2

The New Deal and the
Civil Rights Struggle

*A Case Study of Black Civilian Conservation
Corps Camps in Arkansas, 1933–1942*

Historians have noted the ambiguous and sometimes contradictory impact of the New Deal on black Americans. On the one hand, the federal government programs and reforms that took place during the 1930s gave grounds for hope that things were changing for the better for the black population. The New Deal provided a greater level of federal assistance to blacks that at any other time before. The Works Progress Administration (WPA) employed 390,000 blacks, representing almost 20 percent of its workforce. It also cared for around ten thousand black children every day in its nursery schools. The National Youth Administration assisted thirty-five thousand black students to attend high school and college. It employed five thousand black teachers in the process. The Public Works Administration (PWA) spent four times as much on black schools and hospitals in the southern states from 1933 to 1936 than had been spent on them in the previous 30 years. PWA housing projects provided black employment and built affordable housing, with almost one-third of houses built specifically for black residency. On the other hand, the Depression hit black individuals and families—who were already among the least well-off in the nation—the hardest, with black unemployment running at double the national average. Yet the New Deal did nothing to specifically target their plight but rather, "what the Negroes gained—relief, WPA jobs, equal pay on some federal projects—was granted to them as poor people, not Negroes."[1]

There were distinct regional differences in the impact of the New Deal on blacks. Black southerners faced even more discrimination in New Deal programs since, as historian Tony Badger writes, programs in the South were "run by whites sympathetic to the cultural norms of the communities in which they lived and worked. They ran programs on a segregated basis, routinely paid less in benefits to blacks than whites, and often excluded blacks from participation altogether." Such a situation was not helped by the fact that Hugh Johnson, head of the National Recovery Administration, specifically excluded agricultural and domestic workers from relief rolls. Three-quarters of black southern workers fell into those two categories. In terms of the Federal Emergency Relief Administration, black southerners "found it harder to get on the relief rolls and then received less money than whites when they did get on." The cotton section of the Agricultural Adjustment Administration was headed by "southern whites sympathetic to white landlords and scornful of black tenants," which had a devastating impact, since 70 percent of southern black farmers, representing around two million in total, were tenant farmers.[2] Despite President Franklin D. Roosevelt's perceived commitment to greater racial justice and his much feted "Black Cabinet" of advisers, he did little to challenge the segregation and discrimination rampant in southern New Deal programs. Roosevelt failed to endorse an antilynching bill and he did not propose any civil rights legislation. Barton Bernstein concludes that "Unwilling to risk schism with southerners running committees [in Congress], Roosevelt capitulated to the forces of racism."[3]

Nevertheless, despite all of the New Deal's evident shortcomings, the 1930s are still recognized by historians as a crucial transformative period in the black struggle for freedom and equality. Some of the changes that were set in motion had significant long-term, if often unforeseen consequences. The collectivization and mechanization of agriculture displaced many black farmers, but it swelled the black populations of southern towns and cities. This population shift meant that blacks were less isolated and vulnerable to white attack, and it added to a growing mass urban base for potential mobilization and collective action that would later prove vital to the civil rights struggle.[4] Nancy Weiss points out that in terms of the New Deal itself, "Most black people knew that they were getting less economic assistance than whites, and most of them needed more than they got. But the point was that they got something and that kept many black families from starving."[5] The potential for federal intervention to make a difference in day-to-day life was apparent, even if that potential was too often left unfulfilled. Harvard Sitkoff concludes that as a result of the New Deal, black "expectations rose; black powerlessness decreased [and] white hostility diminished . . . The sprouts of hope prepared the ground for the struggles to follow. Harvest time would come in the next generation."[6]

The complex and multifaceted impact of the New Deal on black southerners is illuminated in this study on the Civilian Conservation Corps (CCC) in Arkansas. Despite being one of Roosevelt's most popular and successful New Deal programs, the role of the CCC, particularly in the South, and especially its impact on blacks, has received little serious academic attention. John Salmond's 1967 book, *The Civilian Conservation Corps, 1933–1942: A New Deal Case Study*, remains the best scholarly monograph on the subject, and it is the only overview of the organization that offers any meaningful analysis of black participation.[7] Salmond's chapter on blacks in the CCC, published separately as an article in the *Journal of American History*, together with a handful of other journal articles, account for almost the entire body of literature on blacks and the CCC.[8] Recently, several monographs have appeared on the CCC's operation at a state level, but none of them deal with southern states, and only one, *The African-American Experience in the Civilian Conservation Corps* by Olen Cole Jr., actually uses the CCC as a vehicle to examine the black experience, but with a focus limited only to California camps.[9] Given the relatively small number of blacks that were enrolled in the CCC—two hundred thousand out of a total of two-and-a-half million enrollees between 1933 and 1942—and the greater impact of other New Deal programs on the black population, the absence of such studies is not entirely unsurprising. However, as this essay demonstrates, the southern black experience in CCC camps offers a valuable insight into the workings of the New Deal and shows the extent to which federal influence touched black lives and challenged southern racial mores in the 1930s, thereby paving the way for changes that would take place in the region in the decades afterward.

The CCC was formed as part of the Emergency Conservation Work Act, signed into law March 31, 1933. Roosevelt's Executive

Order 6101 established the CCC five days later on April 5. The CCC was designed to protect the nation's natural resources through conservation work, but primarily it sought to provide employment for young men between the ages of eighteen and twenty-five who were unemployed, unmarried, from families on relief, and who were physically fit. The mission of the CCC was to engage "in simple work, not interfering with normal employment, and confining itself to forestry, the prevention of soil erosion, flood control and similar projects." Men were given food, shelter, clothing, and medical care in CCC camps, as well as being offered the opportunity to participate in education programs. They were paid thirty dollars a month for their work, twenty-five dollars of which was deducted from their pay and sent directly to their families.[10]

The CCC combined four federal departments whose work was overseen by a national director. The Department of Labor under W. Frank Persons selected CCC enrollees for camps through state and local relief agencies. The Department of War administered CCC work camps, with US Army officers in charge of CCC companies. The Department of Agriculture's Forest Service, and the Department of the Interior's National Park Service, were jointly responsible for organizing and supervising work projects. Roosevelt appointed Robert Fechner, a vice president of the International Association of Machinists, as director of the CCC, ostensibly as a response to concerns that the organization might be construed as an attempt to regiment the work force. Fechner has been described variously as a "tall, slow-spoken, high-booted Tennessean" who was "known widely for his unsympathetic attitude toward the Negro," and who was "firmly devoted to white supremacy and racial segregation." His presence, and his shaping of national policy affecting CCC camps, was a major factor in the organization's persistent discrimination against blacks. Fechner remained as CCC director until his death in December 1939, when he was replaced by his assistant director, James J. McEntee.[11]

The experience of black Arkansans in the CCC largely mirrored national and regional developments.[12] The first obstacle that potential black enrollees faced was actually gaining a place in a CCC camp, despite the organization's clear nondiscriminatory mandate. During the congressional debate over the legislation to form the CCC, the sole black congressman at the time, Oscar DePriest, an Illinois Republican, successfully proposed a clause that stated "in employing citizens for the purpose of this act, no discrimination shall be made on account of race, color or creed."[13] Such a mandate did not prevent local officials from seeking to impose controls over enrollment. In Georgia, state director of selection John de la Perriere concocted a list of excuses for black exclusion, including the assertion that they were not among the "most needy" in the state. Only when W. Frank Persons contacted the state's governor, Eugene Talmadge, to threaten withholding CCC quotas entirely if the state did not enroll blacks, did Georgia begin to make some progress. Pressure and persuasion won similar results in Florida, Alabama, and Mississippi.[14]

It was the National Association for the Advancement of Colored People (NAACP) that first highlighted the exclusion of black enrollees from the CCC in Arkansas, when it complained to Persons about the situation in May 1933. As he had done in Georgia, Persons threatened to withhold all of Arkansas's CCC quotas if the situation persisted. A defensive William A. Rooksbery, state relief director, wrote back to Persons and categorically denied that the state was refusing to appoint blacks. At least three had been enrolled into the CCC already, he pointed out, while promising to improve further on that record in the future.[15] Rooksberry held good to his promise in October 1933, when Arkansas established its first black CCC camp four miles east of Strong, which, like all of the state's black CCC camps, was located in the Arkansas Delta. The Delta was the most logical place to put the camps from a geographic standpoint since the area contained the vast majority of the state's black population. Yet it was also a potentially perilous decision given the region's history of violent race relations. The most notorious example of this violence was a race riot at the town of Elaine in 1919 that left what some estimates put at hundreds of black men, women, and children dead.[16] Nan Woodruff's book on the Delta is entitled *American Congo,* borrowing native Arkansan and NAACP field secretary William Pickens's description of the region in 1921, when he likened conditions there to the barbarism of the African Congo under the rule of Belgium's King Leopold II. "Delta planters did not cut off the head and hands of their African American workers," as in the African Congo, Woodruff writes, "but aided by local law enforcement and politicians, they engaged in peonage, murder, theft, and disfranchisement."[17]

Although there was nothing at all in the national legislation that provided for the establishment of segregated CCC camps, this policy

was employed by all southern states, and it was never seriously challenged for fear of causing uproar among the white populace. Because
of this fear, Roosevelt himself privately acquiesced to Fechner's insistence on segregated camps. In the rest of the nation, a number of
blacks did work in white camps, although usually this was only
because there were not enough blacks to make up a full complement
of two hundred men. In 1934, Fechner extended the southern practice
of segregation to all camps nationwide, and he ordered the repatria-
tion of all black CCC enrollees back to their home states, since some
had been transferred between states to make up the numbers to establish segregated camps. This directive remained in place throughout the
rest of the CCC's operation.[18]

The black CCC camp at Strong was a forestry project involved in
the construction of forest roads, trails, telephone lines, and various fire
protection and suppression measures. It soon became a showpiece for
the state. In February 1934, the state's largest circulation white newspaper, the Little Rock–based *Arkansas Gazette,* wrote a feature article
on "Arkansas's Negro CCC Camp." The article stressed that the "198
Negroes" were "under the supervision of 36 white men," (all supervisory roles at black camps were filled by whites, with the exception of
the educational adviser, and a very limited number of medical officers
and chaplains) and that they were all doing "a splendid piece of work
under the President's New Deal Program." It went on to note that the
existence of the camp proved that "Roosevelt's conservation camp policy makes no detrimental discrimination in class or color," although
that assertion was somewhat undermined by the further observation
that the camp was the only one out of the thirty-nine operating in the
state to employ blacks. The low level of black enrollment was passed
off as being an administrative error whereby "Negroes got lost in the
shuffle" when the camps were first set up. In defense of black enrollment, the article noted that black CCC camps contributed to remov-
ing blacks from the relief rolls and hence lightened the load of the
white taxpayer. It concluded that both blacks and whites at the camp
were "apparently delighted with the life, enthused with the work, loyal
in service and energetically determined to make this particular camp a
model of neatness and efficiency."[19] The conclusion drawn from this
by one observer was that it "brings out forcibly. . . that it is an injustice to the negroes as well as the white boys not to segregate them
especially in the South."[20]

Another obstacle to black enrollment was the question of exactly where segregated camps should be located in the Delta. In 1935, CCC director Fechner complained to Arkansas Senator Joseph T. Robinson that "there is hardly any locality in this country that looks favorably, or even with indifference, on the location of a Negro CCC camp in their vicinity." State governors were integral to the selection process and sensitive to the complaints of voters. Residents objected to the placement of black camps in their locality on a number of grounds, most commonly citing fear of drunkenness and other vices, as well as the safety of women and children in the area. In fact, some of the most vociferous protests against black camps came from northern states and, generally, the most welcoming places for black camps were in the South, although even there attitudes could vary widely. The reason for southern communities embracing black camps more warmly than their northern counterparts appears to be the belief that, given the prospects of a rowdy group of young men being located in their midst, existing formal and informal racial controls would be effective in maintaining law and order.[21]

The experience in Arkansas reveals a mixed attitude among whites to black CCC camps. In August 1941, for example, there was a proposal to replace a white CCC camp in Warren in southeast Arkansas with a black camp relocated from Forrest City in the northeast. The proposal raised a storm of protest and more than eighty residents wrote to their U.S. representative, Oren Harris, to "urge" him to use his "influence to see that personnel of local company remains white instead changed to Negroes." The residents had the backing of Duval L. Purkins, a Warren resident, a circuit judge, and a former U.S. senator, who advised Harris that "in my judgment this would be bad for this community."[22] The move also prompted Arkansas governor Homer Adkins to inform Arkansas U.S. Senator Hattie Carraway that "this is absolutely unacceptable and would be a mistake at any location in the state to disband white company and send Negro company."[23] Meanwhile, Harris assured his constituents that under no circumstances would he allow the relocation of the camp.[24] The CCC district headquarters informed Harris that "colored camps are not transferred to communities where any objection to the transfer exists," but warned that the consequence of this would be "the loss of one company in the state of Arkansas." Warren residents accepted the loss of the camp altogether rather than allow the black camp to relocate there.[25]

Just two months later, Harris received a letter from Carneal Warfield, a county judge in Chicot County, barely fifty miles away from Warren, pleading for the location of "two or more CCC camps for negro boys in this county." Warfield explained, "I have discussed the matter with the directors of Chicot County Drainage District and they think it would be wonderful for the County if we can get the camps and have their labor needed on drainage projects . . . if we can put it over it will mean much to all concerned."[26] This time, Harris found himself pleading with CCC director James J. McEntee for two black camps to be located in the state.[27] However, Harris was informed that the CCC was at that time winding down its operations and that the camps were now being dismantled rather than established.[28]

By that point, Arkansas had already added a further five black CCC camps to the one established at Strong. As part of the nationwide expansion of the CCC in 1935, two black camps were established at Rosston and Ashdown, which were, like the Strong camp, involved in forestry work. Another two black CCC camps, one based at Charlotte, and one based at Forrest City, were both Soil Conservation Service projects that worked on soil erosion measures. The final black camp, at LaGrue, near Dewitt, was involved in work on a migratory bird refuge. After the 1935 expansion, no more black CCC camps were located in Arkansas. In the fall of 1935, Fechner decreed that new black CCC recruits could only be hired to replace existing enrollees as their places became vacant, effectively capping the total number of places available. Roosevelt again privately acquiesced to this decision, calling it "political dynamite" and asking that his name "be not drawn into the discussion."[29]

Notwithstanding the discriminatory practices that severely limited black participation in the CCC, for those blacks who did enroll, it held some of the best opportunities that the New Deal had to offer— another likely reason why whites wanted to restrict black participation as far as possible. One black enrollee from Pennsylvania told historian Nancy Weiss that gaining a place in the camps "was as important as going to Princeton University—they had status."[30] Another declared that "as a job and an experience for a man who has no work, I can heartily recommend it." The figures appear to back up the anecdotal evidence: on average, black enrollment in a camp lasted almost five months longer than white enrollment.[31]

Black CCC camps in Arkansas provided the basic necessities of life such as food and shelter, important contributions in their own right for young black men living in the Arkansas Delta who had survived the catastrophic Mississippi River flood of 1927, followed swiftly by years of drought and economic depression.[32] The camp at Charlotte tellingly reported an average twenty-pound weight gain per man over the course of a year. The camps also provided clothing in the shape of U.S. Army uniforms, which acted as a constant and potent reminder that enrollees were federal employees and under federal jurisdiction. Enrollees also had access to medical care, including the services of white doctors and dentists. They received the same wage as white enrollees for their work, the first time that many of them had achieved such a parity of pay.

In addition to these benefits, one of the most important federal initiatives in the camps was the CCC education program. After 1935, the program was administered by Howard W. Oxley who, in direct contrast to Fechner, enthusiastically pursued his nondiscriminatory mandate. Oxley declared that "It is our policy in CCC education to seek to motivate and develop every enrollee, regardless of race or creed, to the fullest capacity." Moreover, he insisted upon tailoring each education program to the specific needs of the men enrolled in the camp. In black camps, this included hiring a black education adviser to devise and run the education program, a role that provided the one staple nonwhite supervisory post in the camps.[33]

Although education programs at CCC camps were purely voluntary, black participation was extremely high. Nationally, it was reported that 87 percent of black enrollees chose to attend educational programs, and classes taught over thirty thousand blacks to read and write.[34] Some educational advisers in Arkansas camps reported attendance rates running at over 95 percent. A wide range of academic and vocational programs were run in the camps, with educational buildings and facilities supplied especially for them. Each camp had its own lending library of scholarly and leisure reading materials, together with a number of magazines and newspapers. In black camps, these included national black newspapers such as the *Pittsburgh Courier* and the *Chicago Defender*, and most had a number of radios, providing many black enrollees with exposure to local, state, regional, and national black media outlets for the first time. At some camps, blacks produced and ran their own camp newspapers, providing a training ground for budding future black journalists.

CCC classes ranged from basic literacy to elementary, high school, and even college courses. Some enrollees took correspondence classes.

As a result of this schooling, a number of enrollees sat for exams, thereby gaining diplomas and degrees. The CCC camps also encouraged black enrollees to return to school to finish or to further their education, and some received high school and college scholarships to do so. A number of vocational classes were offered, including typewriting, freehand drawing, table waiting, metal work, wood work, and mechanics. Enrollees used the skills they picked up in CCC camps as a steppingstone to find work afterward, with some subsequently taking up jobs in the U.S. Army and U.S. Navy to help in the war effort.[35]

Most important of all, the camps, run by the U.S. Army, provided a code of conduct that treated all men, black and white, as being equally subject to army rules and regulations. This federally organized military framework of discipline was decidedly at odds with the expressly unfair and unequal racialized law of the Arkansas Delta. Under the army code, blacks discovered for the first time that complaints about the conditions they worked in were taken seriously and were even addressed and acted upon. Federal responsiveness to black complaints is evidenced in the official government reports returned by CCC special investigators. In Arkansas, most of these were written by James Sykes Billups. At first glance, Billups's credentials were not the most promising for a racially enlightened approach. He belonged to one of Mississippi's oldest plantation-owning families, and he had himself run the Billups Gate Plantation in Lowndes County for a number of years. Despite this, Billups was scrupulously fair in dealing with racial matters, even demonstrating a degree of sensitivity to black complaints. Precisely why this was the case remains unclear. His actions may have stemmed from a sense of benevolent paternalism developed in running the family business. The fact that Billups was a Methodist rather than a Southern Baptist, the latter denomination being more popular and widespread in the South and having more ardent segregationist leanings, may have meant that he acted out of a religious sense of duty and fairness. Billiups may have simply been honoring the principles of federal and military law in the camps, and he may have held these to be above local, state, and regional authority. Whatever his motivations were, Billups certainly had an impact on race relations in the Delta.[36]

Billups wrote a number of routine CCC camp reports, but far more revealing were the periodic investigations into racial incidents that he conducted. The most striking of these investigations was triggered by events that occurred on July 7, 1938, six miles north of the Delta town of Forrest City. On that afternoon, two groups of men were working at the Cress gravel pit. One was a group of thirteen white men belonging to an Arkansas highway department mainte- nance crew and who were under the supervision of William I. White. The other was a group of nineteen black CCC enrollees who were load- ing gravel onto trucks under the supervision of Jess Weatherford, a white truck driver for the Soil Conservation Service. The black enrollees were helping to gravel the New Castle road from Forrest City to the nearby CCC camp. White highway workers and black enrollees had been working at the same gravel pit for the previous two weeks. On that particular day, the black enrollees in the afternoon were working much slower than those in the morning had. The morning crew had filled nine trucks with gravel, whereas the afternoon crew had filled only three. The truck drivers, who were friends of the white state high- way crew, complained about the slow progress. Some of the white crew pointed out to the black enrollees that the morning shift had filled a water keg and had kept it with them in the gravel pit, instead of walking over to the water pump and taking regular extended breaks. They suggested that the members of the afternoon shift should do the same. The black enrollees clearly resented the interference, since they ignored the advice and continued to frequent the water pump.[37]

At around one thirty in the afternoon, four of the white crew— Maxie Vance, Roy Coffee, Waldo Adams, and Donald Gibbs—were lying in the shade under a tree ten yards from the water pump. Five black enrollees—Elsbery Broadnax, Willie Dandridge, Lennest Walker, Matthew Yates, and Jesse Johnson, the assistant leader of the CCC crew—went to the pump to get water. Gibbs shouted over to Dandridge to ask if the last truck to drive into the gravel pit was a state highway truck or a CCC truck. Dandridge allegedly replied, "God damn you, get up and look for yourself." Maxie Vance shot back, "Don't get smart you black bastard." Elsbery Broadnax then told Vance to "go fuck yourself." Billups later concluded that by that point, "The hard feeling that caused the fight was definitely established." Yet despite Broadnax's challenge, Vance clearly did not fancy his chances against the physically bigger and stronger man. Both sides let the matter rest there, and they left to return to their respective crews.[38]

Back among the white highway crew, working about two hundred yards from the water pump, news of the exchange soon spread. Elmer

Kennedy, a coworker of Vance's, asked him why he had allowed Broadnax to talk to him like that. Vance replied that "he was afraid" of Broadnax, and that "there were too many" blacks at the water pump for him to do anything. Kennedy handed Vance a pick handle and told him, "Maxie you settle with that big Negro and I will see that none of the rest of those Negroes jump on you."[39] Meanwhile, William White, who was in charge of the white crew, complained to Jess Weatherford, who was in charge of the black enrollees, about the incident that had taken place at the water pump. Weatherford told the black enrollees "to get a keg of water [and to] keep it in the pit and to stay away from the pump." However, the enrollees ignored Weatherford's instructions and continued to visit the water pump.[40]

At three o'clock, when Broadnax and others again returned to the water pump, the white highway crew was there waiting for them, armed with pick handles, axes, and kaiser blades. Maxie Vance later claimed that the black enrollees had "large rocks in their pockets," and that "they had come over for trouble." Vance asked Broadnax what it was that he had called him and, without waiting for a reply, charged forward with a pick handle in his hands. Broadnax—consistently referred to as a "big Negro"—took the weapon away from Vance and hit him over the head with it. Another member of the white crew threw a rock at Broadnax, and a gang fight broke out. According to Vance's testimony, one of the enrollees shouted, "let's kill those white sons-of-a-bitches." When it became clear that they were getting the worst of the exchange, the black enrollees retreated, pursued by the white crew, who threw rocks and axes after them. White crew member Elmer Kennedy reported, "It was a serious looking fight for a few minutes and then the Negroes ran . . . there were several very narrow escapes from serious injury."[41]

Back at the CCC camp, Capt. F. T. McQueen, the white commanding officer, convened a joint investigation with Col. Neal M. Snyder, project superintendent, to establish exactly what had happened that afternoon. McQueen and Snyder questioned the enrollees outside of the Soil Conservation Service office with little success. McQueen, along with Snyder, and camp foremen Thomas, Hale, Fischer, Weatherford, and Bradley, then went inside the building and called in the enrollees one at a time for questioning. McQueen thought that the enrollees "seemed to have had their stories pretty well together," with all of them saying that "they didn't know how it [the fight] started, it just started."[42]

One of the enrollees, Phillip Branch, did let slip that fellow enrollee Henry Smith had said something to the effect that "The white boys were meddling." Smith, who had already been interviewed, was called back in. When questioned about the alleged remark, Smith denied saying it. When Branch was summoned to confront Smith, Smith refused to answer whether he had made the remark. The white officers reported that Smith was "very disrespectful and insolent in his answers." He kept saying "What," "What did you say," and "Suh?," and made McQueen repeat several of his questions, "as if," McQueen reported, "he wanted some more time to think it over." McQueen asked Smith if he was hard of hearing. Smith replied, "What?" Then Snyder joined in the questioning, asking Smith, "Boy, you think you are smart don't you?" Smith replied, "No, if I was smart I wouldn't be in the CCC." Foreman Bradley went over to Smith and slapped him, telling him that he was speaking to "a superior officer, his Company Commander and Camp Superintendent." Bradley told Smith to answer only "Yes, sir" or "No, sir." McQueen and Snyder told Bradley to refrain from slapping Smith and, after a further four hours of questioning, they adjourned for the day.[43]

Later that night, Henry Smith sent two telegrams, one to CCC director Robert Fechner in Washington, D.C., and one to Maj. Gen. Stanley H. Ford, commander of the Seventh Corps Area, in Omaha, Nebraska. The identical telegrams read: "Enrollee working under civilian foreman in CO 4734 CCC Forrest City Arkansas come into contact with white WPA workers brought to come office by Captain Project Supt and foreman one beaten by foreman Bradley." It was these telegrams that triggered an official inquiry into the incident.[44]

On the afternoon of Saturday, July 9, Billups, in Hot Springs, Arkansas, received a letter from Charles H. Kenlan, an assistant to Fechner, requesting him to investigate events at Forrest City. Billups had heard about the incident the previous day from the CCC's Arkansas district commander, Maj. G. C. Graham, who told Billups that he intended to hold his own investigation into events. Billups called Graham on Monday morning, July 11, only to discover that he had already sent Maj. S. P. Walker and Capt. J. D. Petty to Forrest City to investigate. Billups set off for Forrest City to conduct his investigation, arriving there before Walker and Petty. He interviewed all of the nineteen black enrollees who had been present at the gravel pit first, "before," he later explained, "they got excited to establish confidence between myself and them. Realizing to get the proper story from them this was absolutely necessary." Upon their eventual arrival, Walker and Petty began their investigation by interviewing the white officers involved.

That evening, Billups met with Walker to tell him that "the investigation was taking an unexpected disclosure and it rather looked to [him] that these were more important than the fight in the gravel pit." Billups informed Walker that he was convinced from the testimony of the black enrollees that foreman Bradley had indeed struck Henry Smith. Walker told Billups that all of the white officers denied this was the case. Billups insisted that he believed the testimony of the black enrollees, and that he would "require sworn statements from all of the [white] officials present."[45]

In the course of questioning the black enrollees, Billups had made further discoveries that he felt directly related to foreman Bradley's conduct and his alleged assault on Henry Smith. The first involved a separate incident that had taken place just a couple of days earlier. On Saturday, July 9, at seven thirty in the morning, Bradley had gone to get his coat from the camp barracks only to discover that it was missing. A black orderly, Charles C. Derden, was in the room making the beds. Bradley asked Derden where his coat was. The orderly said that black enrollee Freeman Montague had removed it earlier. Bradley asked him why he had allowed Montague take his coat. The orderly replied that he had challenged Montague, who claimed that the coat was his, and to prove it he had correctly identified its serial number.[46]

Bradley set off in search of Montague. He found him at the Forrest City train station, along with nineteen other men under the command of Lt. Carlos Emmanuelli. The troops were preparing to travel to Bald Knob, Arkansas, where they were meeting up with another group of black enrollees destined for CCC Company 3760 at Poplar Bluff, Missouri. Bradley told Emmanuelli that Montague had stolen his coat and he wanted it back. Emmanuelli told him that he did not have time to investigate the matter as the train would soon be leaving. Dissatisfied with that response, Bradley went to see medical officer Lieutenant W. A. Regnier. Regnier tracked down Montague and asked him to open his bag in the presence of Emmanuelli and Bradley. Montague pulled out an army issue shortcoat but, as he had previously claimed, it had his serial number on it. "That isn't the coat," Bradley insisted. "I want the one that is missing out of my room." Bradley turned to Regnier and asked him, "What are you going to do about this?" Regnier told him, "Mr. Bradley, you know that I have no command over these boys. Lt. Emmanuelli is in charge." Bradley then traveled into Forrest City to get a civilian officer, who arrested Montague on a charge of petit larceny and placed him in the county jail.[47]

At Montague's trial on Monday, July 11, there were three witnesses: foreman Bradley, black orderly Charles C. Derden, and another man who was there as a "character witness" for Bradley. Justice of the Peace Ed McCutcheon found Montague guilty as charged and handed him a $200 fine and ordered him to pay costs of $25.25, even though the coat had been bought for just $6.28 from the Memphis Army Store. Unable to pay, Montague was sent to Cross Plantation to work off his fine at seventy-five cents per day. Because of his conviction, Montague was handed a dishonorable discharge from the CCC. He spent only a few days at the penal farm before being freed under an appeal bond secured by Coy M. Nixon, an attorney from Pine Bluff, Arkansas, who had been hired by Montague's father. Montague's appeal hearing was set for the first week of September. However, the Montague family, on government relief, did not have enough money to retain the lawyer. Nixon persuaded the judge to lower the fine to ten dollars, an amount the family could afford to pay. Although this got Montague off the plantation, he would still have to pay the fine, he still would be left with a criminal conviction, and he would still be barred from the CCC and unemployed.[48]

When black enrollee Samuel T. Miller, an assistant leader in Bradley's crew, was interviewed by Billups, it transpired that the incident between Bradley and Montague went back to an earlier feud between the two men. It turned out that Bradley had been running an illicit taxi service for black enrollees to and from nearby Forrest City, and that he had been charging them ten cents a ride. This lasted for around two and a half months before complaints from local taxi firms had brought the venture to an end. Montague was one of Bradley's drivers, along with enrollees Ernest Smith and D. W. Thrower, until one day Montague "had the car in reverse and was backing up to get close to the steps and backed into the left hand side next to the porch" of the foremen's quarters. This destruction of his property had apparently motivated Bradley to seek revenge on Montague before he could be shipped out of the camp.[49]

On July 13, Billups requested commanding officer McQueen to allow enrollees with any further complaints to make them known.

Twenty men came forward to complain about Bradley and foreman W. D. Thomas. They said Thomas had been "cursing them, grabbing them by the neck and threatening to whip them, threatening to kick them," and insisted that he "kept them out [on the job] longer than required [by] the CCC." When Henry Smith was interviewed, he revealed that black enrollees Ernest Smith and D. W. Thrower had been beaten by McQueen, Snyder, Bradley, and junior assistant technician Bufford W. Harlan. Smith alleged that he and fellow enrollees Luther P. Brown and Murray Hall he had seen the white men "whip . . . them with rubber hose and a black jack, while Colonel and Mr. Harlan held guns on them." Luther Brown told Billups, "We didn't know what they were doing until they [Ernest Smith and Thrower] started to holler." Did McQueen "know anything about it?" asked Billups. "I don't know sir, I am sure he knows something about it since he was there that night," Brown told him. Other black enrollees corroborated their story.[50]

Another line of inquiry that Billups was eager to follow was how Smith had known who to complain to about his treatment by white officers and how he had managed to compose and send a telegram. This led to the discovery that the black enrollees were not purely at the mercy of white officers, but that they were mobilized and active in their own self-defense. Billups found out that the telegram had been sent with the help and advice of Earl Morris, a black clerk at the camp, who was also the president of an organization to which all black camp members apparently belonged called the "CCC Protectors' Club." Billups was curious about the role and purpose of this club. When Billups questioned Morris, he explained that "it is mostly for social activities. We give dances." Billups asked, "If this is a social club, why do you have the name 'Protectors'?" Morris replied, "We had several names submitted to be voted on for the name of the club, and the name of CCC Protectors' Club was voted on, and that is the one we selected."[51] Harvey McDonald, the black educational adviser at the camp, echoed Morris's story. He said that the Protectors' Club was just a social club. "Has this club been entirely social?" Billups pressed. "Has it has no tendency to bind these enrollees together from a standpoint of anything but social activities?" McDonald replied, "That is all." Despite the steadfast denials, Billups continued to probe. "The statement has been made to me that Henry Smith consulted with Morris on account of his being President of this club, and that Morris furnished him the address that Smith wired to. Could you explain this to me in any way?" he asked. "No," said McDonald, "This is the first time that I have hear[d] about that."[52]

Billups was equally unsuccessful at coaxing information out of Cornelius Summerville, senior leader of the black enrollees. At first, Summerville denied all existence of a CCC Protectors' Club. "Morris . . . tells me that there is an organization of that kind in this camp and that practically all of the enrollees in this camp belong to it, and that you belong to it," Billiups told him. "Is that correct?" Alert to the fact that Billups already knew about the existence of the club, Summerville replied, "Well, now, there is a sort of social committee that looks out for things like that."

"Did you ever hear the name of it, at all?" Billups asked. "Morris tells me that there were names submitted for this club and that the name adopted was the CCC Protectors' Club."

"Well," said Summerville, "I never went to the meetings, because I was always doing something else." Billups followed up, "Is it your opinion, then, that it is just a social club, and you are not thoroughly familiar with the name of it?" Summerville said, "Yes, sir. That is right. They give camp dances. They have a secretary and all, and they look out for the enrollees."[53]

After conducting interviews at the camp for three days, Billups came to a number of conclusions. Acknowledging that "some of the CCC enrollees conduct is not good," Billups nevertheless laid the blame for the fight on white CCC foreman Jess Weatherford who had been wrong to "allow [the enrollees] to work at their pleasure and did not step in and demand order from them." Billups did not "believe either the Arkansas State Highway employees or the CCC enrollees are especially resentful to each other. I further believe that they could be worked in crews side by side without any trouble, provided that each crew was properly supervised." Moreover, Billups pointed out, some of Forrest City's leading businessmen, civic leaders, and politicians had told him that "they would prefer a Colored CCC camp over a white one and that the conduct of the CCC enrollees in the community has been satisfactory." Billups considered the assault on Henry Smith, the arrest of Freeman Montague, and the alleged beating of Ernest Smith and D. W. Thrower to be far "more important" matters.

Billups made a number of recommendations based upon these conclusions. Firstly, he recommended that Elsbery Broadnax should be given a dishonorable discharge for his conduct at the gravel pit.

Secondly, he recommended the actions of other black CCC enrollees should be examined to determine if anyone else should be discharged for their role in events. Thirdly, he recommended that foreman Bradley should be dismissed because of his involvement in various irregularities. Fourthly, he recommended that the Department of Justice should be asked to investigate whether Freeman Montague "had a fair trial and why such an unusual, excessive fine was given him." Fifthly, he recommended that the investigation into the alleged beatings of Ernest Smith and D. W. Thrower be reopened.[54]

After explaining his findings to Dr. Fred Keller, CCC assistant regional administrator, Keller asked Billups to question all of the white officers present at the alleged beating of Henry Smith, since it had been reported to him that "no such occurrence had occurred." Upon Billups's cross-examination, the white officers admitted that Bradley had in fact hit Henry Smith. Bradley was suspended from duty immediately. District commander Major Graham informed Billups that he intended to widen the investigation at the camp and to assess the position of camp commander Captain McQueen. Billups pointed out that "the disposition of everyone was to protect Mr. Bradley and that it has been exceedingly embarrassing for some, since the disclosure [was] brought to light." The situation with Bradley involved further complications. Billups had lunch with a leading attorney in Forrest City who told him that Bradley had contacts with some "higher up politicians," including Senator Hattie Carraway. Bradley's "political friends" were using their influence to keep him in the CCC."[55]

A board of investigation subsequently convened at the camp and made a number of recommendations based upon Billups's investigation and its conclusions. Firstly, the board said that foremen Bradley and Harlan and assistant storekeeper Winston P. Wilson, should "be discharged and that in case they are retained in the service they be reprimanded and transferred to white camps on [Soil Conservation Service] projects." Secondly, Elsbery Broadnax should "be given an administrative discharge for serious misconduct." Thirdly, Jesse Johnson should be demoted from his position as assistant leader, but that he should not be discharged from the CCC. Fourthly, Freeman Montague should be "permitted to reenroll pending the final disposition of his case and that such aid, as the government may properly give, be afforded to him in disposition of his case." Fifthly, "no disciplinary action [should] be taken against enrollees for driving Mr. Bradley's car . . . [since] their actions were condoned by the government's representatives." Sixthly, "Captain McQueen's detail with the CCC [should] be canceled, or in case he is held in service that he be transferred to a white camp."[56]

The decision to remove the white camp commander, while at the same time exonerating a number of black enrollees for their actions, caused a great deal of political controversy in the state. Gov. Carl E. Bailey sent a telegram marked "urgent" to CCC director Fechner, advising him, "It will be a grave error adversely affecting racial relationships of our citizens to remove Captain F. T. McQueen under present circumstances from CCC No. 4734, Forrest City, Arkansas. McQueen and citizens have not been heard. Please give this request your personal attention."[57] Three days later, Fechner's acting director James J. McEntee replied to Bailey's telegram by asserting federal authority in the matter: "Regarding your telegram concerning Captain McQueen, please be advised that the War Department has entire jurisdiction in selecting commanding officers for CCC Camps, direct authority being vested in Corps Area Commanders. This office has not attempted to intervene. The Forrest City matter was thoroughly investigated and the report transmitted to the War Department for consideration and whatever action might be proper. By reason of the authority referred to, the final decision rests with the War Department."[58] The matter ended there. The case against Freeman Montague was later dismissed on appeal and he reenrolled in the CCC at black Company 4735 in Charlotte on September 20, 1938. McQueen was dismissed from his post.[59]

Events at Forrest City provide an intriguing glimpse into the impact of the New Deal on southern race relations. The black CCC camps brought together previously isolated groups of young black men, fed them, clothed them, provided them with a steady wage, health care, and leisure and education facilities, which constituted an attractive alternative to their usual surroundings. As the experience in Forrest City indicates, black enrollees took advantage of these opportunities to the full and, moreover, banded together to ensure their self-protection from unscrupulous white officers and supervisors. When inequalities and injustices beyond their control did flare up, they had access to a body of procedures and laws beyond the immediate locality that they were evidently willing to call upon for restitution. The usually even-handed treatment that followed investigations gave even more confidence to black enrollees to stand up for their rights, and even more faith that federally mandated justice could supersede the highly racialized and discriminatory law of the Delta.

Whites were clearly worried by these developments, which threatened to introduce independent scrutiny of racial practices into the region and to wrest control of the black population out of their hands. White responses to encroaching federal intervention illustrate the double-edged nature of the federal and state power struggle. White southerners clearly preferred not to be beholden to federal power. But as the New Deal demonstrated, the South was, and would increasingly be, dependent upon a federal presence accompanied by federal money to effectively modernize and develop. While white southerners shied away from federal intervention in race relations and other areas, they equally needed that intervention for regional advancement. It became evident in the years that followed the New Deal that the two could not be so easily separated.

Less than twenty years after the incident at the remote Cress gravel pit near Forrest City, the full ramifications of the federal versus state tug-of-war that the New Deal began would be seen in the state capital of Little Rock. In response to the U.S. Supreme Court's *Brown v. Board of Education* (1954) school desegregation decision, Little Rock, Arkansas, and the rest of the South, faced its biggest test in the struggle between federal and state power. Arkansas Gov. Orval Faubus decided to call out National Guardsmen to prevent federal orders for school desegregation from being carried out, and he thereby directly challenged the right of federal authority to take precedent over state rights by interposing himself as head of a sovereign state between the federal government and state citizens. President Dwight D. Eisenhower's subsequent use of federal troops to enforce school desegregation at Little Rock's Central High School brought to a logical fruition the implications of the telegram sent by James J. McEntee to Gov. Carl Bailey almost twenty years earlier. Faubus was fighting a battle that has already been comprehensively lost. The sole question was how long resistance to the inevitable triumph of federal authority would last and how much damage it would cause in the process. As historian Roger Biles concludes: "much of the change in race relations in the 1950s and 1960s began slowly, cautiously, in the 1930s. These modest origins made possible the truly remarkable alterations that followed. . . . The New Deal provided a necessary—if frustratingly small—first step on the road to change."[60]

3

Politics and the Early Civil Rights Struggle

Dr. John Marshall Robinson, the Arkansas Negro Democratic Association, and Black Politics in Little Rock, 1928–1952

One of the most far-reaching effects of the New Deal in the United States was its impact on political party allegiances and voting behavior. President Franklin D. Roosevelt's political "New Deal coalition," which was formed of diverse groups in American society, including blacks, "farmers, blue-collar workers, ethnics" and residents of northern and midwestern cities, provided the votes that kept the Democratic Party dominant in American national politics for almost five decades. Integral to Democratic power at a national level was an unholy alliance with southern Democrats who, in contrast to the liberal stronghold that the national Democratic Party became, were deeply conservative and racist. The South remained loyally Democrat for historical reasons that identified the party with the Confederate cause in the Civil War and its defense of white supremacy. Considering the very different outlook of the national and southern wings of the Democratic Party, the alliance proved to have a good deal of longevity, serving as a pragmatic basis for maintaining party power that largely benefited both groups. Although that relationship was always tentative and parlous, it was only when the national Democratic Party explicitly supported the civil rights movement in the 1960s that the Democratic "solid South" broke decisively apart.[1]

Far more immediate and dramatic than the gradual southern white disenchantment with the Democratic Party was the switch in political allegiances of the black population. Prior to the 1930s, blacks had voted predominantly for the Republican Party as the party of Lincoln and the party of emancipation from slavery—that is, for essentially the opposite reasons that white southerners voted Democrat. Even up until 1932, blacks continued to vote Republican. But from the 1936 presidential election to the present day, blacks have voted Democrat in large numbers at national elections and they have represented one of the most consistent and reliable blocks of national Democratic Party support. Historian Harvard Sitkoff has suggested that the shift in black votes was based on the perceived racial liberalism of the Roosevelt administration and the national Democratic Party since the 1930s, while Nancy Weiss has suggested that it had more to do with the willingness of Democrats to actively pursue socially progressive policies that delivered practical help and support to the black population from the 1930s on.[2] Whatever weight is given to each of these explanations, it is clear that the 1930s marked a significant shift in black politics. Of course, since two-thirds of blacks lived in the South in 1930, and a great many of them were prevented from voting anyway by an array of disfranchisement measures enforced by southern Democrats, it took time to translate black political support into votes and thereby into tangible political power. As the black population in northern cities grew through out-migration from the South, which was particularly pronounced during World War II, a newly enfranchised block of voters began to make their voices heard. A number of commentators point to the 1948 election of Democrat president Harry S. Truman as being the first election in which black votes made a decisive difference in a national election.[3]

In truth, although the 1930s were clearly a watershed in terms of black politics, the move of blacks toward the Democratic Party during that decade was in many ways equally the final chapter in a long goodbye to the Republican Party. With the end of Reconstruction in 1877, and the steady disfranchisement of the southern black population from the 1890s onward, Republicans had for many years been as concerned with placating southern whites as keeping black political support. The record of Republican presidents from the turn of the century up to the 1930s did little to encourage black voters. Theodore Roosevelt (president from 1901–9) did initially provide some continuity with previous Republican ties to black politics by appointing blacks to federal offices, strongly stating his opposition to racially motivated lynching in the South, and relying upon the advice of the foremost black leader of the day, Booker T. Washington, whom he invited into the White House. However, during his second term in office, Roosevelt summarily dismissed three companies of black infantrymen who refused to inform on their compatriots about an alleged shootout in Brownsville, Texas. When Roosevelt ran as a third-party candidate under the Progressive Party banner in 1912, he wooed white southern voters, refused to seat black southerners at the national convention, and refused to consider equal rights measures put forward by black leader W.E.B. Du Bois.[4]

Roosevelt's successor as a Republican president, William Howard Taft (1909–13), also looked to cultivate support among white southerners. He refused to appoint any blacks to office that were not acceptable to local whites, which effectively meant the exclusion of blacks from federal offices in the South. Taft did make some token appointments of blacks in Washington, D.C., in diplomatic and consular positions, but he still neglected issues such as "segregation, discrimination, disfranchisement and racial violence."

The only Democratic president to challenge Republican dominance of the presidency was Woodrow Wilson (1913–21), who extended segregation in Washington, D.C., and demonstrated little desire to win over the black population. In the 1920s, Republican presidents Warren Harding (1921–23) and Calvin Coolidge (1923–29) did little to reverse the actions of Wilson or previous Republican administrations. They failed to address the policy of segregation in the civil service and they appointed few blacks to federal office. Despite the NAACP's campaign for antilynching legislation in the 1920s, neither of the two Republican presidents, nor the Republican-dominated Congresses, supported such legislation. Though both Harding and Coolidge flirted with the idea of forming an interracial commission to address the country's racial problems, neither of them acted decisively upon it.[5]

The election of 1928 provided a glimmer of hope for some black political leverage at a national level. The Democratic nominee for the presidency that year was Alfred E. Smith, the grandson of Irish, Italian, and German immigrants, who had grown up on New York's blue-collar Lower East Side. Smith was the first ever Catholic nominee for president, he opposed prohibition, and he was a product of New

York's Tammany Hall, a political machine that had a reputation for using patronage to build black political support. Taken together, Smith's background soundly alienated Protestant, prohibition-supporting, racist white southern Democrats, and his candidacy held out the possibility that his nontraditional leanings might extend into more progressive racial policies too. Even before receiving the nomination, Smith sounded out Walter White, NAACP assistant executive secretary, about campaigning for black votes on his behalf.

White was initially keen on offering his support, but the Democratic Party convention at which Smith was nominated dented his enthusiasm. The convention had no black delegates and no platform for civil rights. As a sop to the South, Smith chose Arkansas's Senator Joseph T. Robinson as his vice-presidential runningmate. The convention was held in Houston, Texas, in the aftermath of a lynching there. Black alternates at the convention were segregated behind chicken wire "in a separate cagelike enclosure." Nevertheless, White remained on board with the Smith ticket, since the Republican Party offered little better. Its convention in Kansas City also segregated black candidates and showed no sign of reinstating black patronage in the South. White believed that Smith's candidacy was the lesser of two evils compared with Republican nominee Herbert Hoover, and that a move away from the Republicans would be a valuable assertion of black independence. Along with James Weldon Johnson, NAACP executive secretary, White drafted a statement of support for Smith ahead of a promised personal meeting with the nominee to discuss his intentions.

The meeting with Smith never materialized, as the presidential candidate heeded the advice of Joseph T. Robinson and others party members about needlessly antagonizing white voters by identifying too strongly with black leaders. Despite this, the Democrats waged more of a campaign among black voters in the 1928 election than ever before. The Smith campaign established a Smith-for-President Colored League directed by two Boston lawyers, William Gaston, who was white, and Julian D. Rainey, who was black. Black Chicago lawyer Earl B. Dickerson oversaw the campaign in the Midwest; Lawrence A. Walton, black newspaper editor, was director of publicity; and Bishop Reverdy C. Ransom, from the African Methodist Episcopal Church, ran a speakers' bureau. All of the nation's major black newspapers supported Smith, as did black nationalist leader Marcus Garvey, whose United Negro Improvement Association emerged as one of

America's first mass black organizations in the 1920s. Black Smith-for-President Colored Clubs were widespread, large numbers of blacks appeared at campaign rallies, and, for the first time, it became generally acceptable for blacks to speak out against the Republican Party. At the general election, there was a discernable shift in the northern and midwestern urban black vote toward the Democrats because of this, although black voters were still too small in number to make a decisive impact and, in any case, Smith lost the election to his Republican opponent Herbert Hoover. Nancy Weiss concludes that despite loosening traditional political ties, "Smith failed to change the political habits of black Americans. He was intrigued by the prospect of winning black support but unwilling to risk white support to get it."[6]

Political developments in Arkansas mirrored national developments in 1928. Blacks had been active in the state Republican Party since it was first founded in 1867. As elsewhere in the South, during Reconstruction, and in many instances beyond then, blacks held a number of patronage and elected positions through the party. However, from the very outset there was a strained relationship between black and white Republicans as two party factions quickly emerged. One group, the so-called "black and tans," was made up largely of blacks but had some white support. They believed that building black Republican support was the best political response to a white-dominated Democratic Party. Another group were the so-called "lily whites." They maintained that the only way to offer a credible alternative to southern Democrats was to accept white supremacy and to compete with them for white votes. This inevitably meant renouncing black political support. After the 1890s, as disfranchisement spread across the South, arriving comprehensively in Arkansas during the period that race-baiting demagogue Jeff Davis held office as governor between 1901 and 1906, black political fortunes declined in the state as the Republican lily-white forces gained ascendancy.[7]

Black Republicans in Arkansas continued to fight for their place in the Republican Party and they did ultimately succeed in that struggle. Much of this was because of the leadership of Scipio Africanus Jones. Born a slave in Tulip, southwest Arkansas, Jones worked as a field hand after emancipation, moving to Little Rock in 1881. After gaining an education in the city at Philander Smith College, and then Shorter College, he became a self-taught lawyer, opening a practice in Little Rock in 1889. Jones was a talented attorney and he became counsel to many of the black fraternal and Masonic groups in the city, as well as an early advocate for civil rights in the courtroom. In 1919, Jones was employed by the NAACP to defend twelve black men charged for their role in the Elaine Race Riot in the Arkansas Delta, and he successfully managed to win a custodial rather than a death sentence for them. Jones also became the leading black Republican voice in Little Rock and, in 1928, he gained election as a delegate to the Republican National Convention, forcing Arkansas Republicans to acknowledge and accept the legitimacy of black participation in the state organization.[8]

Nevertheless, Jones's was a token victory for blacks. By 1928, political power in the state was firmly entrenched with the Democratic Party of Arkansas.[9] Taking into account the political situation in Arkansas and the national developments in the Alfred E. Smith campaign, the emergence of a black Democratic movement in the state that year was not entirely surprising. Neither was it altogether unprecedented. Black Arkansans had strayed outside of the Republican fold in the past on a number of occasions in search of political influence and power. Two black politicians from Little Rock, Isaac Gillam and Green Thompson, were active in the Pulaski County Greenback Party in the late 1870s, and Elias Rector had been the party's black nominee for the office of Pulaski County Circuit Clerk in 1878. Rector was nominated for the same post by the Populist Party in 1890. P. M. E. Thompson served as a black delegate to the Populist Party National Convention in 1898. A number of prominent black Arkansas Republicans defected to Theodore Roosevelt's Progressive Party in 1912, including Dr. Jefferson G. Ish, a prominent Little Rock physician. Before disfranchisement measures had been passed in the state, the Democratic Party had even successfully courted black support. In the 1879 legislative session a number of white Democrats backed the election of a black chaplain, Little Rock's Rev. John T. Jenifer, in the Arkansas House of Representatives. In the same House session, black Democrat William Hines Furbush held a seat, followed by B. F. Adair in 1891. Isaac Gillam was elected as Pulaski County coroner in 1888 on a Democrat ticket.[10]

At the forefront of a new drive for black representation in the Democratic Party of Arkansas in 1928 was Dr. John Marshall Robinson. Robinson was born in Pickens, Mississippi, in 1879. He attended Rust College in his home state before graduating from Meharry Medical

College in Nashville, Tennessee, in 1904. Before completing his studies at Meharry, Robinson passed the Arkansas Board of Medical Examiners exam, and from 1901 to 1904 he practiced medicine in Newport, Arkansas. In 1904, Robinson completed his medical studies at Knoxville Medical College in Tennessee. He then returned to Newport and in April 1905 he cofounded, along with Little Rock physician Dr. John G. Thornton, the Pulaski County Medical, Dental, and Pharmaceutical Association. In 1906, Robinson opened a medical practice at Seventh and Main Streets in Little Rock. His ambitions to establish a hospital for the association were thwarted, however, and with no hospitals for blacks at all in the city, he was forced to conduct medical procedures, including operations, in his office.[11]

Robinson's life took an unexpected and dramatic turn in 1911. Although married himself, Robinson was conducting an affair with a married woman in Little Rock. In February 1911, he was confronted by his lover's husband. Robinson shot and killed the man. He received a seven-year sentence for manslaughter, although he was released just two years later, apparently for carrying out pioneering medical work while incarcerated. After his release from jail, Robinson resumed his medical career and in 1918 he, along with three other black physicians, founded Bush Memorial Hospital in Little Rock, which was named after the recently deceased prominent black Republican John E. Bush. The same year, Robinson became a founding member of the Little Rock NAACP branch. In 1919, he began work as assistant surgeon at the Missouri-Pacific Hospital, and between 1927 and 1929 he served as Bush Hospital's chief surgeon. Financial difficulties led to the closure of the hospital in 1929.[12]

There are a number of reasons why Robinson emerged as the forerunner of twentieth-century organized black Democratic support in 1928. At a personal level, he had failed to gain a foothold in the Republican Party, which was dominated by more established members of Little Rock's black elite. Robinson served as an alternate delegate to the Republican state convention in 1926, but the prospect of rising further in the ranks seemed remote, not least because of the taint over his conviction for manslaughter. Moreover, Robinson was from a younger generation than existing black Republicans in the state, most of who had been born under slavery or during Reconstruction. Robinson, who was born in the post-Reconstruction era, was both more likely to be out of touch with the older vanguard of black leaders and more likely to seek political independence from the Republican Party. National developments in 1928, with the groundswell of black support for a Democratic presidential candidate, provided the perfect opportunity for Robinson to blaze a new trail for black politics in Arkansas. The choice of Arkansas's senator Joseph T. Robinson for vice president gave added impetus to the movement by injecting direct local interest in the national Democratic Party ticket that year.[13]

Developments in Little Rock also undoubtedly played a role in Robinson's new initiative. In 1927, the city was the scene of horrific racial violence when a black man, John Carter, was accused of attacking two white women on the outskirts of the city. A white mob hunted down Carter and summarily executed him. They shot a fusillade of over two hundred bullets into Carter's corpse and strapped it to the front of a car, driving it into Little Rock as a trophy. When they reached the city, they tied Carter's dead body to the back of the car with a length of rope and proceeded to parade it around the streets for several hours. The lynching party finally ended on West Ninth Street, at the heart of the city's thriving black downtown business district, where they made a makeshift funeral pyre from pews torn from Bethel AME Church and set it on fire, throwing Carter's body to the flames. The mob, which at one point swelled to over one thousand, only dispersed when Gov. John E. Martineau sent in National Guardsmen to quell the disturbance.[14]

Although the barbaric use violence to assert white supremacy was not unusual in the rural hinterlands of Arkansas, displays of such overt hostility in Little Rock were rare. This was due both to the protection of numbers in the black community and the influence of the city's white business leaders.[15] The desire to repair the harm that many businessmen believed the lynching of Carter had done to the city was apparent in their swift and outright condemnation of the affair. At a meeting the day after the lynching they roundly denounced the "cravenly and criminal act" promising "any amount of money necessary" to bring the perpetrators to light. Meanwhile, the *Arkansas Gazette* lamented that the incident would paint an "unjust" picture of the city, ignoring the "thousands of law-abiding men and women" who distanced themselves from such acts. With suitable protestations of remorse on the front pages of the city's newspapers, and a full investigation underway, the grand jury only met briefly before deciding that there was not enough evidence to bring any convictions.[16]

As the black community took stock of events in the aftermath of the Carter lynching, many decided to leave the city altogether.[17] Robinson sent his own son away from the city for protection, but at the same time he decided that his role was to stay and to take a stand against white oppression. On July 18, 1928, Robinson and two hundred and fifty other blacks met at the fraternal building of the Mosaic Templars of America on West Ninth Street to discuss forming a Smith-Robinson Club in support of the Democratic presidential ticket. It was out of this meeting that the Arkansas Negro Democratic Association (ANDA) emerged, with Robinson as its president. Robinson told the assembled group that their debt to the Republican Party had been paid and that the Democratic Party now offered better prospects for black advancement. Robinson described Alfred E. Smith as "an able governor [of New York] and a four-square man of courage, ability, and statesmanship." His running mate Senator Robinson, Dr. Robinson declared, did not have "a blot against his character," and he had served the state with "dignity and honor."[18] Dr. Robinson and other notable black Little Rock politicians, including P. H. Jordan, Isaac Gillam, F. A. Snodgrass, J. C. Gray, and George G. Walker, drew up a constitution stating ANDA's primary goals as being to: "(a) Unite Negroes who believe in the principles of the Democratic Party and who will work to promote its welfare and expansion; (b) Encourage them to qualify as voters; (c) Educate them in the philosophy of government and the mechanics of voting."[19]

The white-dominated Democratic Party of Arkansas (DPA) was wrong-footed by the formation of ANDA. It did not want to eschew its support, but neither did it, as the party of white supremacy, wish to embrace black Democrats. The Arkansas Democratic State Committee (DSC) declined an invitation to send a representative to ANDA's July 18 meeting, although it did invite Robinson and some other members of ANDA along to its day of celebration in honor of Senator Joseph T. Robinson on August 30 at Hot Springs, Arkansas. The segregated arrangements for black Democrats did not dampen Dr. Robinson's spirits, and he quickly set about creating more Smith-Robinson Clubs around the state.[20]

In an election year, ANDA caused considerable controversy, with all of the state's white political factions looking to distance themselves from the new organization as far as possible. Arkansas Republicans looked to make political capital out of ANDA by charging that Alfred

E. Smith's cronies at Tammany Hall were behind the venture and that they were seeking to introduce black political patronage to the state. While trying to unsettle white voters, Republicans also tried to shore up their existing black support by painting Robinson as an "ex-convict" who represented only "the lower class of negroes," and offering the reassurance that the "better class of negroes" still sensibly remained with them. An anti-Smith group of Arkansas Democrats agreed with the Republicans, asserting that ANDA was an instrument of "Northerners" and "Tammyites," hell-bent on introducing race-mixing to the South. The anti-Smith faction thus used ANDA as a further excuse to temporarily defect and support the impeccable credentials of a lily-white Republican Party under Herbert Hoover. The DPA railed against all of these claims, pointing out that Hoover's nomination had involved black delegates at the Republican National Convention, and that only the Democratic Party could be considered the true "White Man's Party."[21]

In keeping with this promise, on November 26, 1928, white DPA officials turned away ANDA members from the party's primary election polls in Little Rock. In response, Robinson and ANDA sued the DPA for the right to vote. ANDA's attack on the white primary built upon regional developments in black activism initiated by black Democrats in Texas who, aided by the NAACP, won an important ruling before the U.S. Supreme Court in *Nixon v. Herndon* (1927). In the *Nixon* case, the court ruled that state laws preventing black suffrage in the Democratic Party primaries were unconstitutional. This victory, however, proved only a partial triumph, since the court did not rule on the constitutional rights of black voters, but rather on the use of state laws to prevent black voting. This left the way open for state Democratic parties, claiming to be private organizations, to introduce rules preventing black suffrage in party primaries. Since the white primary system in Arkansas was identical to that used in Texas, ANDA sought to clarify and extend the *Nixon* ruling. What ANDA wanted was a court decision that would specifically rule out the use of exclusively white party primaries.[22]

Unlike blacks in Texas, however, black Arkansans found it difficult to enlist the support of the NAACP in their struggle. The local NAACP branch in Little Rock was not particularly active and a number of local indigenous political, civic, and fraternal organizations competed more successfully for membership alongside it. Requests from the city for financial and legal assistance from national NAACP headquarters therefore met with a cool response.[23] Walter White, in a memo about the ANDA lawsuit to Arthur Spingarn, president of the NAACP, declared "[a] reason to feel we should not give much, if anything towards this case . . . [is that] we have never been able to get any considerable support from the state." White concluded, in a pragmatic manner, that "we send say fifty or one hundred dollars as a contribution [so that if] it turns out to be the one on which we get the definitive decision, we will at least have given something."[24]

When Robinson and ANDA took their case to court on November 27, 1928, Judge Richard M. Mann of the Second Division Circuit Court, sitting in the absence of Chancellor Frank H. Dodge in the Pulaski County Chancery Court, upheld an application for an injunction against the DPA to prevent it from barring black voters from their party primaries. The injunction restrained election officials from preventing "persons qualified to vote from exercising their right of franchise in the Democratic City primary . . . on account of race, color, or condition of pervious servitude." Yet Mann still ordered the separation of black and white ballots in primary elections pending an appeal.[25] On August 30, 1929, Chancellor Dodge, having returned to court, again revoked black voting rights. Dr. Robinson fumed that "I and my colleagues have been buffed around in a manner unbecoming of democratic citizens. I feel that we who qualify as Democrats have a right to vote in the primary and that anything less is a reflection upon the integrity and confidence of Democracy in Arkansas."[26] Yet ANDA's appeals to the Arkansas and U.S. Supreme Courts both failed to overturn Dodge's decision.[27]

During the 1930s and 1940s, a significant shift took place in the balance of federal and state power. The New Deal began a process of modernizing the South and brining it economically more into line with the rest of the nation. World War II acted as a further catalyst for change. Wartime army bases that located in the South helped its ailing economy, which President Franklin D. Roosevelt recognized as the nation's "number one economic problem," which he tried to fix with twelve billion dollars of investment. Encroaching industrialization went hand in hand with further black urbanization. Blacks pushed hard to win their share of wartime prosperity not only in the South but nationwide. The threat of a mass march on Washington by black labor leader A. Philip Randolph led to the formation of the Fair Employment Practice Committee by Roosevelt to monitor racial discrimination in employment. Even with its shortcomings, the committee contributed to a tripling in the federal employment of blacks. Hundreds of thousands of blacks enlisted to help fight in the war for democracy. They did so with the firm intention of winning support for what the *Pittsburgh Courier* termed the "double V"—victory at home for democracy and equality, as well as abroad. The NAACP experienced a tenfold growth in membership, and a new civil rights organization, the Congress of Racial Equality, was founded in Chicago and began to experiment with nonviolent direct-action tactics to challenge white supremacy.[28]

After its defeat in the 1928 lawsuit, ANDA lay mostly dormant for over a decade, since its members were more preoccupied with surviving the Depression than seeking voting rights. The organization's main achievement during the 1930s was a campaign for the establishment of black Civilian Conservation Corps camps, which, aided by federal pressure on the state, it successfully helped to secure.[29] It was only really with the new interest in voting rights nationwide as the result of wartime black activism, which was taken up enthusiastically in Arkansas by Pine Bluff-based William Harold Flowers and his new civil rights organization, the Committee on Negro Organizations (CNO), that ANDA made a comeback.[30] In December 1940, Dr. Robinson petitioned the new Democratic State Committee to modify its rules to allow blacks to vote in the DPA primaries. Robert Knox, DSC chair, referred the matter to a subcommittee that decided to shelve the matter indefinitely.[31]

The issue of black voting rights again only resurfaced in Arkansas because of developments at a national level, when *The United States v. Classic* (1941) case came before the U.S. Supreme Court. The case, which concerned fraud in Louisiana primary elections, did not deal directly with racial issues, but it did involve the legal question of the constitutional status of primary elections. The court ruled that discriminatory practices in primary elections "may . . . operate to deprive the voter of his constitutional right of choice." The court therefore concluded, "We think the authority of Congress . . . includes the authority to regulate primary elections."[32]

The *Classic* decision appeared to undermine claims by local and state Democrats across the South that their own private rules should govern primary elections. Certainly, the director-counsel of the NAACP Legal Defense Fund, Thurgood Marshall, regarded the decision as "striking and far reaching" in terms of future possible attacks on the white primary system in the South.[33] Robinson echoed Marshall's sentiments, stating that the ruling "distinctly clarif[ies] our position in the coming political agenda." A letter from ANDA to U.S. Attorney General Francis Biddle asked for his support in allowing black Arkansans their legitimate voting rights as inferred in the court ruling. Robinson informed Biddle that the DPA had ignored a petition to secure such rights.[34]

Meanwhile, white Democrats in Arkansas insisted they would still bar blacks from voting in primary elections. June Wooten, secretary of the Pulaski County Democratic Committee, stated that "Under party rules, they [blacks] can't vote in the primary." Democrat Gov. Homer Adkins likewise insisted that it was "Clearly a matter of party regulations," and that the DPA had the "right to make their own rules." Joe C. Barrett, DSC chair, attempted to pass the buck for implementing the decision, saying that he felt the burden of enforcement lay with election judges and clerks in each voting precinct. Making his own position clear, he added, "party rules speak for themselves in the matter."[35]

Robinson's reply from the U.S. attorney general's office reported that "the denial of the right to Negro voters to participate in the primary elections has been the subject of a series of conferences within this department." Encouraged by the news, and despite the ominous warnings from Democratic officials, Robinson informed ANDA supporters that he expected no trouble at the polls from whites in the forthcoming primary elections. Over one hundred ANDA members gathered at Dreamland Hall on West Ninth Street, at a meeting that was broadcast by Little Rock's KLRA radio station, to make plans for voting. J. H. McConico, ANDA secretary, told the members that ANDA was "not asking pity or any special favors, [but was] simply seeking to exercise those rights and privileges guaranteed to free men in a free country."[36]

The decisive test for the *Classic* ruling came the following Tuesday when the Little Rock city primaries were held. Election officials turned away the first black voter, a Baptist minister, from the polling booth at Peabody High School. They even refused the minister's request simply to view a blank ballot. Similar events occurred throughout the city, with an estimated seventy-five to one hundred blacks denied the right to vote.[37]

After the election, Dr. Robinson filed a report of events to Thurgood Marshall. In a mood of resignation, Robinson wrote: "They [white

Democrats] made their decisions and made it stick. We'll just have to let things cool off for a while until everybody gets level headed again." However, indicative of the influence that support from outside organizations could have on sustaining local black protest, discussions with the NAACP's national office brought a more emboldened statement from ANDA. Robinson declared that if Democrats did not allow blacks to vote in the following Tuesday's second primary, ANDA would appeal to the federal courts for relief. At the same time, Robinson sought to maintain good relations with the DPA. In a letter to Harry Combs, DPA state secretary, he pointed out "We hope you understand that this will be a friendly suit, with no financial or penal objectives." Combs bluntly replied, "The same rule that applies to the first primary applies to the second primary."[38]

As the position of stalemate continued at the local level, it took yet another U.S. Supreme Court ruling three years later to stimulate further action. Soon after the *Classic* ruling, Thurgood Marshall launched a test case in Texas in an attempt to get the courts to apply the new precedent in party primaries to black voting rights. The *Smith v. Allwright* (1944) case, similar to litigation existing in several other southern states, finally came down decisively for black voting rights. The U.S. Supreme Court ruled that the all-white Democratic Party primaries were unconstitutional.[39] June Wooten, secretary of the Pulaski County Democratic Committee, conceded that the *Smith v. Allwright* ruling meant that blacks would be able to vote in federal elections. However, he still refused to admit total defeat. He believed that white Democrats could deny blacks the vote in state elections. Even in the federal elections, at which he conceded that blacks were able to vote, Wooten believed that some semblance of segregation could be maintained by providing separate ballot boxes for black and white voters.[40]

There was some encouragement for Dr. Robinson and ANDA when U.S. Assistant Attorney General Cleveland Holland put forward a more liberal interpretation of the Supreme Court's ruling than Wooten's. Holland emphasized the "state and national" clause of the written judgment in the *Smith* case, which, he said, meant that blacks "may be able to vote for state and local offices" as well as in federal elections.[41] With the backing of the federal government, ANDA held another meeting, this time at Little Rock's black Dunbar High School, to discuss plans for voting in the DPA primaries that summer. In his letter of invitation to the meeting, Robinson expressed confidence that ANDA finally had "a definite understanding with the majority group."[42] Such optimism was borne out by the announcement on May 17, 1944, that the DSC would meet the following morning at the Hotel Marion in Little Rock to amend party rules, allowing full participation by blacks in DPA primaries.[43]

Yet, when the meeting convened, a letter from Governor Adkins informed the DSC that the proposal to remove black voting restrictions "does not coincide with my views in any respect." Moreover, Adkins urged the DSC not to act "as it is entirely a matter for the convention and legislature to settle."[44] In the meantime, Adkins pressed for the initiation of further steps to prevent blacks from voting. Seeking to circumvent the *Smith v. Allwright* decision, in June 1944, just before the summer primaries, Adkins advocated barring black voters on another basis than "that of race or color." What he had in mind, he revealed, was a loyalty clause that would refuse blacks the vote because they had previously been loyal to, and participated in, the Republican Party. Joe C. Barrett, DSC chair, suggested the introduction of further membership qualifications along with procedural mechanisms to prevent blacks from voting.[45]

The Democratic State Convention ratified new measures to prevent the casting of black ballots the following month.[46] Shortly afterward, when Dr. Robinson announced ANDA's support for Governor Adkins at the forthcoming election, Adkins replied curtly that the endorsement was "neither wished or solicited by me." Adkins went on to declare that "the Democratic Party in Arkansas is the white man's party and will be kept so. . . . If I cannot be nominated by the white voters of Arkansas I do not want the office."[47] While the DPA waited for the state to sanction their new party rules, it allowed blacks to vote in the Little Rock city primaries. This right was short-lived. In January 1945, the Arkansas General Assembly passed the Trussell Bill, which ratified changes to DPA membership rules, and the Moore Bill, which initiated a complex segregated "double primary" system to disfranchise black voters. The double primary system provided for city and statewide primaries to exclude blacks, and federal primaries at which blacks could vote, but only at segregated ballot boxes.[48]

Following the public renouncement of Robinson's support, white Democrats contrived a direct personal smear campaign against him to discredit black Democrats. In September 1944, Arkansas Secretary of State C. G. Hall claimed that Robinson was not eligible to vote because of his conviction for manslaughter in 1911. Hall asserted that despite Robinson's early release from jail, the absence of a formal pardon for the offence meant that he could not qualify as a registered voter.[49] The blatant attempt to personally intimidate Robinson worked. In exchange for having his citizenship rights fully restored, Robinson offered not only to resign as the president of ANDA, but also to "permanently cease and terminate all my activities, political or otherwise" linked to the organization.[50] Adkins issued a pardon, but only after the elections had gone by, and he had been successfully reelected as governor. The DPA's harassment of the ANDA leader ensured that no more attempts to assert black voting rights were forthcoming from the organization.[51]

Yet Robinson's and ANDA's efforts were not wholly in vain, since they did ultimately pave the way for the demise of the white DPA primaries. In the postwar years, new black leaders emerged to challenge Little Rock's existing black elite to move beyond the interests of the educated few and to push more forcefully for mass black voting. In the vanguard of this movement was Charles Bussey, who led a band of former World War II servicemen to form the Veterans Good Government Association in direct response to "the way we were being treated by the elders of the city of Little Rock—black and white."[52] Bussey helped to form another new group, the East End Civic League, led by Jeffrey Hawkins, to represent the interests of the run down east end of the city, which held a large number of black residents.[53] These new aspiring black community leaders issued a direct challenge to the way the existing black elite addressed racial issues in the city. Typically new arrivals from rural areas and predominantly drawn from lower-class backgrounds, these new black politicians looked to build upon an enlivened constituency of support for change. By drawing upon the perceived changes in federal sympathy for their struggle at a national level, and the growth in registered black voters in the state, they began to issue new demands for black advancement.[54]

Of direct significance for Robinson was the emergence of I. S. McClinton, who launched a challenge to the ANDA leader's existing claim to be the voice of black Democrats in Arkansas. In November 1949, McClinton helped to form, and became president of, a Young Negro Democrats organization. In May 1950, blacks from seventy-five Arkansas counties met in North Little Rock to discuss voting tactics in DPA primaries that year. Pointedly, Robinson was not informed of the meeting, although he turned up with his supporters in tow, demanding to know why he had been snubbed. William Harry Bass, another of the emergent young guns in the black community, whose influence derived from his links with the Greater Little Rock Urban League, told them that it did not matter "who called the meeting or who the officers were," and that finding a consensus for collective action was far more important. Robinson accepted this, telling those assembled that he had been "mighty angry" when he had first heard about their plans, but that he acknowledged they were acting in "good faith," and that "I want·you to know that I am with you in this effort."[55]

Not everyone in the black community saw the emergence of these new postwar black politicians as beneficial. The *Arkansas State Press,* Little Rock's and Arkansas's leading black newspaper, was deeply skeptical about the possibility of meaningful change in this new era of race relations. The owners of the *Arkansas State Press,* Lucious Christopher (L. C.) Bates and his wife Daisy, complained that some blacks posing as leaders were only interested in their own self-aggrandizement instead of advancing the cause of the race as a whole.[56] At best, the newspaper claimed, they still settled for compromise rather than exerting pressure to bring about an end to the existing system of racial discrimination altogether.[57] As the strongest voice of the black community for wholesale changes to the segregated order, the *Arkansas State Press* echoed the increasingly insistent line of the NAACP that nothing short of a complete end to segregation would suffice. *Arkansas State Press* editorials even went so far as to suggest that the new aspiring black leaders were in fact retarding the black community's progress instead of helping it. By still settling for second best, they were in part to blame for the absence of black "parks, playgrounds, enough Negro police, employment . . . and other lacks."[58]

Significantly, it was precisely the political and legal activism advocated by the *Arkansas State Press* that brought one of the most important victories for the black community during the immediate postwar period in the abolition of the DPA all-white party primaries. In May 1950, black minister Rev. J. H. Gatlin, of Little Rock's Metropolitan Baptist Church, announced his intention to stand as a candidate for election as second ward city alderman in Little Rock. Winning nomination for the post meant running in the local DPA primaries. The initial reaction from June Wooten, secretary of the Pulaski County

Democratic Committee, was that he saw "no way under the rules of the State Committee that a Negro would qualify for a place on the state ballot."[59] To run for office, Gatlin had to pay a filing fee to Wooten. An attempt to do so on June 3 resulted in the return of Gatlin's money. Wooten maintained that Gatlin could not run for office since he was ineligible for membership in the DPA.[60] The final deadline for filing in the city race was June 24. On June 7, Gatlin sent a letter prepared by the legal redress committee of the Little Rock NAACP, headed by L. C. Bates, to DSC members. In his letter, Gatlin requested a rule change that would allow his name to go on to the DPA primary election form. Willis R. Smith, DPA chair, then called a meeting of the DSC for the following Tuesday at the Hotel Marion in Little Rock.[61]

At the meeting on June 13, committee members decided that only the State Democratic Convention had the right to vote upon changes to the DPA constitution. Wooten urged members of the committee to think seriously about their actions since in the light of recent court decisions he believed that Gatlin's case stood every chance of victory. He half-heartedly joked, "if I get in jail, somebody bring me a case of cokes." The meeting adjourned with the decision to put the matter to the convention later in the year, after the party primaries had taken place.[62] In response, L. C. Bates indicated that Gatlin was ready to go to court.[63] On June 17, J. R. Booker, a local attorney, and Ulysses Simpson Tate, NAACP Legal Defense Fund southwest regional attorney, filed Gatlin's suit with the U.S. District Court. The attorneys also requested an injunction preventing the exclusion of Gatlin "or any other person qualified . . . on account of race, color, religion, national origin or any other unconstitutional restriction" from the forthcoming Little Rock DPA city primaries.[64]

On July 5, 1950, Judge Thomas C. Trimble upheld the argument of Gatlin's attorneys. Trimble based his decision on precedents set in recent court rulings and finally clarified the status of the primary election. The primary was, Trimble declared, "an integral part of the state election system . . . tantamount to election at the general election." Furthermore, he continued, "it is not sufficient that a citizen have a token exercise of his right and privilege [to vote]."[65] Gatlin became the first black Arkansan to stand under the DPA banner, although he met with defeat at the election. The court victory prompted other black candidates to file for office in other elections, most notably ANDA's Rev. Fred T. Guy, who unsuccessfully made a bid for a position on the Little Rock school board.[66]

The State Democratic Convention changed its rules to allow full black membership of the DPA later that year. Gov. Sid McMath, in his closing speech, declared that he was "proud, and I know you are proud . . . [that the convention] . . . has said the Negro citizen is enti- tled to the rights and privileges of Party membership." McMath's elec- tion in 1948, and his subsequent reelection in 1950, proved an added boost to the campaign for black voting rights. He was part of a region- wide movement that pressed for reform based on a platform pledging better public health, education, and welfare. Collectively dubbed a "GI Revolt" (McMath was formerly a U.S. Marine and many of the other new southern politicians were also ex-servicemen) this group pro- moted economic growth and industrialization as a cure for southern financial and social ills. The GI politicians also recognized that to make a start on tackling poverty and social backwardness in the South inevitably meant including more progressive race relations in their pro- gram of reform. In contrast to previous conservative governors such as Homer Adkins, McMath's liberal administration proved much more receptive to acting upon federal mandates for tackling southern racial injustice. There was just one voice of dissention at the convention, and that came from Amis Guthridge, the only delegate to cast a "nay" vote to allow black membership in the party. Guthridge told the party con- ference that "Sid McMath is all right but is just a man of the moment. You are going to do something here today that you may regret for years to come." Guthridge resurfaced later in the mid-1950s as one of the leading figures in the Little Rock Capital Citizens' Council, an organization that headed opposition to the 1954 *Brown v. Board of Education* school desegregation decision.[67]

Not long after the convention changed the DPA's membership rules, Robinson announced his retirement from politics. "I am tired," he told ANDA members, "I have spent 25 years fighting for my people. I've done my work."[68] The *Arkansas State Press* agreed, concluding that "ANDA and Robinson has served well, but today, its usefulness is ended."[69] Sure enough, in the contest for Robinson's leadership of ANDA in 1952, the young pretender I. S. McClinton and his supporters finally completed their coup. McClinton was elected as president, ahead of Robinson's preferred successor, Pine Bluff attorney Wiley Branton. McClinton and his supporters immediately changed the name of the organization to the Arkansas Democratic Voters Asso- ciation, dropping the "Negro" to pave the way for its assimilation into the DPA.[70]

From 1928 to 1952, Robinson and ANDA provided a vital bridge of activism between a declining black elite based in Little Rock that was influential in state politics through its ties to the Republican Party, forged during Reconstruction and the post-Reconstruction era, and the emergence of mass black political activism, led by W. H. Flowers and the Committee on Negro Organizations, based in Pine Bluff, Arkansas, that would lay the foundations for the modern-day civil rights struggle in the state. Robinson and ANDA were a curious hybrid of the two eras they connected. Although slightly younger than many of the established black leaders in Little Rock in the 1920s, Robinson appeared to share their faith in an ability to work with the white political power structure in the state for black advancement. Likewise, he believed that it was the job of the educated few to represent the black masses and to determine what was in their best interests. Nevertheless, Robinson's efforts to win representation for blacks in the Democratic Party was a truly radical and visionary concept in its day that presaged later local, state, regional, and national developments. Robinson was the first person in Little Rock to seek redress in the courts for black civil rights and to cultivate the assistance of the national NAACP in doing so, both of which were important path-breaking new directions in black activism in the city. It would, admittedly, take a new, bolder, and more assertive generation of black activists to realize the full potential of black voting rights, and further court litigation in the pursuit of more far-reaching racial change. But it was Robinson and ANDA who signaled the way and took the first steps in that direction and in that they proved to be pioneers in the ongoing struggle for freedom and equality in the state.

4

Mass Mobilization and the Early Civil Rights Struggle

"He Founded a Movement": W. H. Flowers, the Committee on Negro Organizations and Black Activism in Arkansas, 1940–1957

Since the 1980s historians of the civil rights movement have moved beyond the exploration of national events, figures and organizations, which much of the initial body of literature addressed, toward a probing of local developments, assessing their impact upon the dramatic social upheavals taking place between the mid-1950s and mid-1960s in American society. These studies have helped set a new agenda of issues. In particular, the growing number of community studies has highlighted the inadequacy of the existing chronology of the civil rights movement. Tracing the origins of black protest back into the 1930s and 1940s, they have stressed that an understanding of developments in those decades is fundamental to fully comprehending changes that occurred in later years.[1]

Building upon work already done in uncovering local movements elsewhere, this essay focuses on the rich and vibrant history of black protest in Arkansas. More specifically, it seeks to highlight the role of W. H. Flowers and the Committee on Negro Organizations (CNO) in the continuing struggle for black rights. At a time when the National Association for the Advancement of Colored People (NAACP) was reluctant to offer help, the CNO emerged as the premier focus for encouraging organized direct-action protest in the state. This essay traces the development of the organization, its changing strategies and agendas, and locates its local campaigns in the context of the New Deal and World War II. Also, the essay explores the complex relationship between Flowers, the CNO, and other centers of power, protest and influence in the state, as efforts were made to assemble a united black front in an "organization of organizations."[2] Above all, it seeks to consider the ways in which Flowers and the CNO established precedents and served as catalysts for civil rights activities that captured national attention only in later years. Both in the way they laid the groundwork for later direct-action protests and challenged black perceptions of themselves and their capacity to resist Jim Crow at the time, Flowers and the CNO played a vital role in the story of black protest in Arkansas.

On March 10, 1940, at the Buchanan Baptist Church in Stamps, Arkansas, six young professional men sat on a raised platform in front of a gathered assembly of around two hundred blacks. These men formed the core of the CNO. W. H. Flowers, a young lawyer and driving force behind the initiative, stood to speak. He charged that there was a "blackout of democracy" in Arkansas. There was, he claimed, no adequate organization to serve the needs of its Negro citizens, to publicize and stand up against the daily racial injustices they were forced to encounter. Realizing the magnitude of the task in filling such a void, Flowers expressed the belief that the young leadership of the CNO possessed "enough brain power and courage to revolutionize the thinking of the people of Arkansas."[3]

William Harold Flowers had been born in Stamps in 1911, son of a businessman and a schoolteacher. His family belonged to a professional elite that formed the upper echelon of black society there. Writer Maya Angelou, who grew up in the same town, referred to Flowers's grandmother as the "aristocrat of Black Stamps."[4] Inspiration to pursue a legal career came early. Trips as a child with his father to watch jury trials at the courthouse had given him his "first peep into the judicial system." Later, at the age of sixteen, he was given an insight into another side of southern justice. On a visit to Little Rock, he witnessed the burning of a lynched black man, John Carter, on the main black downtown business throughfare, on a funeral pyre built with pews plundered from a nearby black church. It was at this sight, he would recall in later years, that he was "truly converted to be a lawyer."[5]

Graduating from Robert H. Terrell Law School in Washington,

D.C., Flowers returned to Arkansas, setting up a practice at Pine Bluff in 1938. Young, eager, and idealistic, with his first-hand experiences of southern injustices toward blacks, from the outset he wished to use his legal talents to further the cause of the race there. Originally, he wanted to work through the NAACP. In October of 1938, Flowers wrote to Walter White, president of the NAACP, emphasizing the fact that Arkansas badly needed organization and leadership, and that it was a fertile field for NAACP activity. Flowers stated that he had returned to his home state "to practice law and render a distinct service to my people." He wished to have the job of organizing Arkansas blacks anew, but needed financial backing for his endeavors. As a novice lawyer, just starting out in practice, he could barely afford to give away time while building up his new business.[6]

No offers of help from the central offices of the NAACP were forthcoming. Instead, further communications came trying to appease Flowers's frustrations. A letter from Charles Houston, one of the NAACP's leading attorneys, empathized with the situation in Arkansas and recognized the fact that Flowers could not take time out of his office without due recompense. However, he also explained that the NAACP worked through local volunteers, which prevented branches from turning into financial rackets. He admitted that this meant protests were sporadic and relied upon the efforts of a few dedicated individuals, but this was the way the NAACP chose to work. Thurgood Marshall, another aspiring NAACP attorney, writing soon after, conceded the fact that not much progress had been made concerning the organization of Arkansas and advised that the matter be left in abeyance until the next NAACP national conference.[7]

The ambivalent attitude of the NAACP had grown out of previous dealings with the state. The first local branch had been established in 1918 at Little Rock.[8] One of the most celebrated cases of the NAACP's early history, the defense of twelve prisoners sentenced to death for their alleged role in the Elaine Race Riot, followed the year after. A lengthy and expensive five years of litigation finally brought a custodial rather than a death sentence for the twelve convicted men.[9] Arkansas's abysmal lynching record meant that there were many more forays for the NAACP into the state. Yet beyond the efforts of a few dedicated black female secretaries, most notably Mrs. Carrie Sheppherdson, who won the Madam C. J. Walker Gold Medal in 1925 for her outstanding fundraising drive, there was very little interest in NAACP activities.[10] As Mrs. H. L. Porter summed up in 1933, "the lawyers, Doctors, preachers and businessmen . . . are just a bunch of egotistic discussers and not much on actual doings," adding that they were "a very slow bunch in turning loose a little money."[11]

Largely, the lack of interest in the NAACP was down to the fact that many local organizations seemed to offer a better forum for racial advancement. The Mosaic Templars of America provide an outstanding case in point. Established in 1882 by John Bush and Chester Keats, two members of Little Rock's black middle class, the organization acted as a fraternity-cum-insurance agency. At the height of its success in 1924 it boasted a membership of 108,000 people in 24 states and combined assets of $280 000. The Templar building, a four-story and particularly ornate downtown edifice, offered a central meeting place for many of the black professional, civic, political, religious, and fraternal associations in the city. In that building, the NAACP occupied one room among many other groups dedicated to advancing the cause of black citizens.[12]

One of the rare applications for NAACP help came in 1928 from Dr. J. M. Robinson, head of the Arkansas Negro Democratic Association, in what turned out to be an unsuccessful challenge to the all-white Democratic Party primary elections. From the outset the NAACP was reluctant to help. The group thought that too much money was being asked to fund the lawsuit, besides which, similar cases were also being argued in Virginia and Texas at the time. But, in a memo to Arthur Spingarn at the head office "another reason to feel that we should not give much, if anything, towards this case" was that "Despite all the money we have spent in the Arkansas cases . . . we have never been able to get any considerable support from the state. For example, the Little Rock branch sent to the National Office during 1928 only $48, and this year only $44.25." A concluding recommendation suggested that "we send say fifty or one hundred dollars as a contribution towards this case so that in the event that it turns out to be the one on which we get the definitive decision, we will at least have given something."[13]

The 1930s increased the need for NAACP assistance. The Depression hit home hard among the black middle classes, heralding the end of many successful enterprises like the Mosaic Templars. By the end of the decade, not only was there a lack of finances to sustain local organizations, but also a new agenda of concerns had moved beyond their capacity to handle. Although the majority of blacks had been hit harder by economic upheaval than the black elite, the potential for change that had been glimpsed in the New Deal, albeit still limited by segregation and discrimination, brought new optimism and raised hopes for further black advancement.

Looking to build upon the promise of change that the New Deal had brought, an enlivened constituency of support for a more aggressive pursuit of black rights developed through the war years. Yet in spite of a potential base for mass support, there was a distinct lack of direction and leadership in the state for such a movement. An entrenched conservative elite still wielded considerable influence and still dominated organizational activities. Compounding these problems was the continuing lack of NAACP interest in the state, which might have given outside help in tackling the local stagnancy of black protest. By 1940 only six local branches existed in Arkansas, with a membership of not more than six hundred people.[14] It was the problem of bridging an activist agenda with a conservative leadership, in the absence of outside help, which Flowers and the CNO sought to address. Half a generation younger than the older, established leadership, this group of professionals recognized the need to harness the support of the masses to bring benefits for the whole of the black population.

By the time the NAACP had rebuffed all requests for help, Flowers had decided he could wait no longer for them to act. At the meeting on March 10 in Stamps, an independent CNO platform had been adopted. The CNO *Spectator,* a bimonthly fly-sheet that kept citizens informed of the group's activities, heralded this platform as the "most forward looking ever . . . touching every field of social activity." The program stated that the CNO's purpose was to provide a "single organization sufficient to serve the social, civic, political and economic needs of the people." It stood for the rights of Negroes to have a say in the government they supported, to fight "un-American activities . . . enslaving the Negro people" and to devise a "system of protest" to remove them. It also outlined its particular areas of concern, which were in education, politics, health, housing, jobs, equal opportunities in the armed forces and wartime industries, provision of truly "equal" facilities for Negroes, and a fair allocation of farm benefits to help remove the "existing evils" in the landlord-tenant relationship. Within each broad area the CNO had specific aims. For example, in education there were demands for equalizing school facilities, equalizing teachers' salaries, and equalizing graduate opportunities, along with calls to appoint Negroes to policymaking boards at state and local levels.[15]

The cornerstone of the CNO's program was to secure widespread, organized political participation. Only through raised political awareness and activity could blacks gain the leverage with the white power structure to have their demands enforced. In Arkansas, unlike many other southern states, blacks were not denied the franchise at general elections. Through the payment of a one dollar poll tax they were eligible to cast their vote. However, since Arkansas was ruled by the Democratic Party, it was the vote in their primary elections that determined who held office.[16] The general election was provided only for the ratification of a usually unopposed Democratic nominee. Blacks were prevented from voting in these primary elections on the grounds that the Democratic Party was a private organization that could draw up its own racially exclusive membership rules.

Attempts at securing black political participation had been in progress since Reconstruction. Scipio Jones had fought a long battle against "lily white" factions in the Republican Party to maintain a black political voice there. In 1928, Dr. J. M. Robinson had filed a lawsuit against local Democrats in order for blacks to gain a say in that party.[17] However, all previous attempts had been by middle-class leaders who wished to win representation in politics so that the educated few, like themselves, could exercise a voice in the parties on behalf of their race. Moreover, this political voice had always been seen as a way of articulating grievances but never actually issuing a wholesale challenge to existing inequalities. Flowers, even though he was a staunch Republican, was attempting to go beyond party politics. He proposed the creation of an independent mass black political organization, representative of the whole of the black population, as a way of tackling the common problems they all faced.

The first step toward political participation was payment of the poll tax. Once blacks began to purchase poll tax receipts and turn up on election day to vote, showing there was an interest and awareness of voting rights among the black population, then it would be easier to challenge white Democrats and push for equal rights. To attain the goal of a mass political mobilization, organization would be needed. This reached the very essence of the CNO's sense of mission. Its central platform was "to seek the endorsement of Negro church, civic, fraternal and social organizations."[18] Only by bringing about unity and direction of purpose, and exerting the sheer strength of numbers in a statewide representative body, could the task of raising a political consciousness be effectively carried out. This would mean creating a coalition in an "organization of organizations," pooling individual and group bases of influence throughout the state. Thus the whole program hinged upon the CNO's ability to gain a wide base of recognition and support throughout the black community.

Although the "independent" program of the CNO was essentially the same as that put forward by the NAACP at the time, it set itself apart in one very important aspect in that it was entirely community oriented. As the NAACP concentrated on winning court rulings that would have a national impact, the CNO focused on the immediate needs of those living in Arkansas. Consequently, the program was attuned specifically to meet local needs and requirements. No one knew these better than W. H. Flowers, and perhaps no one was quite so well equipped to tackle them. Flowers's father had been not only a businessman, but also a leading Mason. His mother was a schoolteacher. He was a lawyer. All had strong links to the church. Theirs was a well-respected and well-known black Arkansas family. With a working, first-hand knowledge of how power was structured in the black community in Arkansas, and direct links to its various strands, Flowers knew just which channels to work through and where success for his endeavors would come from.

After the Stamps meeting, Flowers set off on a speaking tour of the state to raise the profile of the CNO and to muster support from grassroots organizations in the various communities. To do this meant tapping into, harnessing, and redeploying the already existing centers of influence, which resided in different institutions, organizations, and individuals in different places. On April 7, 1940, under the sponsorship of the Hope Interdenominational Ministerial Alliance in southern Arkansas, around three hundred blacks turned out to hear the CNO program explained. The message was reported as "enthusiastically received." At Postelle, in eastern Arkansas, on April 14, approximately six hundred people listened to a meeting held under the auspices of the local branch of the NAACP. On April 16 the Negro Business Club of Morrilton sponsored a mass meeting in central Arkansas of over two hundred citizens. On May 5, the Lewisville Negro Taxpayers Association in southern Arkansas acted as hosts. There, more than two hundred and fifty persons pledged their support to the program. Although not under the direct guidance of the CNO, similar meetings were held throughout the state.[19]

These meetings culminated in the "First Conference on Negro Organization," on September 27, 1940, held at Lakeview Junior High School, a recently completed New Deal project. Located in the Arkansas Delta, the conference exposed the CNO to graphic demonstrations of the kinds of inequalities against which it was fighting. Difficulties were encountered from the outset. The chairman of the local school board, Lester Wolfe, ordered Farm Security Administration officials to prevent the meeting from taking place, claiming he had been "misled" about its true purpose. In spite of black local leaders from the NAACP calling for the conference to be cancelled because of the possibilities of angering whites, Flowers stood his ground and proclaimed that the meeting would take place "even if we have to use the banks of the lake which borders this *United States Government* project."[20]

Local white officials eventually relented and the meeting went ahead. At his opening address, Flowers told the crowd that they were meeting to "devise a program of action" to combat discrimination against Negroes "merely because of the color of their skin." He spoke of organizing Arkansas's half-million Negroes through a program of definite aims and objectives, with a leadership pledged to carry them out. "For six months we have obtained the endorsement of twenty-one organizations with a numerical strength of approximately ten thousand Negro citizens," he informed them. Further, he outlined the achievements of the CNO to date. Thirty-five investigations had been carried out over color discrimination in public works employment. It had brought about the removal of a ban in Jefferson County that prevented blacks from participating in opportunities provided by the National Youth Administration. It had also been responsible for the appointment of a black census enumerator in St. Francis County. Sixteen mass meetings had been carried out successfully, with a total attendance of over four thousand people.[21]

After a successful three-day conference, speaking dates continued. On January 1, 1941, Flowers spoke to the White County chapter of the Lincoln Emancipation League, and urged them to build an organization that would be "truly representative of the people." Moving on to the Salem Baptist Church, he warned that, echoing the NAACP's national slogan, "A voteless people is a hopeless people." Explicitly drawing upon the fight against racism in Europe, and America's possible entry into the World War II, he declared that "the success of our effort to make democracy a way of life for the peoples of the world must begin at home, not after a while, but now." He blamed the existing leadership of professionals, preachers, and businessmen for "the inaction on the part of citizens voting at elections in Arkansas," particularly lambasting "the pussyfooting educators on the public pay roll, who are only submissive to those responsible for their jobs."[22]

Speeches continued throughout the year in a statewide effort to mobilize support. Poll-tax drives began in September 1941 to meet the October 1 deadline for voter qualification. Under the direction of the CNO, Dr. Roscoe C. Lewis, a physician from Hope, promoted poll-tax purchases in southern Arkansas. W. L. Jarrett, an undertaker from Morrilton, supervised in northern Arkansas. Attesting to the ever-expanding base of CNO support, more and more organizations began to assist in the campaign. Among them were the Warren, Phillips County, and Postelle branches of the NAACP; the Morrilton Business Club; the Conway Negro Business League; the El Dorado and St. Francis Negro Civic Leagues; the Lewisville Negro Taxpayers Association; the Camden, Menifee, Crossett, Dermott, and Fort Smith indigenous CNO organizations; the Tau Phi Chapter, Omega Psi Phi fraternity; the Order of the Eastern Star and the Free and Accepted Masons of Arkansas; the Bethlehem District Association of the Missionary Baptist Church; the Phillips, Lee, Monroe, and Desha District Baptist Associations; the Middle Western District Baptist Association; and the Texarkana and Brinkley Negro Chambers of Commerce.[23]

"Drive To Increase Race Votes Is Successful," read the headline in the *Arkansas State Press*, the state's leading black newspaper. A record turnout at the polls was expected.[24] Emboldened by this expectation, the CNO petitioned Gov. Homer Adkins to assist Negro graduate students who were denied an education in Arkansas because the state did not provide graduate school facilities for blacks. "We direct your attention to the growing unrest on the part of the Negro race," Flowers wrote to Adkins. "They no longer are willing to remain on their knees begging for the rights, privileges and immunities of American citizenship."[25] Adkins passed the issue to the State Department of Education, which suggested using the latest increase in funds at Pine Bluff Agricultural, Mechanical, and Normal, Arkansas's only publicly funded black college, to pay for out-of-state scholarships. With the implementation of this plan left to college trustees, no action was taken. Dissatisfied with this, Flowers called together influential Negro educators from throughout the state for a conference with state commissioner of education Ralph B. Jones. A few weeks later, the first of fourteen one hundred dollar awards that year was given to Flowers' brother, Cleon A. Flowers, to help with his studies at Meharry Medical College in Tennessee.[26]

After two years of persistent effort, the CNO could claim a number of concrete achievements. In the same year that the *Arkansas State Press* printed Flowers's photograph with the caption "He Founded a Movement," one of the most important of these, and one of the biggest steps forward for black rights in the state to date, was being taken.[27] In March 1942, Sue Morris, a black Little Rock schoolteacher, initiated a court suit for the right to be paid the same salary as white teachers in the district. It proved to be the first successful attempt by blacks in Arkansas to win equal rights through the courts.[28] Flowers had particularly entreated the teachers, as one of the oldest and strongest of the professional associations in Arkansas, to take a bolder stance in the active pursuit of black rights, and he had regularly chastised them for being more concerned with "dress than redress."[29]

The success of the teachers' salary suit acted as the catalyst for further initiatives that would have a profound effect on the unfolding struggle for civil rights in Arkansas. Thurgood Marshall was in town for the case and his presence raised the profile of the NAACP there. With such a renowned national figure visiting Little Rock, a new interest was awakened in the organization and, according to reports from the local branch secretary, membership dues had taken a dramatic upswing. "He sure did shoot them some straight dope as to their part and membership to be played in the NAACP cause," declared Mrs. H. L. Porter. "Then and there at that meeting we collected $68.50 in membership."[30] In response to this rising local interest—and more money coming in—the national NAACP headquarters began, in turn, to take more of an interest in the state. By 1945 an Arkansas State Conference of branches (ASC) had been created. Soon afterward W. H. Flowers took charge of its statewide recruitment drives.[31]

The year before the ASC came into existence, the U.S. Supreme Court's ruling in *Smith v. Allwright* (1944) outlawed the all-white Democratic Party primaries, which had previously prevented blacks from exercising a meaningful vote at elections. Although white Arkansas

Democrats tried to preserve racial exclusion by instituting a complex system of "double primaries," in which local and state primaries remained segregated, while those for federal office did not, the expense, plus the time-consuming, cumbersome, and bureaucratic procedures involved, soon led to its collapse.[32]

Because of the work of Flowers and the CNO, when blacks could finally reap the benefits of the vote in the late 1940s, they started to do so in significant numbers. From a base level of 1.5 percent of voting-age blacks registered in 1940, the number had expanded to 17.3 percent by 1947.[33] Through poll-tax drives, voter education, and raising political awareness, the CNO had already paved the way for blacks to have an immediate impact on elections.

The CNO gradually became a victim of its own successes. Along with the NAACP moving into the state, the political empowerment of the black community gave rise to a new set of local organizations dedicated to mobilizing the vote and using it as a tool with which to carve direct concessions from the white community. For example, in Little Rock, Charles Bussey's Veterans Good Government Association and Jeff Hawkins's East End Civic League used a black block vote to pressure white politicians into improving street-lighting, roads, and sidewalks in their communities. They also managed to win bond money from the city for the construction of a new black park. These groups, riding on the rising tide of black activism that had been set in motion by Flowers across the state, began to focus on translating a raised political consciousness into action and into concrete gains on a day-to-day basis in their own communities.

Flowers continued as a pioneer in his own right. In the *Wilkerson v. State* (1947) case provided the crowning glory of his legal career. In the case, two black men stood accused of killing two white men. Normally this meant an automatic death sentence. However, in this instance, Flowers managed to get their sentences commuted to jail terms. At the same trial Flowers demanded, and received, some black jurists to sit in on the case, the first time this had happened in Jefferson County since Reconstruction. These achievements were even more remarkable given the fact that Flowers was one of the few black lawyers in the state at the time to represent his clients alone without the counsel of a white lawyer, thereby flaunting established court racial etiquette. Wiley Branton, a leading light in the CNO and later, in the 1960s, executive director of the Southern Regional Council's regionwide Voter

Education Project, recalled that the case had "a major impact on the view of black people . . . that maybe there is justice after all."[34]

In 1948, Flowers personally handled the admission of Silas Hunt to the law school at the University of Arkansas, Fayetteville. Not only was this the first time a black student had attended classes with white students in Arkansas, it was the first time such a situation had existed anywhere in the South since Reconstruction.[35] The following year, Flowers brought the first school case to trial in Arkansas, when he petitioned the De Witt school board to equalize facilities for black and white students. The judgment handed down in favor of the plaintiffs stated that facilities should be equalized "within a reasonable amount of time."[36] The wording of the judgment foreshadowed the same ambiguity of the "with all deliberate speed" clause of the U.S. Supreme Court's *Brown v. Board of Education* implementation order of 1955. The case drew the battle lines for the many courtroom battles over school desegregation in Arkansas that would continue in the decades ahead.

Along with this career of personal achievement, Flowers continued his struggle with the forces of black conservatism within the state. When the NAACP instituted the ASC in 1945, they put Rev. Marcus Taylor of Little Rock in charge of operations, while allowing Flowers to pursue a role as organizer of new branches. Quite early, the mutual antipathy which existed between the two became clear. With no establishment of communications between Little Rock and Pine Bluff, Rev. Taylor began to accuse Flowers of financial wrong-doings, suggesting that he was keeping half of the funds collected from new NAACP branches.[37] Although funds were generally slow in making their way to national headquarters, an investigation into Flowers's activities gave no reason to relieve him of his duties.[38]

In fact, it seemed that activists were beginning to gain an upper hand in the state. In 1948, Flowers was elected as president of the ASC after building up the Pine Bluff NAACP branch to 4,382 members, by far the largest in the state. "I will admit that I may have underrated Pine Bluff and its leadership," wrote Lucille Black, NAACP national membership secretary.[39] When Donald Jones, NAACP regional secretary, attended the ASC meeting in 1948, he reported that spirits were "high and militant." He concluded that "Largely responsible for the fine NAACP consciousness in Pine Bluff and the growing consciousness in the state is Attorney Flowers, who's success in the Wilkerson case and tremendous energy have made him the state's acknowledged leader."[40]

Later the same year in Little Rock, Daisy Bates filed an application to form a "Pulaski County Chapter of the NAACP."[41] The move came out of disillusionment with the local Little Rock branch, which was still in the grip of Rev. Marcus Taylor. The Bateses were good friends with Flowers and came from the same activist ilk. Flowers had written in the *Arkansas State Press* under his grandmother's name of Frances Sampson and considered the Bateses' home his place of residence while in Little Rock. The *Arkansas State Press* provided an effective forum for the dissemination of an activist agenda and reports on the CNO had appeared from the founding of the newspaper in 1941. In response to the application for a new NAACP branch, the head office tried to reconcile the differences between the two existing factions by pointing out that a branch in Little Rock was already operating and suggesting that members wishing to help join up there.[42]

In 1949, the issue of finances reared its head again. The ASC defaulted on its contribution toward the southwest regional conference fund. In response, regional secretary Donald Jones recommended that Flowers be given the choice of either resigning from office or dismissal.[43] The Pine Bluff branch then issued a proclamation deploring the "unrest, discord and disunity now existent in NAACP activities in Arkansas." Moreover, it recommended that the ASC withdraw from the NAACP altogether, to concentrate upon pressing local matters that needed attention. It also suggested that monies already collected be used to fund local battles instead of going to out-of-state concerns.[44] Only after strong letters from leading figures in the NAACP, pleading for the Pine Bluff branch to reconsider its actions, did local activists repent. Disillusioned, Flowers resigned from office.[45]

Flowers was replaced by Dr. J. A. White of Warren, Arkansas. But the resentment of activists still continued to be voiced. Lulu B. White, of the Texas State Conference of branches, reported that "no place in the country is there so much strife and division amongst Negroes as [there] is in Arkansas." Commenting on attitudes there, she wrote that "They say that the work of the NAACP is in charge of a few favorites in the state, who are Lackies, what ever that is, for New York, and New York is not worth a D— to them."[46]

In 1951, Dr. White fell ill and resigned his position. W. L. Jarrett, who had been one of the principal workers in the CNO poll-tax campaigns of the 1940s, became temporary president of the ASC.[47] In 1952, Daisy Bates succeeded him. Ulysses Simpson Tate, NAACP southwest regional attorney, voiced concerns over Bates's election, questioning her ability to work with the existing leadership and raising concerns that she "tends to go off the deep end at times." He concluded, "I am not certain that she was the proper person to be elected [but] I permitted it because there was no one else to be elected who offered any promise of doing anything to further the work of the NAACP in Arkansas."[48]

Bates's election to head the ASC was the culmination of a long struggle. Finally, an activist, who also had a base in the state capital at Little Rock, was leading the NAACP in Arkansas. Bates was therefore in a better position to take on conservative elements within the organization and among black leadership in the state by introducing a more forthright agenda for black advancement. The very year of Bates's election, the first negotiations with white school board members over the desegregation of schools in Little Rock commenced. After a breakdown in talks, Bates was ready for the local NAACP branch to file a lawsuit, but the national office advised her to wait on the outcome of other suits pending in the courts at the time.[49] One of these cases eventually led to the landmark 1954 *Brown v. Board of Education* school desegregation ruling in the U.S Supreme Court.

Although the Little Rock school board had been one of the first to move toward compliance with the *Brown* decision, it soon began to backtrack on its initial plans. The starting date for integration was moved back. Then provisos were added, like the building of new segregated black and white schools in different parts of the city before Central High, near downtown, could be desegregated. By February of 1956 the school board's claims to be acting in "good faith" had worn thin. Daisy Bates, along with an aspiring young black lawyer from the Pine Bluff group of activists, Wiley Branton, formulated a lawsuit to challenge the school board's plans. After a year of wrangling through the courts a ruling was eventually handed down ordering the school board to go ahead with plans to integrate Central High School at the beginning of the fall term on September 3, 1957.[50]

On the evening of September 2, the night before term was about to begin, Arkansas Gov. Orval Faubus surrounded Central High School with National Guardsmen. The next morning as lone black student Elizabeth Eckford tried to enter the school the armed guard turned her away and a gathered white mob began to harass her. Pictures of the scene were relayed all over the world via television and newspaper photographs. Events raised not only a national, but also an international outcry. Only after negotiations broke down between Governor Faubus and President Eisenhower did the latter reluctantly federalize the National Guard and send in the troops of the 101st Airborne unit to uphold the forces of law and order. Finally, under a federal, armed escort, nine black students entered Central High School on September 23, 1957.

Yet as the cameras moved away from Little Rock after the events of 1957, and on to the next dramatic story to capture national attention in the battle for civil rights, the local struggle continued. At the end of the year, Governor Faubus closed all the city's schools. Two years of bitter infighting ensued before they were reopened on an integrated basis in August 1959. Even then, much still remained to be done. Segregation continued to exist at lunch counters, movie theaters, golf courses, parks, swimming pools, and a whole range of other public and private facilities. Blacks still faced discrimination when applying for jobs or obtaining housing, among other forms of prejudice that bolstered the Jim Crow system. The school crisis had been the culmination of one particular phase of the ongoing fight for black rights, but it had also marked the beginnings of another phase, which would bring with it new demands for more wide-ranging changes to take place and a new set of tactics to achieve its goals. Heading into the 1960s, another younger generation of activists was ready to take its place in the continuing story of black protest in Arkansas.

5

Gender and the Civil Rights Struggle

*Daisy Bates, the NAACP, and the Little Rock
School Crisis: A Gendered Perspective*

One glaring omission from Vicki Crawford and associates' land-mark volume *Women in the Civil Rights Movement* is an in-depth look at Daisy Bates's role in the struggle for civil rights.[1] As a central participant in the 1957 Little Rock school integration crisis and head of the Arkansas State Conference of branches of the National Associa-tion for the Advancement of Colored People (NAACP), Bates became one of the earliest women activists in the movement to gain national recognition. Bates won numerous awards and honors from national organizations for her courage in the Little Rock crisis and subse-quently worked for the Democratic National Committee and in Presi-dent Lyndon Johnson's Great Society poverty programs in Washington, D.C. Surely this distinguished career deserves more than the meager two pages of analysis provided in Crawford and colleagues' otherwise wide-ranging book.[2]

One major reason for the absence of an adequate treatment of Bates's civil rights activism is the approaches to women's history that various authors writing in Crawford's book take. Broadly speaking, these fall into two categories. On the one hand there are essays writ-ten from a "contributionist" perspective.[3] This involves writing histo-ries of *what* women, as individuals and as members of institutions and organizations, contributed to traditional patriarchal histories that typically take as their central focus the role played by men and men's organizations.[4] On the other hand, work such as Charles Payne's offers a sociological perspective that seeks to probe deeper into the *how* and *why* of women's participation in the civil rights movement. Payne, for example, seeks to explain the high level of female participation in the movement, analyzing factors such as demographics, religiosity, and the function of social and kinship networks in influencing women's activism.[5] Working in a similar vein, Belinda Robnett has offered an even more analytically rigorous framework for looking at the roles played by women in the movement.[6]

Daisy Bates's brand of activism does not seem to easily fit into either of these approaches. From a contributionist perspective there seems little need to "restore" Bates to the historical record since she is already plainly visible in the more traditional patriarchal histories of the civil rights movement.[7] Since Bates is presented as the "leader" of the Little Rock black community during the school crisis, traditionally prescribed as a "masculine" role, this ensures her place in a traditionally masculine gendered history. From a sociological perspective, Bates does not fit into the framework of analysis that has typically examined the role of the "majority" of women in the civil rights movement who operated largely in traditionally defined "feminine" roles, such as organizers, supporters, and nurturers through women's social and kinship networks. Bates, therefore, appears to fall between the methodological cracks of studies of women in the civil rights movement.

This essay seeks to provide a gender perspective on Daisy Bates's activism that attempts to overcome the limitations of existing contributionist and sociological approaches, while incorporating their valuable insights. Taking as its base a contributionist perspective by focusing on one particular individual, it also seeks to apply a sociological perspective at a personal rather than group level in order to look at why and how Bates's experiences as a woman were important within the context of the segregated South.

What is immediately striking about the documentation of Bates's life through her personal papers, her memoir *The Long Shadow of Little Rock,* newspaper articles, film footage, and photographs, is the massive imbalance between what we know about her public and personal life.[8] Bates's public career is almost exclusively foregrounded, whereas much of her personal life remains elusive. Few scholars of the civil rights movement are probably aware, for instance, that Daisy and her husband Lucious Christopher (L. C.) Bates had a foster son living with them from 1951 to 1957, who they were forced to return to his former family in order to escape the violence directed at the Bateses' home during the school crisis.[9] Neither are the strains in the marriage between Daisy and L. C. Bates, as a result of the school crisis—which led their divorce and remarriage in 1962—apparent in most commentaries.[10] Yet surely these intense personal traumas make up a significant part of the broader picture of Daisy Bates's public life. As Sara Evans has suggested, the distinction between the "personal" and "political" (or "public") sphere is an artificial construct and what happens in one cannot easily be separated from what happens in the other.[11]

Our lack of knowledge about Bates's personal life is partly because of historians having imposed their own (typically masculine) reading of her role in the movement and concluded that what is important about Bates is her role in public life. This has led to historians ignoring or marginalizing how Bates experienced the civil rights movement on a personal level. The situation has been reinforced by the fact that Bates's own accounts of her activism, most notably in her memoir, do not challenge but rather reflect the assumption that her public persona is somehow privileged above, and more important than, her personal life.

The vast majority of chapters in *The Long Shadow of Little Rock* comprise a narrative by Bates about events happening around her, but only rarely are those events in the public realm related to her own private life and feelings. There is one notable exception to this, in chapter 2 of her book, entitled "Rebirth." Here, we find the only chapter that Bates devotes entirely to a focus on her personal life and on her own private thoughts and feelings, concerning her relationships, experiences, and interactions with other people, black and white, male and female.[12] Largely ignored by scholars, this chapter provides us with a precious insight into Bates's own reflections and representations of the impact of racism on her life.

Significantly, "Rebirth" deals with Bates's early experiences from childhood in Huttig, Arkansas, through to the death of her father, followed shortly afterward by her marriage to L. C. Bates and their move to Little Rock. It appears that Bates feels more comfortable talking about herself within the context of her "pre-activist" life, before she became joint editor of a crusading newspaper and NAACP leader, since there then remains a clear distinction between her private life in Huttig and her public life as a civil rights activist in Little Rock. Bates seems to offer her early biography merely as a prelude to her more "important" later work, devoting one chapter to it out of a total of sixteen. Yet the chapter provides important insights into Bates's later activism. Embedded within the narrative of Bates's early personal life are indications of the powerful emotions and experiences, particularly with regard to gender, which fundamentally shaped and influenced Bates's later public career as a civil rights leader. For this reason, a discussion of the influence of gender on Bates's later life must be rooted in a close reading of how Bates chooses to represent her earlier experiences of race and gender consciousness.

Bates's chapter "Rebirth" deals with her childhood discoveries about the existence of racism in Huttig during the 1920s and 1930s. At the heart of the chapter is Bates's reaction to the news she learns when just eight years old, that three white men murdered her biological mother when Daisy was just an infant.[13] Shortly afterward, she learns the identity of one of her mother's killers, a local drunkard who hangs around Huttig's downtown square, whom Bates refers to throughout simply as "Drunken Pig." Daisy proceeds to run a war of attrition with "Drunken Pig," constantly tormenting him by her presence for the evil deed he has done. "Drunken Pig" becomes the embodiment of everything that Daisy hates about racism in the South and as such is accorded little status as a person in his own right. Rather, the impact of Daisy's biological mother's death is reflected more in her accounts of other relationships that influenced and shaped her early life.

In Bates's mind there seems little doubt that the most influential relationship in her early years was with her adopted father—although she never actually refers to him as such—Bates always simply calls him "Daddy." Bates's father represents the main source of love, tenderness, comfort, and affection in her early life, notably the kind of emotions more usually associated with a "mother" figure. When Daisy has her first encounter with white hostility at the age of seven, after she is given sub-standard produce at the local white butcher shop because she inadvertently attempts to get service in front of a white girl, it is her father who stops her tears when he "lifted me in his arms and smiled."[14] When Daisy learns of the circumstances of her biological mother's death, it is again her father who is on hand to comfort her. Bates recounts her father saying "'It's time to go home darling' . . . He reached out in the darkness and took my hand . . . He lifted me tenderly in his arms and carried me home."[15] On another occasion, during a walk in the woods near their home, her father tries to explain why her biological mother's death occurred, within the context of the racist South of the time. "He began in tones so soft I could barely hear the words," Bates recalls, revealing, "I was always happy on these excursions with Daddy."[16] Later, when Daisy is coming to terms with the death of Drunken Pig and the final part of her childhood trauma is laid to rest, it is her father who is again on hand: "my daddy heard me crying. He came in to comfort me. He sat on a chair next to my bed and took my hand in his."[17]

This tender and loving relationship between father and daughter is drawn together in a moving scene that closes the chapter when Daisy lends comfort to her father as he dies of cancer. As she tries to deny her father's inevitable death, he raises a hand to stop her. "He knew I knew," Bates recalls, "and to deny it would make meaningless the honesty we'd always held to in our lifelong relationship with each other." On his death bed, Daisy's father passes on to Daisy "a priceless heritage—one that was to sustain me throughout the years to come." Presumably, this heritage rests in an earlier passage where her father delivers his daughter a lesson on hate. "You're filled with hatred," her father warns:

> Hate can destroy you, Daisy. Don't hate white people just because they're white. If you hate, make it count for something. Hate the humiliations we are living under in the South. Hate the discrimination that eats away at the soul of every black man and woman. Hate the insults hurled at us by white scum—and then try to do something about it, or your hate won't spell a thing.[18]

The meaning of this "heritage" is left equivocal. Rather than telling Daisy not to hate, which would presage the nonviolence associated with the civil rights movement, her father appears to advise Daisy not to allow her hatred to become self-destructive. This implies an acceptance of hatred as an emotion that may be turned to good use, a view that is markedly at odds with a message of nonviolence.

On his death bed, Daisy's father laments that he could find no outlet for his smoldering resentment of the humiliations he suffered as a black man in the white South. Before he dies, he recalls one of the most degrading episodes in his life. On the day of Daisy's biological mother's funeral "three young white hoodlums" accosted him and mocked him as a "dressed-up ape" and one of them painted a red stripe down his best suit. He recalls that "if I touched one hair on his head I could be lynched." Helpless, Daisy's father appealed to a deputy sheriff who belittled him, saying that his assailants were "just having a little fun. Turpentine will take the paint out of your coat." With clenched fists, Bates's father's last words to his daughter are: "I ought to have died the day they put paint on my coat. I should have taken those guys and wrung their necks like chickens. But I wanted to live—for what, I sometimes wonder."[19]

Certainly, Daisy Bates inherits her father's resentment. Her deep-felt affection for her father only serves to increase her anguish that he was never able to stand up against whites as the "real" man he so yearned to be. Bates laments:

How I loved this strong man who all his life had not been able to use his strength in the way he wanted to. He was forced to suppress it and hold himself back, bow to the white yoke or be cut down. And now that his life was ebbing, he was trying to draw on that reservoir of unused strength to give me a lasting inheritance.[20]

Hand in hand with the legacy of her father's tenderness, throughout the text there is an ever-present empathy with the demoralization and anger her father felt at never being able to achieve full "manhood" on an equal basis with whites. After the episode at the butcher shop, when he has comforted Daisy and she finally tells him what has happened to upset her, "his smile faded . . . I could feel his muscles tighten as he carried me into the house."[21] Later, when he tries to explain "the words just wouldn't come. I stood there, looking at him and wondering why he was acting so strangely. Finally he stood up and the words began tumbling from him." With Daisy still unable to fully comprehend, her father

dropped to his knees in front of me, placing his hands on my shoulders, and began shaking me and shouting.

"Can't you understand what I've been saying?" he demanded. "There's nothing I can do! If I went down to the market I would only cause trouble for my family."

Poignantly, she asks "Daddy, are you afraid?" In reply, he

> sprang to his feet in an anger I had never seen him in before. "Hell no! I'm not afraid for myself, I'm not afraid to die. I could go down to that market and tear him limb from limb with my bare hands, but I'm afraid for you and your mother."[22]

On another occasion, Daisy and her father have been walking in the woods and he has been explaining her biological mother's death in terms of the "timeworn lust of the white man for the Negro woman—which strikes at the heart of every Negro man in the South," and she notices that "my daddy looked tired and broken."[23]

In marked contrast to her father, Daisy's "adopted Mother"—as she actually refers to her at one point—is given short shrift.[24] Even in the snippets of information we are given, there seems little of the closeness that her relationship with her father engenders. Daisy's mother sends her to her first encounter with racism at the butcher shop because she is "not feeling well" enough to go herself. When she returns, her mother tells her to "Go on out to the porch and wait for Daddy," to handle the dilemma.[25] In another instance, when Daisy picks a wilting single red rose that reminds her of her biological mother, her adopted mother exclaims, "I can't understand that child, crying over a dying flower." But Daisy's father makes the connection, telling his wife "Let her be. It just takes time."[26] When Daisy is in mourning for her biological mother, her adopted mother's solution is to "send Daisy away for a visit to her grandmother," confessing "I wish I knew what was going on in that mind of hers." When she protests, it is again her father who intercedes by saying "All right, darling, if you don't want to go to grandma's you don't have to."[27]

In addition, Bates often represents her mother as a repressive force in her life. Curiously, it is her mother who Bates associates with discipline, traditionally the more "masculine" role of the father within the family unit. "I was often clobbered, tanned, switched and made to stand in the corner," she tells us. In part, at least, Bates ascribes this to her mother's religion, since "she believed every word in the Holy Bible—including that passage, 'Spare the rod and spoil the child,' which I later learned wasn't in the Bible at all."[28] Daisy's mother also stops her from playing "for keeps" at marbles with the neighborhood boys on religious grounds since "That's gambling and gambling is a sin."[29] Bates curtly notes that her father is allowed to gamble on Saturday nights so long as he seeks forgiveness for it on Sunday mornings. One morning, she impudently asks Daddy in front of her mother, "Daddy, why don't you go to church and ask God to forgive you for a whole month? Then you won't have to go to church every Sunday." Bates tells us, "Mother fanned my tail and sent me off to Sunday school. After that I left it to Mama and God to worry about Daddy's sins."[30] When her mother finds young Daisy has been "playing for keeps" yet again "[She] didn't allow me to wait for Sunday. She dragged me off that evening for Wednesday night prayer service, so I could ask God to forgive me for my sins."[31]

The association of the church and religion with punishment and oppression are clearly bound up with Bates's feelings about her mother's treatment of her. Bates appears to have little time at all for religion and the church, identified by scholars as a central focal point of black women's networks and socialization in many southern communities.[32] She views religion as a site of white oppression rather than black liberation. The scene where Daisy finally appears to turn her back on the church is particularly poignant. This occurs when she is asked by one of the "church ladies" to play the part of "an angel hovering over the straw crib of infant Jesus" in the Christmas nativity play. Daisy replies "*No!* I won't . . . I don't want no part of that play about a dead white doll . . . All the pictures I ever saw of Jesus were white . . . If Jesus is like the white people, I don't want any part of him!" Her mother, "shocked" tells her daughter "I won't have that kind of talk . . . You stop that kind of talk this minute!" Nevertheless, Daisy holds firm and "Nothing more was ever said about my appearing in the Christmas play. While my friends and family attended the Christmas pageant, I spent a lonely evening with my dog and colored doll."[33]

Daisy further mocks the "Church Sisters" in a more light-hearted scene, as they pray at her bedside while she is ill after hearing the truth about her biological mother's death. As "They knelt around my bed and prayed for my soul," Bates's mind fixes on "the fat knees of one praying lady." Daisy then proceeds to release the guinea pigs she has been hiding in a box under her bed covers. She describes the ensuing scene of chaos:

One of them ran across the fat lady's leg. Unable to lift her weight up on the chair beside her, she lumbered around the room, screaming hysterically. The other ladies, managing to keep a few paces ahead of her, joined in the wild demonstration.

The whole scene leaves Daisy "Helpless with laughter." Predictably, the event ends with Daisy having her "behind properly spanked" by her mother. At this spectacle, "The ladies, although convinced that I certainly needed prayer, decided to do their praying for me elsewhere."[34]

Despite her evident shows of disrespect for religion and church women, Daisy does indicate that she is aware of and appreciates their dedication to their faith. When she describes the "two church buildings" with "drab exterior[s]" in Huttig, she does note that it is the "Sisters of the church" who keep them "spotless inside."[35] However, Bates decides, that this is not a direction that she could follow.

Even outside of the church, Daisy seems to have little time for the black women in her community. At one point, she declares herself "engaged in open warfare with the neighborhood adults." Although "adult" is a not gender specific here, it is clear from Bates's narrative who the enemy is:

> I felt they were a lazy, conniving bunch of porch sitters who were always chasing us kids around town on errands for them. I resented their rewarding us with stale pound cake and soggy homemade cookies.
>
> One afternoon, after lugging a gallon of milk six blocks for Mrs. Coleman, I watched her reach for a piece of cake from her red-and-white cake pan.
>
> "Thank you, Daisy, for fetching the milk. I always seem to be tired these days," she said, handing me my reward.
>
> "Shucks, I get tired too," I said. "And you are always chasing me all over town and then giving me nothing but that old cake. I don't want it—I've been throwing it in the ditch anyhow."
>
> "Well, did you ever!" said the shocked Mrs. Coleman. "The nerve! I'll certainly see your mother hears about this!"
>
> It was my last feud with adults. My mother had seen to that.[36]

Daisy's experiences of racism seem to play an important role in her rejection of the "feminine." Certainly, in terms of religion for example, this is clearly apparent. Yet there are other very subtle "defeminizing" codas to many of her stories about discovering the nature of black oppression. In her first experience at the butchers shop, she begins "I put on one of my prettiest dresses and my mother brushed my hair." The episode ends, "That night when I knelt down to pray, instead of my usual prayers, I found myself praying that the butcher would die."[37] Again, when Daisy has the identity of her mother's killer confirmed in an overheard conversation between three white men in a department store, a similar transition takes place. "I was standing behind them, admiring a big colored doll," Bates tells us, when one of her mother's killers walks in. The men discuss the killer among themselves:

> You heard about that colored woman they found in the mill pond a few years ago? I heard he was involved . . . leastwise, he started to drink about then, and he's been getting worse and worse ever since. He's about hit rock bottom. Too bad, 'cause he had a good job at the time."

She "stood motionless listening. Now that I was sure of what I suspected I lost all interest in the doll."[38]

Most striking of all is the episode in which Daisy finds out precisely how her biological mother died. At the outset, she is picking flowers:

> I passionately loved all blooming things. In the woods I hunted out the first of the cowslips and spring beauties, and from the open fields, the last of the Indian paintbrush. I was always bringing home bouquets . . . All of the neighbors knew that the flowers in our yard were my garden, not Mother's.

Within one page of text, after Daisy's father has explained the death of her biological mother to her, the soft feminine tones and activities halt and suddenly become more masculine, hardened and embittered, as her mind turns to vengeance:

> Dolls, games . . . held little interest for me after that. Young as I was, strange as it may seem, my life now had a secret goal— to find the men who had done this horrible thing to my mother.

So happy once, now I was like a little sapling which, after a violent storm, puts out only gnarled and twisted branches.[39]

We know little of Daisy's biological father, other than he "was as light as a lot of white people" and that he "was so hurt" at the murder of his wife than he left town, never to return. Daisy's biological father is notable only as an absence, rather than a presence in her life.[40] Although we receive little information about her biological parents, it is Daisy's mother to whom she clearly feels closest, no doubt because many people have told her that she is "the living image of her."[41] Appropriately, it is Daisy's father, who acts as a surrogate mother in gender terms for her, and who relates the information about Daisy's biological mother to her, saying "your mother was very pretty—dark brown with long hair."[42] There is also bitterness on Daisy's father's part that he was unable to prevent or subsequently secure justice for her killing. As Daisy's father briefly narrates the death of her biological mother, he says "your mother was not the kind to submit . . . so they took her."[43] As readers we are left with the curious juxtaposition of Daisy's biological mother, who resists humiliation at the hands of whites and is killed for her efforts, and Daisy's father who accepts the humiliation of the three white hoodlums on his way to the funeral and survives. There is a great deal of ambiguity over meaning here, especially what this tells us about the relative costs of "protest" and "accommodation" and how these are relevant in terms of the roles played by (and expected of) black men and women in the Jim Crow South.

Daisy's early experiences of racism affect not only her relationships within the black community, but also her relationships with whites, male and female. Not all whites are demonic in Bates's narrative. There is, for example, an "elderly and retired mill worker who was now nearly crippled with arthritis" who "knew all the children, both white and Negro" and sat in the town square, often handing out free candy to those who passed.[44] The old man witnesses the daily war of attrition between Daisy and Drunken Pig and is always silently on hand to help safeguard Daisy in these encounters.[45] It is the old man who finally informs Daisy that Drunken Pig has died and tries to comfort her.[46] Yet Daisy cannot fully accept the old man's friendship because he is white. When a friend suggests that they go and get some free candy one day, she responds "If I want candy, I have some money to buy it . . . I don't want anything from white people."[47] After this episode, her friendship with the old man sours. "The old man had not spoken a word to me since the day I refused his candy," she later informs us.[48]

Similarly, Daisy's experiences of racism affect her relationships with her female friends. One day, soon after finding out about the death of her mother, Daisy is approached by a white girl "with whom I had been friends a long time." The white girl prods her in the back and calls, "Look, Daisy, I have two pennies. Let's buy some candy and I'll tell you about my vacation." Daisy's anger and frustration is vented on the girl, who she slaps across the face: "Don't you ever touch me again" Daisy cries, "I don't want your penny!"[49] When she arrives home she feels guilt and remorse for what she has done:

> I wanted badly to go back and tell her I was sorry, and that I didn't really hate her. During our friendship we had often met at the store and shared our pennies. We would have so much fun shopping with our pennies. If I bought winding balls, she would buy peppermint sticks and we would divide them. How could I explain to her that. . .[50]

At that instant, Daisy realizes the significance of her action: "Suddenly I was afraid. Suppose she went home and told her people that I had hit her? Suppose they came for me or my daddy that night?"[51] Within the context of a firmly drawn line of racial etiquette, even a childhood squabble threatens both her life and the lives of her family. she decides to keep quiet about the incident. Fortunately there are no reprisals, but Daisy ends up losing one of her best friends and further realizes the significance of minor indiscretions in a racialized world.

Bates's early life presents a confused world of ambiguous, mixed metaphors with regard to gender. By her own admission she wears pretty dresses, picks flowers, and has braids in her hair. She relies upon her male cousin, Early B., to protect her from bullies. She is squeamish about "bugs and spiders," while declaring herself "a regular tomboy" who enjoyed "competing with the neighborhood boys," climbing trees, gambling with marbles, and keeping guinea pigs in her bed, with only her adopted mother stopping her from keeping hogs in there with her too.[52] Bates appears to be a product of a childhood that has produced no strong or convincing gender orientation: she neither accepts the "feminine" gender referents offered her, nor rejects them totally for "masculine" referents, which also appear to have their flaws and weaknesses.

Daisy's marriage to L. C. Bates demonstrates that the ambiguous gender roles inherited from her childhood persisted into her adult life. Daisy met her future husband when she was fifteen and L. C. was twenty-one years her senior.[53] Although L. C. did the wooing with gifts from his travels as an insurance man, and made the first move in the relationship by holding Daisy's hand in the movie theater one night, it was Daisy who made the decision that "I would one day marry him," without revealing her "plans to L. C." She reaches this decision despite the fact that "Daddy had often declared that a girl should not consider marriage until she could cook and sew. And I could do neither."[54] It was also Daisy who sued for divorce in 1962 on the grounds of "abuse, contempt and studied neglect," and confirmed their remarriage to the press several months later.[55] By all accounts, Daisy Bates was the active and dynamic partner in the marriage.[56] Bates's own memoirs insist that she played an equal role in the founding and running of the *Arkansas State Press*.[57] She also learned how to run the business side of the newspaper, studying business administration and public relations at North Little Rock's Shorter College. Around the same time, L. C. only just managed to talk Daisy out of taking flying lessons on the grounds that the insurance premiums would be too high.[58] It was Daisy who became the public figure in the partnership, first as president of the Arkansas State Conference of branches and later, nationally, as a result of her role in the Little Rock crisis. Although L. C. was the "husband" in the marriage, his role in gender terms was more typically that traditionally assigned to a "wife," as a supporter from the sidelines. Like many other "wives" in history, L. C. Bates has never really received due recognition for the considerable part he played in the civil rights movement in Arkansas.[59]

Daisy Bates's rejection of the "masculine" as both the site of white male oppression and black male powerlessness, and the "feminine" as a perceived delimiting sphere that revolved around church groups and seemed apathetic ("a lazy conniving bunch of porch sitters"), rather than overtly political, produced an obvious dilemma. Where, if not in either of these gendered frameworks of expression, would Bates find an outlet for her anger against whites and against the incapacity of black networks to issue that challenge?

One immediate answer was the *Arkansas State Press* newspaper. Through its pages, Bates was able to have a "say" in community affairs without working through existing networks of black activism. Yet, at the same time, the newspaper had an important impact on those groups, and could stir them to take action. Bates's reporting of the shooting of black army Sgt. Thomas P. Foster by a white city police officer in downtown Little Rock in 1942, for example, created such an outcry that the normally complacent, male black leaders were forced to investigate the incident through a Negro Citizens' Committee. The newspaper's impact, not only upon the city but also throughout the state, was demonstrated by the massive turnout at the First Baptist Church in Little Rock on Sunday, March 29, when blacks from all over Arkansas gathered to hear the committee declare that Foster had been unlawfully killed.[60] Although Foster's white killer escaped punishment in the courts, the *Arkansas State Press*'s ongoing crusade brought some concessions. The first nine black policemen were enrolled into the city's police force soon after.[61]

Bates utilized the *Arkansas State Press* not only to launch an attack on the wrongdoings of the white community but also to criticize what she viewed as the shortcomings of the black community, in particular lambasting the influential male-dominated leadership. This criticism sharpened, especially during the postwar era, when a new black leadership began to emerge in Little Rock. Since Reconstruction most of the city's black influential public figures had been drawn from the ranks of a small but thriving business community. With the impact of the Depression, which crushed many black businesses, and the U. S. Supreme Court's 1944 *Smith v. Allwright* ruling, which outlawed racial exclusion in state and local Democratic party primaries and led to an increased concentration on voter registration, a new politically oriented black leadership began to develop in the city. In the vanguard of this revolt against older leaders was Charles Bussey who, with a band of black GIs, formed the Veteran's Good Government Association. Bussey also had a hand in forming another new group, the East End Civic League, led by Jeffrey Hawkins, which concentrated specifically on representing the interests of the run-down, heavily black populated east end of the city. I. S. McClinton, another prominent member of this new band of black leaders, formed the Young Negro Democrats group, which later became the Arkansas Democratic Voters Association. These new leaders looked to harness the political potential of the black vote in order to use it as leverage with whites to press for improvements in the black community.

Bates remained skeptical about the methods and intentions of these new political leaders. In the pages of the *Arkansas State Press,* she complained that some who were posing as leaders were only interested in their own self-aggrandizement. They delivered black votes for white politicians rather than advancing the cause of the race as a whole.[62] Even those who she deemed sincere were portrayed as misguided in settling for a bargaining of votes to improve conditions within the bounds of segregation, rather than exerting pressure to end racial discrimination altogether.[63] The *Arkansas State Press* demanded nothing short of a complete end to segregation. "Arkansas needs leadership" ran one typical editorial in 1950. "Arkansas cities need leadership . . . the Negro needs leadership which will stand up and be counted . . . and above all, Little Rock, Arkansas's capital city, needs leadership badly."[64] In another editorial, male leaders were blamed directly for the inadequacies in the black community's facilities. Their failure, the *Arkansas State Press* claimed, was "a sounder explanation of our failure to get parks, playgrounds, enough Negro police, employment on the Negro side of the employment office, and other lacks, than any amount of white opposition."[65] Ominously, another 1950 editorial concluded it was "about time for a general showdown on the leadership in Little Rock."[66]

For that "showdown" Bates would need a different vehicle than the *Arkansas State Press.* Although the newspaper could effectively provide a voice of protest, it could not provide a base from which to mobilize a direct and comprehensive assault on segregation. Even if Bates had wanted to form her own political organization, which from her comments she clearly did not, the gender constraints of that male-dominated world would probably have prevented her from doing so with any degree of success. Neither had Bates discovered any attachment to or affection for the female-dominated networks in the city that revolved around clubs, associations, and institutions such as the National Council of Negro Women, the Young Women's Christian Association, and the church. Bates was a member of many of these organizations but was a "joiner" rather than a "joiner-inner." She played no prominent part within any of these groups. Indeed, she still showed a private disdain for women's networks. One of Daisy Bates's closest friends in the white community, lawyer Edwin E. Dunaway, vividly remembered the time he approached Bates and asked her to sit on the board of the Greater Little Rock Urban League. The league, established by black schoolteacher Amelia B. Ives in 1939, was an interracial group in which women were heavily represented. The Urban League looked to address the problems that blacks faced in the city, albeit strictly within the bounds of existing Jim Crow laws. Bates rejected Dunaway's approach, insisting that the executive board of the Greater Little Rock Urban League was "just a bunch of niggers who want to sit next to white folks once every two weeks."[67]

Bates ultimately found that the most effective vehicle for her anger at the conditions blacks faced was the NAACP. In many ways, it was the perfect organization for Bates since it too was neither fully incorporated into existing male or female networks in the city. The local branch of the NAACP in Little Rock, formed in 1918, confirmed Charles Payne's hypothesis that "men led, women organized," yet it remained unclear what role was seen as the most important and who actually held authority within the organization. Most of the city's prominent black male leaders were members of the NAACP board, but none of them played an active role. Rather, it was left to black women to keep the branch afloat, which was done with consummate success. In 1925, for example, Mrs. Carrie Sheppherdson won a national NAACP award, the coveted Madam C. J. Walker Gold Medal, for her fundraising efforts.[68] Still, those women who were active in the Little Rock NAACP remained exasperated at the lack of effort by the men. As Mrs. H. L. Porter, one in a line of female local branch secretaries, summed up in 1933 "the lawyers, Doctors, preachers and businessmen . . . are just a bunch of egoistic discussers and not much on actual doings."[69]

Active interest in the NAACP in Arkansas only really took root during the 1940s. Fittingly, it was an initiative led by an organization in which women were in a majority, the Little Rock Classroom Teachers' Association, that sparked that interest. Throughout the 1930s the association had followed the teachers' salary equalization suits championed by NAACP attorney Thurgood Marshall. The success of the *Alston v. School Board of the City of Norfolk* (1940) case in Virginia convinced Little Rock teachers that they should pursue a similar action. A Salary Adjustment Committee was organized and Miss Solar M. Caretners, its secretary, wrote to both Melvin O. Alston, the plaintiff in the 1940 suit, and Walter White, president of the NAACP, to ask for advice about "the method of procedure and techniques of bringing about equal salaries for teachers."[70] With preparations in place, Sue Morris, head of the English Department at Dunbar High School in Little Rock, was nominated as lead plaintiff for the suit, filed in the U. S. District Court on February 28, 1942.[71] After numerous appeals, the Eighth Circuit Court of Appeals at St. Louis finally decided the suit in favour of Morris on June 19, 1945.[72] The victory marked a significant triumph both for the local and national NAACP. Historian Mark Tushnet describes the Little Rock teachers' salary suit as the "most important of its kind."[73] Certainly, the national NAACP was overjoyed at the outcome, evident in their triumphant press release that proclaimed "NAACP WINS DOUBLE VICTORY IN ARKANSAS TEACHERS SALARY CASE."[74]

The success of the teachers' salary suit led directly to the formation of the Arkansas State Conference of branches (ASC). This stirred a great deal of controversy in the state over the direction of black activism. The national offices of the NAACP divided responsibilities for the ASC between the young activist William Harold Flowers from Pine Bluff, who became chief organizer of branches, and the Reverend Marcus Taylor, an older and more conservative figure from Little Rock, who became ASC president. Animosity between the two as a result of their conflicting styles of leadership soon became apparent. With no real communication between the two rival power bases, two factions, one activist and one more conservative, quickly formed within the organization. Jealous of the support Flowers began to receive, Taylor fired accusations of financial mismanagement at the younger leader, even suggesting that Flowers was keeping half of the funds he collected from the establishment of local branches for himself.[75] An investigation launched by the NAACP to investigate the situation found Taylor's accusations to be untrue.[76] Indeed, Flowers's popularity continued to grow alongside the rapid expansion of NAACP branches and membership throughout Arkansas. The battle within the NAACP was finally resolved in 1948 when Flowers was elected as ASC president.[77]

There was no doubt as to which side of the activist versus conservative argument Daisy Bates was on. Both Daisy and L. C. were friends of Flowers. The *Arkansas State Press* had publicized Flowers's voter registration efforts in the early 1940s as head of the Committee on Negro Organizations, an indigenous organization whose activism predated the NAACP's expansion in the state. Moreover, Flowers wrote a regular column in the *Arkansas State Press* under the pseudonym of Frances Sampson and considered the Bateses' home a welcome stop-over during his visits to Little Rock.[78] In contrast to other male politicians, Bates remembered in later years, Flowers was the only truly "effective" protest leader of the time.[79]

Flowers's election as president of the ASC inspired Daisy Bates to attack the lethargy of male leaders in the Little Rock NAACP. Her difficulties were compounded by the fact that the capital city was the center of black conservatism in the state. Rather than engaging with existing NAACP in-fighting in the city, Bates attempted to set up her own separate sphere of influence in a rival group, filing application for a "Pulaski County Chapter of the NAACP" in 1948.[80] By forming a countywide NAACP chapter, Bates hoped to undercut the authority of older male leaders such as Reverend Taylor and provide a new dynamism for the organization. In her application for charter, Bates included fifty membership subscriptions, plus the branch-founding fee, and nominated herself as president. Wise to what Bates was attempting to do, the national headquarters of the NAACP turned down the application. In a curt reply, Gloster B. Current, national director of NAACP branches, pointed out there was already a branch in Little Rock and that if people were interested in helping the organization they should join up there.[81]

After Bates's unsuccessful attempt to displace Taylor, unrest continued in state NAACP activities. In 1949 when the ASC defaulted on its annual contribution to the NAACP's Southwest Regional Conference fund, the national office demanded Flowers's resignation under threat of dismissal.[82] Flowers resigned but, as a result, talk of mutiny by grassroots members grew. Only the interventions of Roy Wilkins, executive secretary of the NAACP, and assistant executive secretary Walter White, prevented a wholesale defection. Nevertheless, the deep dissatisfaction of local NAACP activists persisted.[83] Many were extremely reluctant to accept Flowers's replacement, Dr. J. A. White, who represented the old guard of black leadership and was imposed upon them by national headquarters. Dissension within Arkansas NAACP ranks caused much concern. Mrs. Lulu B. White, a member of the Texas NAACP State Conference of branches, observed "no place in the country is there so much strife and division amongst Negroes as [there] is in Arkansas."[84]

The internal wrangling was finally resolved in 1952 when Daisy Bates won election as ASC president. She came into office after Dr. White fell ill and resigned in 1951, resulting in the first popular election of a leader by local NAACP members since Flowers's resignation. Undoubtedly, Bates's connection with W. H. Flowers helped her to win the office. In contrast to many other organizations in the black community, the issue of Bates being a woman and leader of the ASC never seems to have been broached. This reflected the fact that, at the state level, the NAACP was perceived neither as an exclusively "male" or "female" sphere of influence. Of more concern than Bates's gender was her forthright stance. Ulysses Simpson Tate, NAACP southwest regional attorney, who had been present at Bates's election, questioned her ability to work with older, more established leaders in the state, and was wary of her tendency "to go off the deep end at times" in a forceful pursuit of black rights. However, he concluded apologetically, "[although] I am not certain that she was the proper person to be elected I permitted it because there was no one else to be elected who offered any promise of doing anything to further the work of the NAACP in Arkansas."[85]

As ASC president, Daisy Bates began to exercise a more direct influence on day-to-day affairs of the black community in Little Rock. In particular, the U.S. Supreme Court's 1954 *Brown v. Board of Education* school desegregation decision helped to garner support both for Bates and the NAACP. With existing male and female networks unable to handle such a contentious issue as school desegregation, the NAACP filled a void in a black community which saw the *Brown* decision as a signal that "the time for delay, evasion or procrastination was past."[86] As head of the NAACP, Bates spearheaded attempts to press the Little Rock school board, as well as other school boards in the state, into compliance with the court ruling.[87]

As school desegregation descended into crisis in Little Rock during September 1957, Bates's backing from the black community, solidified. A 1958 study by sociologists Tilman C. Cothran and William Phillips Jr., titled "Negro Leadership in a Crisis Situation" confirmed Bates's commanding position. Twenty-two out of twenty-six existing black leaders in Little Rock described Bates as "the most influential Negro in the community" while twenty-four out of twenty-six named her as "the most influential Negro in determining policy on educational desegregation." One interviewee described Bates as "the only outspoken Negro leader," adding, "the other Negro leaders have remained silent and have allowed her to become spokesman [sic]." A parent of one of the nine black students undertaking the task of desegregating Central High School agreed that "the NAACP President is the only leader who has stood up for these children. She has been more helpful than anybody." The parent, adding her thoughts on the rest of the black leadership in the city, declared "We have a shortage of leaders . . . There are a lot of would-be leaders, but the problem is that when the trouble starts they won't stand up and be counted."[88]

Although Bates was clearly the sole voice of leadership in the city during the school crisis, her position, working outside of existing male and female networks of influence, remained tenuous. Despite her leading role, Bates was still considered an outsider. One black woman later uncharitably referred to Bates as "sort of an opportunist." Ozell Sutton, who was hired as the first black reporter on the white *Arkansas Democrat* newspaper in 1948 to cover the news in the black community, and after the school crisis became a major figure in the civil rights struggle in city and state, explained:

> Daisy Bates was a leader for the Negroes in the contending forces concerned with integration, but there was definite disagreement within the Negro community over her tactics and personality. However, there was never any public disagreement because of the unanimity of commitment to desegregation. Because the community power was centred in Daisy Bates, she made arbitrary decisions.[89]

Bates also soon discovered that, outside of the immediate problem surrounding Central High School, she was isolated from the rest of the community. Bates became the target of white segregationists after the 1957 school crisis. Missiles were hurled at her home, and she was arrested by the state authorities for refusing to hand over NAACP membership lists. Few in the black community were prepared to take an open stand in her defense.[90] Likewise, the NAACP received little local support for its efforts. In fact, when the organization was attacked by the state authorities through harassing lawsuits, membership figures dropped to an all-time low. When the *Arkansas State Press* was forced out of business in 1959, through a campaign by segregationists to force advertisers to withdraw their support, Bates's anger at her isolation became clear. In one editorial in April 1959, the *Arkansas*

State Press declared that too many blacks in Little Rock were apathetic, too many satisfied with "the master-slave relationship which the whites called good race relations" and therefore lacked the determination to fight for their constitutional rights.[91]

Bates's final disillusionment came when she played a part in organizing sit-ins with students from Little Rock's Philander Smith College. Following the wave of sit-ins across the South in early 1960, Bates met with black students who staged their first demonstration in downtown Little Rock on March 9 at the F. W. Woolworth lunch counter.[92] City authorities were quick to have students arrested and the courts handed down both harsh fines and long jail sentences.[93] White and black leaders condemned the sit-ins as harmful to race relations. Only the local NAACP and, later, the local branch of the National Council of Negro Women, actively supported the students. The city's more conservative black newspaper, the *Southern Mediator Journal*, older black leaders, and especially Dr. Lafayette Jones, president of Philander Smith College, all strongly dissented. Indeed, Jones had to be persuaded by white college-board members not to expel immediately all of the students involved.[94] As the students were passed from court to court, deliberately log-jammed in the legal system, local black support for their cause remained virtually nonexistent. As a result, further demonstrations ground to a halt. Lack of support proved to be the final straw for Bates. She left Little Rock to concentrate upon national appearances, writing, and then promoting her memoirs. She also supported the "Dollars for Daisy" campaigns run by various black communities across the United States to raise money to revive the *Arkansas State Press*. From 1960 to 1963 she spent most of her time out of Little Rock.[95]

Although Bates left Little Rock under a cloud of disillusionment, her impact on existing black leaders and black networks in the city was palpable. As those who had been leaders in the community before Bates tried to reassert their authority, factional conflict between different individuals and organizations erupted. Many in the black community began to openly express their dissatisfaction with the pre-Bates leadership. "Disunity among Negro leaders," wrote an observer from the National Urban League, "proved to be of more concern than the school crisis."[96] Young black city lawyer John Walker, who was associate director of the interracial Arkansas Council on Human Relations, described black leadership as "virtually nil" while adding that "the masses of Negroes are anxious for more progressive leadership from new people."[97] Bates had managed to successfully disrupt existing lines of leadership, which older leaders subsequently struggled to restore. However, since the crisis had brought a change in their former constituencies of support that demanded a more active and dynamic approach to racial issues, older leaders generally failed to live up to the new standards required by the masses. Increasingly, many in the black community felt there was a need to find a more assertive and capable leadership that could adapt to a more innovative strategy for the pursuit of black advancement.

Initial signs that a new leadership was struggling to establish itself came in the first school board elections after the Central High crisis in November 1959. Dissatisfaction with the newly established pupil assignment system, which limited desegregation at the discretion of the all-white school board, led to a delegation from the black community launching an appeal to abandon the system altogether.[98] When these appeals were ignored, Dr. Maurice A. Jackson, a young black physician, declared his intention to stand for the school board. Over one thousand black residents signed a petition in support of the action. Although threats from the white community, coupled with disparaging remarks from older black leaders, ultimately prevented Jackson from running, the campaign marked the beginning of a new era of black leadership.[99] Through the offices of the Arkansas Council on Human Relations, working in tandem with the black community, a new forum for leadership emerged. This was rooted in a visit in 1960 by John Wheeler, a black leader from Durham, North Carolina, who explained how his community had organized a "Council on Community Organizations," with various groups pooling their resources to focus on a common goal of black advancement. This paved the way for the formation of a similar group in Little Rock called the Council on Community Affairs (COCA).[100]

COCA became the most effective vehicle for local black protest in Little Rock during the 1960s. Formed as a collective body of existing centers and networks of community influence, COCA proclaimed its intention to "give the Negro community a untied voice in all matters concerning their welfare."[101] Significantly, this pooling of community influence began to break down the hitherto clearly defined "male" and "female" roles and spheres of responsibility for black activism. Moreover, the core leadership of the new group, who were all physicians, included a woman, Dr. Evangeline Upshur. She, along with Dr. William H. Townsend, Dr. Maurice A. Jackson, and Dr. Garman P. Freeman, represented the new breed of leadership in Little Rock and provided tangible links to Daisy Bates. Upshur was Bates's next door neighbor and family practitioner and had been one of her few determined supporters throughout the school crisis.[102] Yet COCA remained careful to incorporate older leaders into the new structure of community activism, thereby utilizing various avenues of organizational strength and influence, while at the same time deploying the group's energies into new areas of activism.[103] In so doing, COCA proved an effective voice for the black community. It was COCA, for example, that, in 1963, linked up with representatives from the Student Nonviolent Coordinating Committee and local students to put an end to segregation in Little Rock's downtown area through direct-action protests and negotiations with the city's white businesses leadership. COCA continued to forge links with white moderate and liberal groups in the city, male and female, and to build important community coalitions that helped to shape the future of race relations in Arkansas's state capital.[104]

Daisy Bates's involvement with the struggle for black freedom and equality demonstrates the importance of gender as a potent force in shaping reactions to white oppression in the Jim Crow South. Moreover, it highlights the interconnectedness of the "personal" and the "political." Through an analysis of Bates's activism from a gendered perspective, we can also see that women played multiple roles in the civil rights movement and that, contrary to Charles Payne's hypothesis, they served as both leaders and organizers, including many varieties of involvement within these two categories. Although, as sociological studies have highlighted, the majority of women who participated in the civil rights struggle played their own part through women's networks and spheres of influence, clearly not all did. We need to understand the "uncommon" experiences of women alongside these more "typical" experiences if we are to comprehend the multifaceted roles that women played in the movement. Exploring why some women made an impact in a male-dominated world helps to shed light on why others did not. Contributionist histories do not satisfy the complexities and nuances of women's experiences in the civil rights movement *as* women and not simply as "honorary men." Overlooking the experiences of black women in the civil rights struggle who operated outside of a traditional women's sphere of influence, and failing to recognize that that sphere was itself a product of choices influenced by gender, risks losing sight of the important role played by some of the most influential women in the movement. To be marginalized simply because they were successful against the odds would be an unjust legacy for women, like Bates, to bear.

6

White Opposition to the Civil Rights Struggle

Massive Resistance and Minimum Compliance: The Origins of the 1957 Little Rock Crisis and the Failure of School Desegregation in the South

Two assertions are central to this avowedly revisionist essay, which uses the case study of white reaction to the 1954 *Brown v. Board of Education* school desegregation decision in Little Rock, Arkansas, to suggest a new framework for understanding the emergence of white resistance to *Brown* in the South. The first assertion is that gradualism and tokenism employed under the banner of "minimum compliance" played a far greater role in the development of southern resistance to the *Brown* decision than has previously been acknowledged. With its defiant rhetoric and radical stance, massive resistance grabbed more headlines than minimum compliance, but it was precisely the latter's low-key and surreptitious approach to school desegregation that made it far more effective in undermining the *Brown* decision in the long run. The dangers of gradualism and tokenism were not lost on civil rights movement participants, including Martin Luther King Jr., who in his 1963 "Letter From Birmingham City Jail," written almost nine years after *Brown*, noted that he had "almost reached the regrettable conclusion that the Negro's great stumbling block in his stride toward freedom is not the White Citizen's Counciler or the Ku Klux Klanner, but the white moderate . . . who paternalistically believes he can set the timetable for another man's freedom. . . Lukewarm acceptance is much more bewildering than outright rejection."[1] King also anticipates my second assertion in his 1967 book *Where Do We Go From Here: Chaos or Community?*, when he notes that the Supreme Court's 1955 implementation order for *Brown*, which became known as *Brown II*, was "a keystone in the structure that slowed school desegregation down to a crawl."[2] Although the *Brown* decision has received a great deal of attention from commentators and historians, far less had been written about the significance of *Brown II*. Yet it is my assertion that *Brown II* had a much greater impact on the development of white resistance to school desegregation than the first *Brown* ruling.

In shifting the focus from massive resistance to minimum compliance, and from *Brown* to *Brown II*, this essay encourages a rethinking of the emergence of southern resistance to school desegregation and the long-term impact of that resistance. One important point to note at the outset is that this study focuses on an upper South city, which had a black population (about a quarter of Little Rock's one hundred thousand residents were black) that was smaller than many lower South cities, and smaller than that of many southern rural areas as well. Different parts of the South offered different levels of resistance to school desegregation, and that resistance often developed quicker and more determinedly in places that had larger black populations, where whites felt more threatened by racial change.

Nevertheless, upper South cities such as Little Rock played a pivotal role in the white southern reaction to *Brown*. When the Supreme Court handed down the two *Brown* decisions it very probably did not expect lower South states such as Mississippi and Alabama to rush to desegregate their school systems. It did, however, very probably expect upper South states such as Arkansas and North Carolina to set the pace for school desegregation, and thereby to place pressure on surrounding rural areas, and for those rural areas to in turn place pressure on neighboring lower South states. In practice, the court probably envisioned what might be described as a southern school desegregation domino effect. The fact that the process of school desegregation stalled at such an early point and so dramatically in a prime, progressive upper South city like Little Rock was catastrophic for the strategy of school desegregation that the Supreme Court embarked upon, and its reverberations reached far beyond Little Rock.

The existing historical record of the 1957 Little Rock school crisis paints a picture of a moderate upper-South city hijacked by massive resistance. Little Rock appeared to be at the forefront of compliance with the *Brown* decision when the school board declared that it would work toward the peaceful desegregation of the city's schools. However, the night before the all-white Central High School was due to accept nine black students in September 1957, Gov. Orval E. Faubus called out the National Guard to prevent the implementation of the desegregation plan, ostensibly on the grounds of preserving the peace. When President Dwight D. Eisenhower eventually persuaded Faubus to withdraw the state soldiers, a white mob frustrated attempts by the nine black students to attend Central High. This finally prompted Eisenhower to send in federal soldiers to ensure the safety of the black students. Central High spent one school year desegregated under armed guard. When the federal troops were withdrawn, Faubus closed all of the city's schools to prevent desegregation. Only when the white business community mobilized to gain control of the city school board did Little Rock return to a path of moderation, when it desegregated schools on a token basis.[3]

In tracing the origins of the Little Rock crisis to the early formation of local school policy in response to the two *Brown* decisions, and in particular to the development of a policy of minimum compliance, this essay offers a significant corrective to existing accounts of the school crisis and a suggestive framework for understanding the development of resistance to school desegregation throughout the South. In line with similar tactics used in other upper South cities, minimum compliance was a policy that sought to employ gradualism and tokenism to delay and to limit the implementation of school desegregation for as long as legally possible. The driving force behind minimum compliance was that it theoretically placated those who did not want school desegregation by limiting integration to the bare minimum. At the same time, it allowed school districts to maintain that they were in fact implementing the law. Advocates of minimum compliance viewed such a stance as "moderate" in relation to the "extremes" of meaningful integration and the outright opposition to school desegregation offered by those who advocated massive resistance. Yet in fact, minimum compliance turned out to be simply a more diluted form of massive resistance that on the face of things offered a less harmful way of frustrating the process of school desegregation but that actually wreaked chaos. Therefore, although massive resistance and minimum compliance at first appeared to be quite different, their differences quickly narrowed in the years following the *Brown* decision, as they combined to under-mine the process of school desegregation in Little Rock, in other upper South cities, and ultimately throughout the South.[4]

Many of the observations and findings about the Little Rock cri-sis in this essay echo those of Numan V. Bartley's summary of events in his book *The Rise of Massive Resistance*. The most important dif-ference is that Bartley attributes the failure of school desegregation in Little Rock to "an accumulation of failures by well-meaning leaders," whereas I identify the policy of minimum compliance as a much more calculating and premeditated attempt to circumvent the *Brown* deci-sion.[5] In contrast to the civility that William H. Chafe identifies in the upper South city of Greensboro, North Carolina, Little Rock instead exhibited cynicism in race relations. Certainly, the architect of mini-mum compliance in Little Rock, superintendent of schools Virgil T. Blossom, demonstrated little of the "personal grace that smooths con-tact with strangers and obscures conflict with foes," which Chafe cites as a hallmark of civility. Neither did he seem to possess "a way of deal-ing with people and problems that made good manners more impor-tant than substantial action" or evidence much "abhorrence of personal conflict, courtesy to new ideas, and generosity toward those less fortu-nate than oneself" in his dealings with Little Rock's black community. Blossom single-mindedly pursued a policy of minimum compliance and rode roughshod over any dissenting voices. His express aim all along was to frustrate the process of school desegregation by drawing up an implementation plan that purposefully pushed the law to its furthest limits. Meanwhile, those most likely to practice civility in Little Rock, the city's white business elite, stood by silently and did nothing.[6]

Blossom's intention to pursue a policy of minimum compliance with the *Brown* decision in Little Rock became apparent just four days after the Supreme Court ruling. As he started to outline the school board's plans to an expectant delegation from the black community, Blossom noticed that the "high spirits" with which the meeting began transformed in a "rapid [loss of] enthusiasm." Blossom told the black delegation that the school board did not intend to move ahead with desegregation immediately. Instead, it would wait for the expected announcement of the Supreme Court's implementation order the fol-lowing year. In the meantime, Blossom indicated that he would take on the job of drawing up plans for what might happen if the court forced Little Rock schools to desegregate. After Blossom finished his speech, Lucious Christopher (L. C.) Bates, owner and editor of the Little Rock-based *Arkansas State Press,* the state's leading black newspaper, stormed out of the meeting in outright disgust at the school board's perceived lack of commitment to implement a desegregation program. Others stayed, but the widespread disappointment in the black delegation was clear. Blossom tried to reassure them that he was not proposing to "delay for delay's sake, but to do the job right."[7] Privately, Blossom told whites of his intention to design a school desegregation plan that would provide "the least amount of integration over the longest period."[8]

Unhappy with the school board's response to the *Brown* decision, the black community, spearheaded by the Little Rock branch of the National Association for the Advancement of Colored People (NAACP), pressed Blossom for a definite declaration of plans for desegregation. At a subsequent meeting, Blossom told Little Rock NAACP representatives that before any desegregation took place, the school board intended to build two new schools. Horace Mann High School would be built in the predominantly black eastern part of the city, and Hall High School would be built in the affluent white suburbs of the west. Blossom insisted that the two new schools, in black and white residential areas, respectively, would not have a set racial designation. Rather, Blossom assured local NAACP members, the school board planned to desegregate all three of the city's high schools, Horace Mann High, Hall High, and Central High, along color-blind attendance zones in 1957. Elementary schools would follow some time around 1960.[9]

The so-called Blossom Plan divided members of the Little Rock NAACP's executive board. L. C. Bates opposed the Blossom Plan, as he believed that it was "vague, indefinite, slow-moving and indicative of an intent to stall further on public school integration." Nevertheless, a clear majority supported the Blossom Plan and cautioned against pushing the school board too hard. Most felt that Blossom and the school board should be given a chance to prove their good intentions, that the plan they had drawn up was reasonable, and that, importantly, it would be acceptable to the white community. The local branch therefore decided against immediate action and instead awaited further developments.[10]

In April 1955, the Little Rock NAACP held a meeting in anticipation of the Supreme Court's implementation order. The main speaker was a field worker for the NAACP's Legal Defense Fund, Vernon

McDaniels, who had spent six months in Arkansas assessing the school desegregation situation. McDaniels admitted that different communities would offer different degrees of resistance to school desegregation. Yet, he insisted, with increased efforts by blacks across the state to urge local school boards into compliance with the *Brown* decision, Arkansas represented the "brightest prospect among the southern states for integration."[11]

This upbeat assessment followed encouraging developments in the state after the *Brown* decision. A few school districts in the predominantly white northwest Arkansas had already moved to desegregate, whereas in many other southern states there was no progress at all. No widespread, organized campaign of resistance to school desegregation had developed as had happened in other states. Moreover, the state legislature had delayed the one direct attempt to circumvent the *Brown* decision. State representatives from heavily black populated eastern Arkansas introduced a Pupil Assignment Bill to the 1955 Arkansas General Assembly that was designed to evade school desegregation by assigning black students to black schools and white students to white schools on grounds other than race.[12] A divided assembly agreed to delay the implementation of the measure until after the Supreme Court had announced its school desegregation implementation order.[13] The opposition to legislation designed to circumvent *Brown* indicated the presence of law-abiding influences in Arkansas that could hold at bay attempts by militant segregationists to align the state with massive resistance elsewhere in the South. Although the situation over school desegregation remained somewhat ambiguous, there were grounds for cautious optimism that a more definite timetable for desegregation would consolidate the state's position of moderation.

Yet to those who held faith in the ability of the Supreme Court's implementation order to clear a path for compliance with *Brown*, the words of the justices on May 31, 1955, came as a major blow. Instead of following up on its initial conviction, the court equivocated. The court's implementation order, which became known as *Brown II*, ambiguously told school boards that they must make a "prompt and reasonable start" to desegregate "with all deliberate speed." No definite deadline was set for when integration had to begin and there was no indication of what exactly constituted compliance with the *Brown* decision, in terms of how many students were to be integrated and at what grades. Indeed, the court even listed the "local problems" that might be given as reasonable excuses for delay. The court decentralized the task of administrating school desegregation by handing this responsibility to federal district judges and to local school boards. The overall message to the South seemed to be that it could take as long as it wanted to desegregate schools. To many, this meant never.[14]

The reasons behind the Supreme Court's indecisiveness were complex. Rumors abounded that in exchange for unanimity over *Brown* some southern justices had managed to win the South the benefit of the doubt in awarding a lenient implementation order. The lack of political backing also seems to have played a major role. President Eisenhower continually refused to support the *Brown* decision strongly in public. In private, he admitted that he feared catastrophic massive resistance in the South if its racial mores were put so quickly and directly under threat. Southern leaders, emboldened by the delay between the school desegregation decision and its implementation order, warned of impending violence. Playing upon the fears of massive resistance voiced by the president, they warned of the need not to alienate the white population through forcing racial change too fast. White southerners increasingly sought to demonstrate the fears articulated by their leaders. Reluctance to implement the *Brown* decision quickly began to crystallize into direct opposition to it. Due to a perceived lack of support from other branches of the federal government and the public at large, together with divisions within its own ranks, the court climbed down from its original lofty stance for racial change. Instead, it offered an ambiguous and confusing compromise.[15]

Brown II proved an important turning point for school desegregation in Arkansas. Whites such as Blossom who advocated a policy of minimum compliance saw the court implementation order as a mandate for further measures to limit the impact of *Brown*. In turn, this paved the way for the beginning of a movement toward outright defiance of the law and total opposition to school desegregation. Before the Supreme Court implementation order, the most outspoken opponents of school desegregation in Arkansas had looked to find a way to circumvent school desegregation through legal means. Encouraged by the reluctance to enforce the *Brown* decision, the first calls for resistance by any means came from an organized band of segregationists. This hardening of sentiment against desegregation among whites helped, in turn, to strengthen the resolve of blacks as their earlier optimism that whites would implement the *Brown* decision vanished.

The feeling that *Brown II* meant that school boards could take as long as they liked to desegregate was evident when Virgil Blossom announced plans to modify his original school desegregation proposals. The most important development was the introduction of a transfer system that would allow students to move out of their assigned school attendance zones. Under the original Blossom Plan it was clear that new schools were being strategically placed to provide attendance areas that would ensure a majority black Horace Mann High and a majority white Hall High. The assignment of black students to Horace Mann High, although they lived closer to Central High, had confirmed the intentions of the school board to pursue a policy of minimum compliance and to limit the impact of desegregation as much as possible.[16]

Even so, the minimum compliance of the original plan still allowed for integration that involved several hundred pupils. The new plan, however, reflected the belief that *Brown II* allowed minimum compliance to be taken even further. Thus, the modified Blossom Plan allowed whites to opt out of attendance at Horace Mann High without giving blacks the right to choose to attend Hall High. Furthermore, it allowed only token integration at Central High. To encourage the shift of white pupils from Horace Mann High, the school board clearly designated it as a black institution by assigning an all-black teaching staff there. The school board then declared that it intended to open Horace Mann High as a segregated black school in February 1956, a move that would establish a clear precedent for black attendance the year before the school was supposed to desegregate.[17]

The revised Blossom Plan incensed members of the Little Rock NAACP's executive board, even those who had been willing to accept the superintendent's original proposal for school desegregation.[18] To add insult to injury Blossom did not even bother to consult the NAACP about the changes. When local NAACP representatives met with the school board to request the immediate integration of the city's schools, the school board rejected the proposal outright.[19] Little Rock's stance set the pattern for the three other largest municipal school districts in the state. Fort Smith, North Little Rock, and Hot Springs all drew up plans that purposefully delayed any desegregation of schools until the state capital made the first move.[20]

The fact that *Brown II* encouraged not only backpedaling but also helped to create an active movement of opposition and resistance to school desegregation was first in evidence at Hoxie, a small settlement in northeast Arkansas. With a population of just over a thousand, Hoxie was close enough to the Arkansas Delta to have a split school term to allow for the cotton-picking harvest. Yet it was atypical in that, with only fourteen black families living there, it did not reflect the density of the black population in other Delta areas.[21] On June 25, 1955, the school board at Hoxie voted, largely for financial reasons, to desegregate.[22] On July 11, the first day of integrated classes, a small group of disgruntled local men gathered outside the school to witness proceedings. Some parents voiced their misgivings, with one, a Mrs. John Cole, worriedly telling newspapermen that her eight-year-old daughter Peggy "feared Negroes." However, despite the apprehension surrounding integration, the consensus was that "we have to obey the law." Although there was some tension in classes at first, teachers soon made black students feel welcome, and normal school life quickly resumed. At noon recess, black and white boys tried out for the school baseball team together, and photographers even caught the fearful Peggy playing and walking arm in arm with black female students.[23]

Ironically, the very success of school desegregation at Hoxie made it the rallying point for massive resistance forces in the state. *Life* magazine reporters were present to document the event, producing an article that included a collection of pictures showing the mixing of black and white students.[24] Whereas other school boards were generally at pains to avoid the glare of publicity, desegregation at Hoxie became a national story. With the help and encouragement of segregationists in other states, particularly the closely neighboring Mississippi, local whites held a meeting in Hoxie. There, they elected Herbert Brewer, a local soybean farmer and part-time auctioneer, as chair of a new pro-segregation group.[25] Brewer and the Hoxie Citizens' Committee picketed and petitioned the Hoxie school board in an effort to persuade its members to reverse their decision to desegregate. The school board held firm in its conviction and rebuffed the demands of segregationists. However, to provide a cooling off period, the board closed the school two weeks before the scheduled end of term.[26]

The concession to close the schools early proved unfortunate, since it encouraged further disruption from segregationists. The gathering storm also helped to draw support from other segregationists across the state. White America, Inc., a Pine Bluff-based organization, sent the attorney Amis Guthridge from Little Rock to stir up the popu-

lace. James D. Johnson, head of the newly formed segregationist faction the White Citizens' Councils of Arkansas, followed soon after. The
meeting of segregationist factions at Hoxie led to a pooling of resources
and the formation of the Associated Citizens' Councils of Arkansas
(ACCA). The ACCA became the main vehicle for white resistance to
school desegregation in the state after the Hoxie campaign.[27]

Yet, for all the bluff and bluster of segregationists at Hoxie, they
only met with a protracted defeat. The school remained desegregated
the following term, and the courts issued an injunction to prevent any
interference.[28] Unlike other such white activists in the South, Arkansas'
White Citizens' Councils remained distinctly lacking in kudos. In some
other southern states, the Citizens' Councils could count merchants,
bankers, landowners, and politicians among their brethren. They
could exert economic, political, and social influence alongside the
angry rhetoric at mass rallies. In Arkansas, the militant segregationist
voice came from those who had little community standing.[29] Membership figures underscored white Arkansans' lack of interest in the
Citizens' Councils. Whereas Mississippi boasted three hundred thousand members, Arkansas recruited, at the highest and most likely over-
stated estimate, only twenty thousand members.[30]

Despite the ACCA's overall lack of credibility, the NAACP was
keenly aware of the potential dangers of growing organized white
resistance in Arkansas. The standoff at Hoxie prompted an increased
urgency within the Arkansas State Conference of NAACP branches
(ASC) to step up the pressure for school desegregation before similar
tactics spread to other parts of the state. In December 1955, Little
Rock's NAACP executive board members voted to file a lawsuit
against the Little Rock school board. They contacted the NAACP's
Legal Defense Fund southwest regional attorney, Ulysses Simpson
Tate, who had worked with them previously, for advice on how to
proceed. The Little Rock NAACP was especially concerned about
plans to open Horace Mann High as a segregated school in February
1956. Tate cautioned against seeking an injunction to prevent the
opening of Horace Mann High. Instead, he urged the branch to take
the positive step of petitioning for the admission of black students to
white schools when Horace Mann High opened.[31]

On January 23, 1956, thirty-three black students applied for
admission to four different white schools in Little Rock. All principals
of the schools refused entry to the students and referred them to

Blossom. Daisy Bates, president of the ASC and wife of L. C. Bates, accompanied nine of the black students to Blossom's office. There, Blossom explained that he had to "deny their request . . . in line with the policy outlined [by the school board]." Blossom was adamant that school desegregation would take place, as planned, in 1957. Daisy Bates told reporters after the meeting "I think the next step is obvious. We've tried everything short of a court suit."[32] On February 8, 1956, the ASC's attorney, Wiley A. Branton, filed suit in the U.S. District Court against the Little Rock school board for desegregation on behalf of thirty-three students under the title of *Aaron v. Cooper.*[33]

At the trial in August 1956, the U.S. District Court backed the modified Blossom Plan. To a large degree, however, this reflected confusion within NAACP ranks about the nature of the trial rather than the persuasive arguments of school board attorneys or the soundness of Blossom's proposal. The Little Rock NAACP built its case on very specific terms that asked only for the enforcement of the original Blossom Plan. In order to reinforce the strength of its argument, branch members went to great pains to select individual examples of black students who faced particular hardship under the modified plan. Ulysses Simpson Tate had different ideas about the case. As previous dealings between the national, regional, state, and local NAACP had revealed in Arkansas, each often had its own agenda of concerns that could cause conflicts of interest and misunderstandings. Tate did not confer with local branch officials before the trial. When he flew into Little Rock the day before the scheduled hearings in the case, he claimed that he was too tired to take instructions and immediately retired to his room to rest. The next morning, Tate ignored the case built by the Little Rock NAACP and proceeded to argue the national NAACP line for the immediate and complete integration of all schools. This was the same line taken by the national NAACP in all of its other sixty-five integration suits against school boards in the upper South at that time.[34] Since Tate was senior to Branton in the NAACP legal hierarchy, the local attorney deferred to him.[35]

Tate's line of argument lost the lawsuit by playing straight into the hands of the school board. Tate did not demand that the school board should live up to the promises it had already made. Rather, by demanding wholesale immediate integration, he allowed school board attorneys to contend that their clients were acting in accordance with the "with all deliberate speed" guidelines laid down by *Brown II.*

Judge John E. Miller upheld their argument. Offering a shred of con-solation for the local NAACP, Miller retained federal jurisdiction in the case to make sure that the school board now carried out the Blossom Plan along the lines it had indicated in court.[36]

The Little Rock NAACP branch was naturally disappointed at the outcome of the lawsuit. In consultation with their attorney, Wiley A. Branton; Thurgood Marshall, director-counsel of the NAACP Legal Defense Fund; and Robert L. Carter, special counsel to the NAACP, they decided to appeal.[37] The Court of Appeals at St. Louis heard arguments in *Aaron* v. *Cooper* on March 11, 1957. Again, the Court upheld the modified Blossom Plan, saying that the school board was indeed operating within a timetable that was reasonable, given the local problems of desegregation in the South. However, the court reaf-firmed Judge Miller's ruling that the school board was now obliged to carry out its modified plan, beginning with the desegregation of high schools in September 1957.[38]

Wiley A. Branton reported that in spite of the court defeat he was pleased by some aspects of the decision, particularly the affirmation that desegregation must take place the following school term. Branton felt that the ruling offered an important "cloak of protection against some die-hard, anti-integration groups who might still try to delay integration."[39] In a letter to the head of the school board attorney team, Archibald F. House, Branton insisted that "the plaintiffs feel just as strongly about the issues." Yet, he added, "time has made many of the problems moot and the opinion of the appellate court clarified some of the issues more favorably for us." Branton believed the court deci-sion left room for "give and take" that could "make for a spirit of goodwill and harmony among the students and patrons in the initial phase of school desegregation at Little Rock."[40]

Branton's optimistic outlook, despite the court defeat, came within the context of continuing positive developments in Arkansas. In the schools, with Little Rock under federal court order to desegregate, four other major municipal school districts—Pine Bluff, Hot Springs, North Little Rock, and Fort Smith—all drew up integration plans for September 1957.[41] By then, all of the publicly state-supported colleges and universities had begun to admit black students. In politics, six blacks were appointed to the Democratic State Committee by Gov. Orval Faubus, two blacks were elected to the city councils of Hot Springs and Alexander, and two blacks were elected to school boards at Wabbaseka and Dollarway. Local groups and associations across the state made goodwill gestures promoting interracial harmony. Several religious groups integrated and an interracial Ministerial Alliance formed in Little Rock in 1956. Some county medical societies also integrated their memberships, along with the American Association of University Women chapters in Conway and Fayetteville and the Little Rock League of Women Voters.[42]

The most striking development came in April 1956 when four municipalities—Little Rock, Pine Bluff, Hot Springs, and Fort Smith—successfully desegregated their public transportation systems. This occurred after a misunderstood Supreme Court ruling in *South Carolina Electric & Gas Co. v. Flemming* (1956), that many national newspapers reported as heralding the end of segregation in public transport. Amid the confusion, several bus companies in upper South cities took the initiative to desegregate.[43] Even after discovering the mistake, the policy continued in Arkansas. All interstate waiting rooms for bus and rail transportation desegregated without incident.[44] This was in direct contrast to Montgomery, Alabama, where it took a much-publicized bus boycott led by Martin Luther King Jr., and yet another U.S. Supreme Court ruling, *Browder v. Gayle* (1956), to compel the city to desegregate its buses.[45]

Despite these promising signs, the issue of school desegregation swiftly reached its denouement at Little Rock in the latter half of 1957. During the summer of that year, Blossom drew up attendance zones for admission to Central High that included two hundred black students. He then asked Leroy Matthew Christophe and Edwin L. Hawkins, the principals of the black Horace Mann High and Dunbar Junior High, to determine how many of their students wanted to apply for transfer. Thirty-two pupils from Horace Mann High and thirty-eight from Dunbar Junior High indicated an interest in attending Central High. Blossom asked the principals to screen each student individually and to make a judgment as to their suitability for selection. This was based upon a range of factors, including intelligence (Blossom insisted that all those selected must posses an IQ of over 100), personality traits, and social skills. When this process was completed, the principals forwarded the names of suitable candidates to Blossom for further screening.[46]

Blossom forged ahead with the plans for attendance zones and screening without bothering to consult the Little Rock NAACP. The organization only learned of the new plans through the black community grapevine. Upon hearing the news, Daisy Bates contacted the principals of the two black high schools, who confirmed that the selection process was already underway. The principals suggested that Bates contact Blossom for an explanation of his actions. When she contacted Blossom, he agreed to meet with local NAACP officials.[47]

At the meeting, Blossom explained his actions by comparing the situation in the schools to the desegregation of baseball, where Jackie Robinson had been selected as the first black player because of his high personal standing, conduct, and morals. Similarly, Blossom said, "I feel that for this transition from segregation to integration in the Little Rock school system, we should select and encourage only the best Negro students to attend Central High School—so that no criticism of the integration process could be attributed to inefficiency, poor scholarship, low morals, or poor citizenship."[48]

Questioned by local NAACP officials, Blossom admitted that he could not legally turn down an application from a student simply because he or she did not meet his own personal criteria. However, Blossom made it clear that he would do everything possible to discourage such a candidate. With regard to the new attendance zone, which further limited the pool of potential black applicants to Central High, Blossom told the Little Rock NAACP that he was prepared to invoke the state's pupil assignment law if any complaints were raised. Furthermore, Blossom asserted that he would make any final decision on transfers to Central High. "I know it is undemocratic, and I know it is wrong," Blossom told them, "but I am doing it."[49]

Blossom's continuing manipulation of the school desegregation process angered Little Rock NAACP members, particularly as the court suit seemed to rule out any further adjustments to the already modified Blossom Plan. Efforts to screen candidates, they complained, "seem[ed] to carry pursuasion [sic] and possibly pressure" and served only to instil "a feeling of inferiority, fear and intimidation" in black students. Moreover, they pointed out, the threat to use the pupil assignment law clearly contradicted the "good faith" compliance demanded by ongoing court jurisdiction. Blossom responded that he had already discussed these matters with the judge and insisted that all the changes would stand.[50]

Since it was now too late to challenge the new measures in court, the Little Rock NAACP reluctantly accepted the further changes to the

Blossom Plan. When the two black principals recommended thirty-two of their students to Blossom, he rigorously interviewed each of them again. As predicted by the Little Rock NAACP, Blossom used the selection process to further dissuade students from attending Central High. In one case, he reduced a prospective female student to tears by declaring that she lacked the right "scholastic background and emotional responsibility." When two talented black high school football players turned up at his office, Blossom warned them that their careers would come to a premature end if they attended Central High. Blossom ruled, adding yet another new proviso to school desegregation, that no black students would be allowed to participate in any of the social or sports activities at Central High. Upon hearing this, both students withdrew their applications.[51] Finally, after a grueling ordeal, the number of students permitted to integrate Central High School stood at seventeen. After further black students withdrew, the number went down to just nine students. They were Minnijean Brown, Elizabeth Eckford, Ernest Green, Thelma Mothershed, Melba Pattillo, Gloria Ray, Terrance Roberts, Jefferson Thomas, and Carlotta Walls.[52]

In August 1957, as the prospect of desegregation at Central High drew closer, the Capital Citizens' Council in Little Rock launched a last-gasp attempt to halt the process of school desegregation. It filed a number of lawsuits that attempted to force the state to uphold its segregation statutes to prevent integration and invited two high-profile segregationists, Georgia Gov. Marvin Griffin, and the former speaker of the Georgia House of Representatives, Roy V. Harris, to speak in Little Rock. At the meeting, Griffin lauded the 350 present as "a courageous bunch of patriots." Harris told them that Griffin would use the highway patrol to resist school desegregation if necessary, and if that failed, he would enlist "every white man in Georgia."[53]

Although clearly unhelpful, neither the litigation nor the speeches by Griffin and Harris were serious enough to derail the desegregation process. The real bombshell came on August 27, when a newly formed segregationist group, the Mothers' League of Central High, filed suit in the Pulaski County Chancery Court.[54] Acting as spokesperson for the group, Mrs. Clyde Thomason claimed that recent events caused "uncertainty of the law, conflicting court decisions and a general state of confusion and unrest." This would lead to "civil commotion" if the school board implemented its desegregation plan. At face value, the Mother's League suit appeared to be yet another futile bid to prevent desegregation. However, the league dramatically called Governor Faubus as its star witness. On the stand, Faubus testified that he believed violence would occur if plans for school desegregation went ahead, citing unsubstantiated reports of increased weapons sales in the city and the recent confiscation of revolvers from both white and black students.[55]

Chancellor Murray O. Reed, a Faubus appointee, ruled in favor of the Mothers' League and issued a restraining order against the school board, preventing its desegregation plan from going ahead. Attorneys for the school board promptly petitioned the U.S. District Court, asking it to forbid the implementation of Reed's order. On Friday, August 30, Judge Ronald Davies upheld the school board's petition and ordered school desegregation to proceed as planned the following Tuesday. Davies, from Fargo, North Dakota, was a temporary assignment to the bench because of an unfilled vacancy and was therefore a newcomer to events. Since Arkansas was the only southern state that belonged to the Eighth Circuit Federal Court district, temporary replacements often came from northern and midwestern states. Davies was detached from the southern mores and local politics that governed issues of school desegregation and simply followed the letter of the law in his ruling.[56]

Upon hearing of Davies's decision, Faubus met with William J. Smith, his legislative counsel, and mooted the idea of calling out the National Guard to prevent school desegregation from taking place. Smith counselled against doing that until serious violence and disorder actually developed.[57] However, at nine in the evening on Monday, September 2, the evening before Central High was due to desegregate, armed National Guardsmen began to cordon off the school buildings. At quarter after ten Faubus broadcast a speech, carried by all local television and radio stations, claiming he had evidence of impending violence in the city. Therefore, he had called out the National Guard "to maintain or restore order and to protect the lives and property of citizens."[58] Shortly after Faubus finished his speech, the school board issued a statement that "In view of the situation . . . no negro students [should] attempt to attend Central or any white high school until this dilemma is legally resolved."[59] From that point on, events unfolded inexorably. When black students attempted to enter Central High, National Guard soldiers turned them away. The courts then ordered the troops removed from Central High and for school desegregation to proceed as planned. When Faubus removed the state soldiers, attempts by black students to study at Central High were frustrated by scenes of mob lawlessness. Finally, President Eisenhower acted decisively by sending in federal troops to preserve law and order and to ensure the safety of the nine black students.[60]

The eventual unravelling of school desegregation in Little Rock was rooted in a flawed policy of minimum compliance. In 1954, Blossom and the Little Rock school board drew up plans to desegregate three city high schools that would have involved a substantial number of students attending formerly segregated schools. During the three years after *Brown*, Blossom continually modified his plan to limit the impact of desegregation as much as possible, at each step undermining efforts to ease a path for peaceful integration. Thus, by September 1957, the difference between minimum compliance with and massive resistance to *Brown* had narrowed to the barely distinguishable question of whether nine black students or whether no black students at all should attend just one city high school. As Blossom and the school board backtracked, the confidence and influence of massive resistance forces in the state grew. When the final push to halt school desegregation came from a small but dedicated band of segregationists in September 1957, the inherent flaws of the Blossom Plan became apparent. In concentrating school desegregation at only one city school, Blossom allowed Little Rock segregationists to marshal their slim resources to maximum effect. The fact that Central High was located in a working-class neighborhood injected class antagonisms into the already fraught question of school desegregation. Blossom sold his plan to a great number of social and civic groups, but almost all of these were exclusively white and middle-class. Little attempt was made to engage wide-ranging community support or consensus, even for minimum compliance with the law. Indeed, Blossom was extraordinarily autocratic in taking control of school desegregation to the extent that Little Rock's school desegregation plan even bore his name. Blossom earned his much-desired recognition from the city's elite for this—he was named Little Rock's "Man of the Year" in 1955—but it did nothing to prepare the wider community for school desegregation.[61]

Blossom's targeting of Little Rock's white business elite, evidenced in the groups to which he sold his plan for minimum compliance and the award he received for it, made them complicit in that policy. Elizabeth Jacoway characterizes the white business elite in Little Rock as "taken by surprise" by the events of September 1957. Jacoway contends that these men ultimately came to the rescue of the community by eventually, prodded by their wives' formation of the Women's Emergency Committee to Open Our Schools, mobilizing to defeat segregationist school board members and to reopen closed schools in August 1959. Such an account does not convincingly answer the crucial question of why the white business elite allowed the school crisis to occur in the first place. Viewed over the longer term from 1954 to 1957, the description of the white business community might more accurately be summed up as "struck dumb." After all, as Jacoway points out, the white business elite was a tightly knit and impressively organized group that had successfully waged campaigns in the postwar period to profoundly shape the economic and political future of the city.[62] Moreover, in stark contrast to the events of September 1957, in the first six months of 1963, the white business community, pressured by protest and demonstrations in the black community, moved swiftly and decisively to end segregation in virtually all public and in many private downtown facilities.[63]

There seems little doubt that the white business elite held the ability to facilitate the peaceful desegregation of schools in 1957. That they chose not to intervene can in part be attributed to their own ambivalence toward desegregation and in part to the fact that the Blossom Plan allowed them to ignore the integration controversy altogether. Under the Blossom Plan, the white elite received its own, segregated Hall High School, built in the affluent suburbs of the western part of the city. The decision of the white business elite to wash its hands of school integration was a grave error of judgement that cost the community dearly both in economic and in educational terms. Other business communities in other southern cities were left to learn from the mistakes of Little Rock. Some responded positively, while others still blindly followed a similar pattern of recalcitrance, and many subsequently paid a similar price.[64]

Ironically, it was Governor Faubus who proved one of the most effective combatants of massive resistance up until September 1957. Faubus held his own particular take on minimum compliance. In contrast to Blossom's brand of minimum compliance, which involved doing the legal minimum to enforce school desegregation, Faubus's minimum compliance involved doing the political minimum to keep segregationists happy while pursuing a policy of non-interference over school desegregation. Faubus's stance on school desegregation prior to September 1957 was wholly consistent with his personal and political background. Faubus was born in the Ozark Mountains of northwest Arkansas in 1910 and raised in a poor white farming family. His early political development was strongly influenced by his father, Sam, an ardent socialist. In 1935, Sam actually persuaded his son to enroll at the leftist Commonwealth College in Mena, Arkansas, where Orval spent several months. As a youth, Faubus worked variously as an itinerant farm laborer, lumberjack, rural schoolteacher, postmaster, and editor and publisher of the weekly *Madison County Record*. In 1942, he entered the U.S. Army and served as a commissioned officer in Europe during World War II. Upon his return to Arkansas Faubus began to pursue his political ambitions in earnest. In 1949, he joined the liberal reformist administration of Gov. Sid McMath, sitting on the state highway commission and later becoming director of highways. Hailing from northwest Arkansas, Faubus had limited experience of interaction with blacks, yet he solicited the help of influential black political figures and actively sought black votes during his campaigns for governor.[65]

On the campaign trail in 1954, Faubus largely eschewed the politics of race and played down the impact of *Brown*, insisting that the matter should rest at a "local level with state authorities standing ready to assist in every way possible."[66] Throughout his first term in office, Faubus stuck by his decision not to interfere with school desegregation and steered clear of racial controversies. Although this stance did nothing to actively implement school desegregation, Faubus's refusal to become embroiled with segregationists prevented the efforts of Arkansas's White Citizens' Councils to give the race question mainstream political exposure.[67] When directly challenged for the office of governor in 1956 by the head of Arkansas's White Citizens' Councils, James D. Johnson, Faubus did take on the segregationist mantle to win votes. However, he simply adopted and then diluted all of the measures proposed by his opponent to prevent segregation, and then painted Johnson as a "purveyor of hate."[68] Faubus thereby successfully gained reelection at a time when taking the most extreme segregationist stance appeared mandatory for electoral success in the South. The Citizens' Councils remained critical of him, lampooning him in their publications as "Awful Faubus" and demanding that he declare himself "either for the white folks or for the NAACP."[69] Neither was the population at large sure of Faubus's segregationist credentials. As one bemused *Arkansas Democrat* reader declared in 1957, "I consider the governor without peer in the art of carrying the water of segregation on one shoulder and the water of integration on the other without spilling a drop of either."[70]

This questioning of Faubus's intentions seemed quite justified when, shortly after the 1956 election, he sought to drop the segregationist mantle as quickly as he had donned it. Faubus failed to implement any of the prosegregation legislation that he had sponsored in the 1957 Arkansas General Assembly in order to win segregationist support for his own reformist agenda. He refused to make appointments to the State Sovereignty Commission, which formed the cornerstone of the state's prosegregation program. Without a quorum, the commission was unable to act upon any of the prosegregation measures passed by the General Assembly. Eventually, segregationist politicians had to file a lawsuit to force Faubus to fill the places on the commission.[71] Faubus's delay effectively undermined the prosegregation measures, since the commission was not able to hold its first meeting until August 30, just a week before school desegregation was due to occur.[72] Faubus's relapse to a more moderate stance on school desegregation once the immediate political necessity to adopt segregationist rhetoric had passed was also evident in his dealings with the Citizens' Councils. They repeatedly petitioned Faubus to use his authority as head of a sovereign state to prevent school desegregation from taking place. Faubus scoffed at any notion that he might intervene, telling the press "Everyone knows no state law supersedes a federal law" and that "If anyone expects me to use them to supersede federal laws they are wrong."[73]

Faubus's final decision to thrown in his lot with the segregationists in September 1957 came within the context of the failure of minimum compliance. In the lead-up to school desegregation, segregationist litigation and the speeches by Griffin and Harris exerted pressure on the process of integration. It became increasingly clear that Blossom and the Little Rock school board, whose stance all along had been that school desegregation was a necessary evil and that they would do all they could to minimize its impact, had fostered little actual support for desegregation to combat this pressure. Faubus made no attempt to solicit concrete support for desegregation, since he quite rightly perceived this as political suicide. What he did do was to follow a policy of noninterference, believing that he was offering protection from militant segregationists for local communities to get on with the process of desegregation. When the local community in Little Rock, in the shape of Blossom and members of the white business elite, came to Faubus at the eleventh hour to ask him to take a stand to help enforce a weak and insubstantial plan for school desegregation, the governor felt that they were asking him to take risks that they were not prepared to take themselves and asking him to sacrifice his political career in the process. Refusing to do this, and in the absence of any convincing groundswell of support to make school desegregation work in the city, Faubus chose to side with the segregationists, which he saw as the only viable choice for political survival.[74] Indeed, as it turned out, Faubus was right. He was reelected to an unprecedented third term of office in 1958 and for a further three terms after that. As Faubus tasted the fruits of success through his opposition to desegregation, his actions became more reckless and cavalier. Moreover, his electoral victories meant that Arkansas inherited a prosegregationist governor whose political career long outlasted the momentary influence of the Citizens' Councils and who proved a future obstacle in efforts to return a moderate image to Little Rock and to Arkansas after the school crisis.[75] Thus, the policy of minimum compliance turned a potential moderate ally into a potent enemy.

When Little Rock's schools eventually reopened in August 1959 after the white business community moblized to wrest control of the school board out of the hands of segregationists, the policy of minimum compliance was resumed. Only four black students attended formerly segregated schools, with two assigned to Central High and two assigned to Hall High. Token integration prevailed until further federal intervention in the mid-1960s, this time by the U.S. Department of Education, which drew up more stringent desegregation guidelines. As with many other cities, Little Rock used a variety of further methods to limit integration, including so-called "freedom of choice" and "zoning" plans. An equally familiar pattern of busing and resegregation followed in the 1970s and 1980s. The impact of the policy of minimum compliance therefore continued to have a much greater long-term impact on school desegregation in Little Rock than massive resistance.[76]

Events in Little Rock demonstrate that the impact of the two *Brown* decisions in southern communities needs careful scrutiny. Many of the assumptions, expectations, and foundations for what was to follow solidified during that period. One reading of those years might well insist that white resistance was an inevitable outcome of the Supreme Court directly threatening long-established southern racial mores. Another might, as I do here, insist that white southern massive resistance to school desegregation was not inevitable, particularly in upper South states such as Arkansas. Rather, massive resistance emerged within a context of missed opportunities, a failure to mold community consensus, and a failure to cultivate respect and support for the law. When massive resistance failed, self-styled moderates used the furor it created to justify their already established policy of minimum compliance with the law. Yet it was the policy of minimum compliance that helped to bolster massive resistance in the first place. It was also the ongoing policy of minimum compliance after massive resistance had subsided that far more effectively undermined the process of school desegregation in Little Rock, in other upper South cities and states, and eventually throughout the South.

7

White Support for the Civil Rights Struggle

The Southern Regional Council and the Arkansas Council on Human Relations 1954–1974

Many histories of the civil rights struggle have centered on what the press in the 1960s labeled the "Big Six" organizations: the National Association for the Advancement of Colored People (NAACP), the National Urban League (NUL), the Brotherhood of Sleeping Car Porters (BSCP), the Congress of Racial Equality (CORE), the Southern Christian Leadership Conference (SCLC), and the Student Nonviolent Coordinating Committee (SNCC).[1]

However, as sociologist Aldon D. Morris demonstrated in his 1984 study, *The Origins of the Civil Rights Movement,* the civil rights struggle was composed of a complex, often interrelated network of organizations, which operated on a number of different levels.[2] One of those tiers of organization was made up of indigenous black community organizations that have been extensively documented through various local and state studies.[3] Another less familiar tier of organization is what Morris refers to as "Movement Halfway Houses." These organizations provided an important link between national and regional civil rights organizations and indigenous black community organizations, lending "a battery of social change resources such as skilled activists, tactical knowledge, media contacts, workshops [and] knowledge of past movements." In contrast to other organizations, Morris points out, "What they lack is broad support and a visible platform." Morris lists Highlander Folk School in Tennessee, the Fellowship of Reconciliation, the Southern Conference movement (including the Southern Conference on Human Welfare and the Southern Conference Education Fund), the American Friends Service Committee, the War Resisters League, and the Southern Regional Council as examples of movement halfway houses.[4]

One distinguishing hallmark of movement halfway houses is that, in contrast to other more familiar civil rights organizations, they were predominantly staffed by whites. Thus, Morris argues, "The focus on halfway houses of the civil rights movement also reveals the organized efforts that certain courageous and committed white people gave to the civil rights movement."[5] These movement halfway houses and the courageous and committed white people who staffed them—who I will refer to here collectively as white activists, which I define as those whites who broadly shared the aims of black activists in striving to bring about greater black social, political, and economic freedom and equality—remain largely overlooked in the civil rights struggle of the 1950s and 1960s.

In contrast, the role of what is more often referred to collectively as "white southern liberals" prior to those decades is a far more familiar story. Two good surveys for that period exist in Morton Sosna's *In Search of the Silent South: Southern Liberals and the Race Issue* and John Egerton's *Speak Now Against the Day: The Generation Before the Civil Rights Movement in the South*. There are also a number of studies of white liberal organizations, with, for example, three on the Southern Conference movement alone. From the mid-1950s onward, such cohesive treatments of white activism tend to disappear. What we are left with is a collection of autobiographies and biographies of white activists and little sense of what connects them.

Earlier studies of white southern liberal activism tend to suggest that this historiographical incongruity is actually a reflection of historical reality. The collapse of white liberal activism in the 1950s is ascribed to three factors. The first is the rise of McCarthyism in an oppressive Cold War climate, which decimated left-leaning organizations and activists, white southern liberals among them. The second is the segregationist backlash to the U.S. Supreme Court's *Brown v. Board of Education* school desegregation ruling and the rise of massive resistance, which swept away any influence that white southern liberals might otherwise have had. The third is the emergent wave of black activism, which superseded white southern liberal activism and made it both redundant and irrelevant.[6]

One notable study that has provided an analysis of the roles played by white southerners in the civil rights movement, including white southern liberals—or what he terms "white dissenters"—is David Chappell's 1994 study *Inside Agitators: White Southerners in the Civil Rights Movement*. Yet Chappell in many ways confirms rather than challenges the prevailing paradigm of a fragmented and isolated response of white southerners to the civil rights movement. Central to his analysis, drawing upon the model of the community studies used so effectively by civil rights historians to explore local and state-level black activism, are studies of four southern cities. Although instructive, a major problem with these case studies is that each offers only a year-long snapshot of white southern activism in communities in crisis—Montgomery during the 1955–56 bus boycott, Tallahassee during the 1956–57 bus boycott, Little Rock during the 1957–59 school crisis, and Albany during the 1961–62 Martin Luther King-led demonstrations. Chappell effectively demonstrates the involvement and role of white dissenters in these places but, as in the larger literature, they often appear to be isolated individuals offering individual responses rather than collective action or coordinated support. He thus concludes: "Given the weakness and disunity of southern white dissent, it is hard to say exactly what it consisted of." Chappell ascribes a greater role to pragmatic southern white moderates—those whites who were moved to reform racial practices when their own, usually economic self-interests were placed under threat by direct action demonstrations—than he does to idealistic white southern liberals/dissenters/activists in influencing the course of the civil rights movement.

A closer examination of Chappell's city-based case studies reveals the potential for a different sort of approach and analysis. One link between all four communities, for example, is the mention in each of the Atlanta-based Southern Regional Council's affiliate branches, the state Councils on Human Relations. The Human Relations Councils were established in 1954 as part of the Southern Regional Council's restructuring of local branches after the *Brown v. Board of Education* school desegregation decision. Anticipating the state and local struggles to implement the decision, the group created the councils to encourage new dynamism in state affiliate branches and to provide local grassroots support for communities that faced great upheavals in race relations. The Human Relations Councils were soon after made legally autonomous bodies, enabling them to shape their own agendas for action according to local circumstances.[7]

The existence of such a white activist infrastructure across southern states after the mid-1950s holds out the possibility of further investigating the roles played by white activists at local and state levels during that period, as well providing a basis for state and regional comparisons of their effectiveness. Moreover, the interaction between these state affiliates and other white activist organizations potentially lays the foundations for constructing a more coherent narrative of white southern activism in the civil rights movement from the "bottom-up." Such studies hold the potential to transform our understanding of white southern activism in the civil rights struggle, in much the same way that state and local studies of black activism over the past quarter of a century have fundamentally altered our understanding of the nature of black activism.

This essay provides a case study of how this new history of white southern activism can be constructed, by looking at the Arkansas Council on Human Relations (ACHR) and reexamining precisely one of those communities, Little Rock, Arkansas, where David Chappell previously claimed to find little evidence of coordinated or effective white dissent. Formed in December 1954, the ACHR existed for almost twenty years before merging with the Greater Little Rock Urban League in May 1974.[8] It functioned as a typical movement halfway house as defined by Aldon Morris. Indeed, its founding 1954 mission statement uncannily anticipated Morris's later definition by declaring the ACHR's intent "to be a service agency; a clearing house disseminating information, funded experience, suggestive of action to local groups; supplying counsellors for officials and administrators, speakers and resource materials on group relations; correlating the efforts of individuals and organizations working for better human relations in Arkansas."[9] Moreover, as the ACHR's first executive director, Nat R. Griswold, explained, also echoing Morris's description, "We have not claimed to be a mass movement or force or power and have never attempted to be."[10]

Contradicting the received wisdom about the perceived failures of southern white liberals, the ACHR played a prominent role in the civil rights struggle in Arkansas. Although national and regional organizations were present at pivotal moments in the struggle to force change in the 1950s and 1960s, it was often the ACHR that gave a sense of continuity to that struggle and that provided essential grassroots assistance to national and regional organizations while helping to nurture local black activist leaders and organizations. At various points, the ACHR provided moral and legal support for embattled school officials who sought to uphold the law after the *Brown v. Board of Education* decision; it provided an important hub of communication between blacks and whites through a period of racial polarization during the 1957 Little Rock crisis; it exerted pressure on reluctant white moderate business leaders to embrace peaceful racial change; it nurtured local black leaders and organizations by providing positions of leadership responsibility and acting as a forum for intra- as well as interracial contact; and it played a major role in organizing black voter registration efforts in the 1960s.[11]

The first chair of the newly constituted board of the ACHR was Fred K. Darragh Jr., a native Arkansan, the chair of Darragh Company Agribusiness, and a millionaire businessman and philanthropist. Darragh was a war hero who flew planes with military provisions over the Himalayas from India to China during World War II. Throughout his life, Darragh committed his personal funds to many different causes. These ranged from personal acts of kindness, such as helping to fund the college education of the son of Tenzig Noray, the sherpa who climbed Mt. Everest with Sir Edmund Hillary in 1953, to later founding and financing the Arkansas branch of the American Civil Liberties Union.[12] In keeping with the biracial policy of the Southern Regional Council, the first ACHR vice chair was Rev. Charles C. Walker, the black pastor of Little Rock's First Congregationalist Church.[13] However, it was the second vice chair, Harry S. Ashmore, executive editor of the *Arkansas Gazette,* who alongside Darragh proved the most influential force in the founding of the organization. Ashmore, a native of Greenville, South Carolina, joined the *Arkansas Gazette* in 1947. He already had a number of years of experience as a journalist and was working as editor of the *Charlotte News* in North Carolina when approached by the *Gazette's* owner, J. N. Hieskell, to take over as editor. Like Darragh, Ashmore was a war veteran. He had taken part in European campaigns with the U.S. Army and rose to the rank of lieutenant colonel during World War II. As with many other returning GIs, Ashmore urged the building of a more progressive South. His editorials at the *Arkansas Gazette* supported two-party politics, racial and religious tolerance, the right of blacks to vote, and higher pay for teachers. These editorials enhanced the importance of the newspaper as a significant force for modernization in Arkansas and counterbalanced the more conservative bent of its major competitor, the *Arkansas Democrat*.[14]

The two most important posts within the ACHR were those of executive director and associate director, since they were the people charged with the organization's day-to-day running and program development. The first executive director, and the most influential guiding force in the ACHR's first decade, was Nat R. Griswold. A native Arkansan and an ordained Methodist minister, Griswold was educated at Henderson-Brown College in Arkadelphia, Arkansas, and then at Northwestern and Columbia universities. He taught for twelve years as associate professor of religion at Hendrix College in Conway, Arkansas, and served as director of community activities at Arkansas's Japanese American Relocation Centers during World War II. In 1954, he took a job in Austin, Texas, as secretary of peace education for the American Friends Service Committee in the Southwest. Soon after, he moved to take up the post of ACHR executive director.[15] Griswold reported that he was "quite excited about work in Arkansas. It [would] be a privilege to be associated with [Arkansans] in the effort to relieve tensions and to 'oil' the process of integration in the state."[16]

Christopher C. Mercer was appointed associate director. A native of Pine Bluff, Arkansas, Mercer was among the first group of black lawyers to graduate from the University of Arkansas Law School in Fayetteville after it desegregated in 1948 under pressure from NAACP-sponsored litigation and demands from local black activists.[17] After graduation Mercer moved back to Pine Bluff, where he worked in the same law practice as fellow black University of Arkansas Law School graduate Wiley A. Branton. It was Branton, an ACHR board member, who successfully persuaded Mercer to accept the position of associate director.[18]

The ACHR used Mercer's home address at 211 Izard in Little Rock as its headquarters from 1955 to 1957. Frederick B. Routh, Southern Regional Council assistant director for state organizations, approved the choice of two "highly qualified people" and Griswold and Mercer began work on April 15, 1955.[19] In July 1955, Darragh, Walker, and Ashmore incorporated the ACHR under Arkansas law as a nonprofit organization.[20] The total ACHR membership at that time stood at seventy-two, most of who were based in Little Rock.[21]

Helping to ensure a smooth and peaceful process for school desegregation in the state was the first major task that the ACHR faced. ACHR vice chair Ashmore had greeted the *Brown* decision with optimism. "Looking out over the debris this morning, I'm right proud of the South," Ashmore wrote the day after the decision was handed down. "[Georgia governor] Herman Talmadge exploded on schedule, but virtually every other southern politician of standing took the high ground. . . [I]f I had to define the prevailing feeling here—and I believe this is generally true all over the South except for the really hot spots— I would say that it is one of relief that the other shoe has finally dropped. I think I can see the beginning of the time I have always dreamed of—when you can conduct a conversation in the South without it having to degenerate into an argument over where a man should sit in a street car."[22]

Ashmore's optimism was based in part on the state's previous record of progress. In 1948, the University of Arkansas had become the first university in the South to desegregate. The state capital of Little Rock had instigated a number of what were, within the context of the times, significant, if still tentative and limited, racial reforms. The city's public library was already desegregated. Blacks had also gained admission to a selected few of the city's segregated public parks, although the use of swimming pools and golf courses was prohibited. The Little Rock Zoo began to admit blacks, but only on Thursdays, and with use of the amusement park and picnic areas discouraged. Pfeiffer's, a downtown department store, built a segregated lunch counter to cater to black clients who were previously refused service altogether. Other establishments took down the "white" and "colored" signs from their drinking fountains, but still stringently enforced segregated restrooms. Downtown hotels began to relax their policy of segregation by allowing interracial groups such as the Greater Little Rock Urban League to hold meetings at their facilities, but still seated blacks and whites at different tables for lunch. By the early 1950s, hotels were accepting group bookings of visiting black sports teams, while still prohibiting any black individuals from occupying a room. The *Arkansas Gazette* and *Arkansas Democrat* changed their policies of denying courtesy titles of "Mr." and "Mrs." to blacks, by dropping "Mr." altogether except for members of the clergy (black and white), and applying "Mrs." equally. The first press pictures of blacks in white newspapers began to appear. The *Arkansas Democrat* even hired Ozell Sutton, the first black reporter to work for a white newspaper in the state, to write a weekly column about news in the black community.[23]

Initially, Arkansas appeared to live up to its reputation as a progressive upper South state. Several school districts in northwest Arkansas, where there was only a very small black population (the whole of the northwest part of the state contained less than 5 percent of the state's entire black population of around half a million people) immediately moved to desegregate, since it was cheaper to provide an integrated education for their few black students. In contrast, many other southern states saw no progress toward desegregation at all. Also, unlike many other southern states, no widespread, organized campaign of massive resistance to school desegregation developed. New governor Orval E. Faubus won election in November 1954 without taking any firm stance on the issue of school desegregation. Moreover, the state legislature delayed the one direct attempt to circumvent the *Brown* decision. State representatives from eastern Arkansas, which contained most of the state's black population (over 90 percent of the black population in Arkansas resided in the thirty-five counties in the Arkansas Delta area) introduced a Pupil Assignment Bill to the 1955 Arkansas General Assembly that sought to evade school desegregation by assigning black students to black schools and white students to white schools on grounds other than race. A divided assembly agreed to delay the implementation of the measure until after the U.S. Supreme Court had announced its school desegregation implementation order. The opposition to legislation designed to circumvent *Brown* indicated the presence of law-abiding influences in Arkansas that could hold at bay attempts by militant segregationists to align the state with massive resistance elsewhere in the South.[24]

The first real test of the *Brown* decision in Arkansas came in 1956 when the school board at Hoxie, a small settlement in northeast Arkansas, decided to integrate. With a population of just over a thousand, Hoxie was close enough to the Arkansas Delta to have a split school term to allow for the cotton-picking harvest but atypical in that, with only fourteen black families living there, it did not reflect the density of the black population in other Delta areas.[25] On June 25, 1955, the school board at Hoxie voted to integrate its 25 black students with 1,050 white students because, the school board declared, it was, "right in the sight of God," unconstitutional not to, and cheaper.[26] Nat Griswold wrote to superintendent of schools K. E. Vance "to congratulate you and your Board of Education for your prompt decision. . . The newspaper accounts indicated not only the right attitude, but sound wisdom in the way you did it. We were pleased at the first reason you gave . . . that it is in accord with the will of God." Griswold sent Vance a copy of the Southern Regional Council publication the *New South*, which contained reports about church support for school desegregation.[27] On July 11, the first day of integrated classes, a small group of disgruntled local men gathered outside the school to witness proceedings. Some parents voiced their misgivings, with one, a Mrs. John Cole, worriedly telling newspaper reporters that her eight-year-old daughter Peggy "feared Negroes." However, despite the apprehension surrounding integration, the consensus was that "we have to obey the law." Although there was some tension in classes at first, teachers soon made black students feel welcome and normal school life quickly resumed. At noon recess, black and white boys tried out for the school baseball team together and photographers even caught the fearful Peggy playing and walking arm in arm with black female students.[28] The school board reported that during the first three weeks of term there was "Not a single incident. Not a single case for discipline."[29]

Ironically, it was the very success of school desegregation at Hoxie that made it the rallying point for a massive resistance movement in the state. *Life* magazine reporters were present to document the event, producing an article that included a collection of pictures showing the mixing of black and white students.[30] Whereas other school boards were generally at pains to avoid the glare of publicity, desegregation at Hoxie became a national story. With the help and encouragement of segregationists in other states, particularly the closely neighboring Mississippi, local whites held a meeting in Hoxie where they elected Herbert Brewer, a local soybean farmer and part-time auctioneer, as chair of a new pro-segregation group.[31] Brewer and the Hoxie Citizens' Committee launched a concerted campaign of intimidation against the Hoxie school board including "anonymous phone calls at all hours, abusive language hurled at members of their families, petitions calling for members to resign, law suits threatened and filed charging violation of Arkansas school laws" in an effort to get its members to reverse their decision to desegregate.[32] With the school board facing immense provocation, Griswold wrote to fortify its resolve, asking its members to "stand firm. . . I want you to know that we stand ready to help at any time."[33] Encouraged by this support, the school board rebuffed the demands of segregationists, although many of its members threatened resignation, insisting "We may have to leave it with them [the segregationists]; we can't take anymore. But we'll not change our action: we'll not send the Negro children back to that rat hole [the old school house]."[34] Instead of resigning, however, the school board closed the school two weeks before the scheduled end of term to provide a cooling off period in the hope of diffusing existing tensions.[35]

The concession to close the schools early proved unfortunate since it only encouraged further disruption from segregationists. The gathering storm also drew increasing support from other scattered segregationists across the state. Soon after, they banded together to form the Associated Citizens' Councils of Arkansas under the leadership of lawyer James D. Johnson.[36] Yet for all their bluff and bluster, segregationists only met with a protracted defeat in Hoxie. While they made all the headlines, the ACHR was busy mobilizing support behind the scenes. The ACHR rallied assistance from Forrest Rozzell, the executive secretary of the Arkansas Education Association, who backed the school board's decision; from Harry Ashmore, who wrote editorials offering strong support for the school board in the *Arkansas Gazette;* and from E. B. Williams, a well-respected Methodist minister in Hoxie, who appealed to local whites to uphold the law. Most important of all, the ACHR arranged practical legal help for the school board. Few lawyers were prepared to come to the school board's aid, but Griswold persuaded ACHR member William Penix, along with his father Roy Penix, who both practiced law in Jonesboro near Hoxie, to provide the school board with legal representation. All of this was done outside of the media glare and not once was the ACHR mentioned in the newspapers. The school at Hoxie reopened integrated the following term and the Penix attorneys won a landmark court ruling from a federal district judge who issued an injunction to prevent any further interference from segregationists.[37]

Heartened by this significant victory in eastern Arkansas, the ACHR turned its attention back to school desegregation in Little Rock. With the state's strongest record of progressive racial change, there was great optimism that successful school desegregation in the capital city would send a firm signal for compliance with the *Brown* decision to the rest of the state. As one concerned superintendent of schools from Union County in south central Arkansas put it, "I don't like to see a leading community like Little Rock take the lead too fast. . . In the end, other communities will have to follow suit."[38] Initially, it appeared that Little Rock would indeed lead the way. The day after the *Brown* ruling was handed down Little Rock superintendent of schools Virgil T. Blossom announced that the school board intended to comply with the decision and to desegregate all of the city's high schools in September 1957, thereby signaling both his and the city's "moderate" stance. However, as the Blossom Plan for school desegregation unfolded, the superintendent arbitrarily introduced a number of caveats along the way, each of which limited the number of black students eligible to apply for admission to white schools.[39]

The ACHR found Blossom's approach extremely frustrating. Nat Griswold noted a "great lack of planning for bi-racial meetings of parents in small groups in preparation for integration," exactly the sort of area where the ACHR was eager to lend assistance and felt that it could be most helpful.[40] However, Blossom "did not confer in the ordinary sense," Griswold explains. "He fervently explained and defended a position, *his*. In response to any thoughtful contrary opinion, usually he said something like this: 'You have a right to your view, but this is our plan.'" There were distinctly insidious undertones to Blossom's obstinacy. According to Griswold, Blossom believed that he had found "the admissions device by which the requirements of the courts could be met, and, at the same time, by which only a few Negro students would be enrolled in formerly white schools. Th[e] intent of the plan [was] to guarantee an extended life to the dual school system. . . . He was the author of one of the earliest plans for school desegregation in the South [and] he was at the same time guardian of its built-in, submerged features which provided a way for schools in the South to avoid the dreaded consequences of integration."[41] While the ACHR sought to persuade Blossom to take a more constructive approach to school desegregation, the NAACP, headed in the state by Daisy Bates, who with her husband Lucious Christopher (L. C.) Bates co-owned the Little Rock-based *Arkansas State Press* newspaper, took a more direct approach and launched a lawsuit to compel Little Rock schools to desegregate. The courts, however, upheld the much-revised Blossom Plan and ordered that it should be put into effect as scheduled in September 1957.[42]

As the date for school desegregation in Little Rock drew closer, the ACHR submitted a proposal for renewed funding to the Southern Regional Council. It described the situation in the state as "mixed . . . We have the same defying forces here that operate in other sections of the South; but progressive affirming forces have their roots deep in the state's history and culture." The proposal concluded, "the defying forces and the affirming forces just now seem squared off for a tussle . . . In the matter of school desegregation this may prove a fateful year."[43] The summation proved prophetic, although the eventual, decisive source of resistance to school desegregation came as a surprise.

In September 1957, the night before Central High School was due to desegregate, Governor Faubus dispatched National Guard troops to encircle the school building. When the nine black students that Blossom finally allowed to enrol attempted to enter Central High, the soldiers turned them away. Up until that point Faubus had remained ambivalent on the question of school desegregation. During his first term of office from 1954 to 1956, Faubus had steered clear of taking any firm stance on the issue. Challenged by head of the Associated Citizens' Councils of Arkansas, James D. Johnson, for office in 1956, Faubus donned the segregationist mantle to win re-election only to drop it again once he had been safely returned to office. Under pressure from segregationists in the run up to school desegregation in Little Rock in August 1957, Faubus finally decided that taking a pros-egregation stance best served his political interests. He was right: it subsequently earned him an unprecedented six consecutive terms as governor. When Faubus's actions were challenged in court, he was ordered to remove troops from Central High. The courts decreed that school desegregation should then proceed as planned. When Faubus removed the National Guard, attempts by the nine black students to study at Central were frustrated by an unruly white mob. Finally, President Eisenhower sent federal troops to Little Rock to uphold law and order and to ensure the safety of the black students. Central High spent one school year desegregated under armed guard. When the federal troops were withdrawn, Faubus closed all of the city's schools to prevent desegregation. Only when the white business community mobilized to gain control of the city school board, spurred on by some of the city's influential white middle-class women who formed the Women's Emergency Committee to Open Our Schools, did Little Rock schools reopen on a token integrated basis in August 1959.[44]

During the years of the school crisis in Little Rock the ACHR acted as an important local contact for outside groups, especially the American Friends Service Committee, which Griswold had previously worked for, and the Fellowship of Reconciliation. In a climate of increasing racial polarization in the city, both organizations sent representatives to Little Rock in an effort to exercise their influence to resolve community conflict.[45] C. H. Yarrow, American Friends Service Committee association secretary, reported "I found that the office of the [ACHR, from December 1957 located at 1220 West Capitol Avenue] was a center for mobilizing thinking people to come to the support of desegregation in the schools and for upholding the principles of law and order." He added, "The Council has . . . avenues of approach and ways of bringing constructive ideas to the attention of persons in authority in the government and to persons of influence and importance in the community. The Council also has strategic importance as a center where communication can go on with freedom and equality between white and negro communities in Little Rock."[46]

Yet the following year, Yarrow lamented the lack of receptivity by white moderates to the ACHR's overtures. "It is sad to hear of all the excellent opportunities that are passed up by officials and organizations who might make a constructive approach to the problem," Yarrow observed. "It almost appears as if they wanted the experience of the nine students to be uncomfortable and defeating."[47]

The American Friends Service Committee sent staff member Thelma Babbitt to Little Rock. The ACHR coordinated with Babbitt to hold several "Conferences on Community Unity" and a variety of other meetings and workshops that attempted to strengthen lines of communication between the black and white communities.[48] The ACHR also liaised with Fellowship of Reconciliation representatives such as Rev. Glenn Smiley, who had advised Martin Luther King Jr. during the 1955–56 Montgomery bus boycott, and Rev. James Lawson, who became a leading figure in the 1960 sit-in movement and the subsequent formation of SNCC, to promote nonviolent methods to resolve the conflict.[49] The American Friends Service Committee noted that "As other interracial groups are experiencing decline of both Negro and white participation, th[e ACHR] seems to evidence unique vitality."[50] Membership figures reflected that fact. Whereas the Arkansas NAACP and Urban League had seen membership figures plummet as a result of the crisis, ACHR membership actually grew to 216, with 80 of those members based in Little Rock.[51]

When Little Rock schools finally reopened in 1959 the ACHR took the opportunity to try to build on the white community's acceptance of limited school desegregation. To do this, it targeted the white businessmen who had acted to reopen the city's schools. The ACHR hoped they would now be more proactive in other areas of community race relations to avoid a repetition of the events of the school crisis that had proved so socially and economically damaging to the city.[52] Shortly after the schools reopened, the ACHR showed a film titled *Dallas at the Crossroads* to white business leaders. The film charted the smooth process of racial change in that Texas city because of cooperation between various groups in the black and white community. Only ten out of seventy-five invited members attended and there was little progress in the discussion after the meeting. The new president of the school board and director of industrial development for the Chamber of Commerce, Everett Tucker, summed up the white business community's attitude: "The best thing for Little Rock to do now is nothing."[53]

Faced with stonewalling from white businessmen, the ACHR quickly realized that it would need to help build an effective base for protest in the black community that in turn could exert direct pressure for change on white businessmen. The NAACP and its state president Daisy Bates, who had provided leadership for the black community in the crisis years, were now left beleaguered because of segregationist harassment. More established black leaders proved incapable of inspiring a new surge in black activism.[54] National Urban League director of community services for the southern field division, C. D. Coleman, on a visit to Little Rock, noted "the one great problem facing Little Rock [is] the lack of unity, confidence and cooperation between Negro leaders and the lack of regular and orderly lines of communication between Negro organizations. . . Disunity among Negro leaders [is of] greater concern than the school crisis."[55] The young, new, black associate director of the ACHR, John Walker, who replaced Christopher C. Mercer in 1958, observed early in 1960 that "Negro leadership is virtually nil . . . the 'masses' of Negroes are anxious for more progressive leadership from new people."[56] Walker's appointment as associate director was itself an important step toward developing a new black leadership in the city. When Griswold recommended Walker's appointment he noted that Walker was "disarmingly modest but as sharp as a briar. We think he can open up some new areas for us with Negroes and students."[57] Walker remained in the position only until

June 1960, when he left to take up a place at New York University.[58] Griswold encouraged Walker to "give thought . . . to getting legal training. The law offers opportunity for a direct attack on injustice . . . As you are aware all work with Negroes for fair treatment very soon involves one in questions of law."[59] Walker later returned to Little Rock, where he developed into a leading civil rights lawyer and took forward continuing school desegregation litigation. Walker's case was one of many instances where the ACHR provided a position of leadership and responsibility that nurtured a subsequently important black community leader.

The ACHR tried to stimulate discussion in the black community about the need for leadership and organization. In 1960, Griswold wrote to John Wheeler, a black leader who had been instrumental in forming a Council on Community Organizations in Durham, North Carolina, to coordinate the struggle for civil rights there. Wheeler was a member of the executive committee of the Southern Regional Council and a board member of the North Carolina Council on Human Relations.[60] Griswold hoped that Wheeler could persuade black leaders in Little Rock to work "together in the interest of all Negroes and . . . shift their focus above the petty views of individual[s]." Initially planned as a day visit, Griswold persuaded Wheeler to stay for a week.[61] Yet nothing did happen as a result of the meetings. Divisions within the black community remained, with each black leader still reluctant to surrender his own sphere of influence to work as part of a collective push for civil rights. As Griswold summed up, "Each wanted a united voice—his."[62]

The full ramifications of disunity in the black community were brought home when the student sit-in movement began to sweep across the South in 1960. In Little Rock, the first sit-ins by black students from Philander Smith College were held March 10 and continued intermittently for several months. Local and state courts handed out harsh fines and stiff sentences that swiftly ground the movement to a halt.[63] The movement resumed later in the autumn led by Worth Long, a twenty-four-year-old Philander Smith student who worked at a nearby air base. According to an observer in the ACHR, Long had a "good public relations sense," which resulted in the demonstrations being "well coordinated and managed."[64] The ACHR held a forum to encourage the continuation of student protest in October 1960, in which Long featured prominently.[65] "We wish to add our word of appreciation to the many we have heard for your contribution to our panel discussion," Griswold wrote Long afterward. "We sincerely hope this is the beginning, not the end, of genuine helpfulness to the students in their move against segregation as a moral evil."[66] With the help of the ACHR and the Southern Regional Council, four Philander Smith students attended workshops on nonviolence in Atlanta.[67] Still, a major obstacle to effective protest remained the lack of support from the black adult community which, Griswold reported, was "showing its usual fragmentation and divisiveness." With momentum for demonstrations again lost, and wary of the position of their friends who were still involved in protracted courtroom battles and facing large fines and long jail sentences, again protests came to a standstill.[68]

Without any immediate pressure for change, Little Rock's white business community still refused to act. When Gustave Faulk, southwest regional director of the American Jewish Committee, inquired why the ACHR was not doing more to work with the white business community to effect racial change, it drove a wilfully restrained Nat Griswold to distraction. Griswold replied:

The basic premises are these: (1) at this time it is not possible to work *with* the power structure in Little Rock to end segregation; (2) it is possible to work *on* it . . . We are sure what is needed is not the 'how' to move from segregation to desegregation. At the moment what is needed by the men of decision is the 'will.' Efforts to establish the will to change through dialogue, through conferences, through committees has met with cold rejections. There is no sense among the powerful that anything affirmative needs to be done. Thus, they must be worked *on*.[69]

A further attempt to use direct action to bring pressure for change came in the form of Freedom Rides. On July 10, 1961, an interracial group of five members of the St. Louis branch of CORE rode into Little Rock to test bus terminal facilities. They were arrested upon arrival. Wanting at all costs to avoid adverse national headlines after trying to rebuild the city's progressive image after the school crisis, the city tried to dispatch the Freedom Riders as quickly as possible. Judge Quinn Glover in Little Rock's Municipal Court handed each of the Freedom Riders the maximum sentence of a five hundred dollar fine and a six-month prison term, but he agreed to suspend their sentences if they left Arkansas. The riders agreed to those terms. However, when they discovered that the terms actually meant that they would have to return to St. Louis and could not continue on to test facilities in Louisiana as planned, they submitted themselves to rearrest. The leader of the group, Rev. Benjamin Cox, told reporters that he would "much rather be dead and in my grave" than be "a slave to segregation" and threatened to go on hunger strike while incarcerated. Griswold visited the Freedom Riders in jail, reported their arrests to the U.S. Attorney General's office, and approached business leaders in Little Rock to try to resolve the impasse.[70] For the first time since the school crisis, the Freedom Ride fiasco brought action from the city's white businessmen. Thirteen business leaders met at the downtown First National Bank to discuss the situation and formed an ad hoc Civic Progress Association to handle the matter. In a statement to the press, the business leaders diplomatically backed the city authorities in their handling of the matter. At the same time, they suggested that the city could learn from the incident in dealing with similar matters in the future. The following morning Judge Glover relented and allowed the Freedom Riders to continue their journey.[71]

Although the Freedom Ride failed to make the desired impact of forcing concessions for change, it did act as an important catalyst for a significant new black community initiative. Dismayed by the events of the sit-ins and embarrassed by the city's treatment of the Freedom Riders, a young cadre of black medical professionals including Dr. William H. Townsend, Dr. Maurice A. Jackson, Dr. Garman P. Freeman, and his wife, Dr. Evangeline Upshur, decided to act. The four had recently banded together to set up their own practice in the city. Under the leadership of Townsend, who was also ACHR treasurer, a Council on Community Affairs (COCA) was set up to coordinate the activities of existing black organizations in the city to lobby for change.[72]

The ACHR's imprint on COCA was palpable. The organization's name appropriated that of John Wheeler's black community action group in Durham, North Carolina. Many members of COCA held positions in, or were affiliated with the ACHR, particularly its "Community Unity" group of black professionals that had developed within the organization. In effect, COCA represented an assertion of independence from the ACHR to act as an autonomous black community organization, although it continued to maintain close links and overlapping membership with the ACHR.[73]

Griswold was hopeful that the formation of COCA might prove a turning point in the city's race relations, reporting it as "the most promising organization of Negro leaders with a broad base" to emerge in Little Rock since the ACHR began to operate there.[74] Initial efforts by COCA to engage in a dialogue with the white business community met with little success. Ozell Sutton, at that time both John Walker's replacement as associate director of the ACHR and COCA's public relations director, wrote to Burke Marshall, director of the civil rights division of the U.S. Department of Justice, reminding him that they had previously "discussed the need for the Justice Department to use its influence to persuade the 'power structure' of Little Rock to take some role in initiating progress. [Sutton] accepted [Marshall's] commitment to this and hope[d] a start [could] be made in the very near future."[75] Just over two weeks later on March 8, 1962, twenty-two members of COCA filed a collective suit in the U.S. District Court for the desegregation of "public parks, recreational facilities . . . and all other public facilities." [76] Although conceding the inevitable eventual success of the COCA lawsuit, the white business community still insisted that it would draw out the process of desegregation for the longest possible amount of time.[77]

It was the ACHR that moved to break the deadlock. Griswold telephoned SNCC headquarters in Atlanta to ask for assistance in reinvigorating black protest in the city. SNCC responded by sending seasoned white civil rights worker, Bill Hansen, to Little Rock.[78] In 1961, Hansen had participated in a CORE-sponsored Freedom Ride from his home in Cincinnati, Ohio, to Montgomery, Alabama. He was arrested en route in Mississippi and spent one and a half months in jail. In 1962, Hansen had been in Albany, Georgia, helping SNCC and the SCLC to organize mass demonstrations there. He was jailed and beaten by local police officers, resulting in four broken ribs and a broken jaw. The Little Rock assignment was to be Hansen's rehabilitation back into the movement.[79] When Hansen arrived at the ACHR office in Little Rock, he spoke with Griswold and Sutton. They explained that the city was ready to capitulate to demands for desegregation if blacks could apply sufficient pressure. Playing upon the businessmen's fear of unwanted publicity after the school crisis was, they believed, "the most vulnerable point in Little Rock's armor." The only drawback was the lack of direct action in the city that might persuade white businessmen to act. Griswold and Sutton told Hansen that they hoped he might be able to use his organizational skills to help revitalize the student movement at Philander Smith and provide a much-needed catalyst for change.[80]

Hansen contacted students at Philander Smith and generated enthusiasm for a concerted campaign of direct action that eventually brought Little Rock's white businessmen to the negotiating table. Demonstrating the ability of Little Rock's white business community to initiate change if sufficient pressure was applied, in concert with COCA they quickly drew up a schedule for desegregation during the first six months of 1963. By the end of 1963, without drama or fuss, Little Rock desegregated most of its public and some of its private facilities.[81] Black reporter John Britton wrote a feature-length story in *Jet* magazine about peaceful desegregation in Little Rock that contrasted events there with violence in other communities across the South, such as Birmingham, Alabama, where in the same year that Little Rock desegregated, Police Commissioner T. Eugene "Bull" Connor used police dogs and spray from high-power fire hoses to break up demonstrations.[82] In the article, executive secretary of SNCC, James Forman, heralded Little Rock as "just about the most integrated [city] . . . in the south." Both Dr. William Townsend and Ozell Sutton agreed that the major change in the city since 1957 was the newfound unity within the black community.[83]

The desegregation of public facilities and accommodations in Little Rock was the crowning achievement of the ACHR's efforts since 1954. Membership was up to over six hundred and the organization had established itself as one of the most respected forces for racial change in the state. However, in a ten-year retrospective in the *Arkansas Gazette* under the heading "Arkansas Council on Human Relations Looks Back on a Long, Difficult Decade," both Griswold and Sutton refused to rest upon their laurels. "The operation now is harder," Sutton explained. "We have moved from outright defiance to circumvention, which is more difficult to deal with." Both Sutton and Griswold described the task that lay ahead principally as "Opening Doors" to new opportunities. From battle-hardened experience, Griswold noted, "It would be good to have the heart converted but if that doesn't work we try something else."[84] During its next decade, the ACHR continued its pursuit of civil rights, pressing for desegregation of schools and facilities in Little Rock and throughout the state. As more SNCC workers, followed by War on Poverty agencies, moved into the state, the ACHR acted as a liaison point for those outside organizations. The ACHR also expanded its mission to include campaigns for desegregated housing, black employment opportunities, fair treatment of prisoners, and the reform of Arkansas's archaic penal system, among other causes.[85] To take on these new tasks, the ACHR appointed a new, black executive director, Elijah Coleman, to take over from Griswold. Coleman was a native of Smackover, in south central Arkansas, and had worked in the nearby oilfields of El Dorado before enlisting in the U.S. Army during World War II. After the war, Coleman attended Philander Smith College, assisted by the "GI Bill," which provided funds for the education of war veterans. Coleman became involved in civil rights activism while at Philander Smith and attended Progressive Party rallies in the state when white liberal candidate Henry Wallace ran for the presidency in 1948. Coleman worked as a high school principal at Stuttgart in eastern Arkansas before taking on the job of ACHR executive director.[86]

At the very forefront of its post-1965 activities, "the most consistently active and productive program of the ACHR," as Coleman put it, was its involvement in the Arkansas Voter Education Project (AVP).[87] The AVP was part of a regionwide Voter Education Project (VEP) run under the tax-exempt auspices of the Southern Regional Council with the support of all the major national and regional civil rights organizations of the time. The ACHR's stamp on the VEP was assured from the outset since former board member and native Arkansan Wiley A. Branton was the VEP director.[88] The ACHR likewise played an influential role in the AVP, with former ACHR associate director Ozell Sutton as the AVP director and Dr. W. H. Townsend as the AVP chair. The AVP coordinated with other groups such as the NAACP, SNCC, COCA and a "Democrats for Rockefeller" organization made up of white Democrat supporters of the Republican candidate, Winthrop Rockefeller, the grandson of Standard Oil founder John D. Rockefeller, to assist in his successful bid for election as governor in 1966.[89] Rockefeller's campaign was helped by incumbent Gov. Orval Faubus's announcement that he would not stand for reelection in 1966, and the Democratic Party of Arkansas's choice of former head of the Associated Citizens' Councils of Arkansas, James D. Johnson, as their candidate for governor. From the outset, Johnson made it quite clear that he would not be campaigning in the black community and he even refused to shake hands with blacks on the election trail.[90]

Funds from Rockefeller's own considerable fortune and changes to the voter registration law significantly aided the AVP's effort to increase the number of black voters. In 1964, the passage of the

Twenty-fourth Amendment to the U.S. Constitution outlawed the use of the poll tax in federal elections. In 1965, Arkansas abolished the poll tax as a requirement for voting and introduced a permanent personal voter registration system. This new voter registration system simply required a free, one-off registration to vote that in most cases lasted a lifetime. Qualifying to vote therefore became much easier and the number of black and white electors in Arkansas rose rapidly.[91]

Rockefeller's election and subsequent reelection as governor in 1968, when he polled 88 percent of the state's black vote, marked an important sea-change in Arkansas politics. Before the Democrats recaptured the office in 1970, the Democratic Party of Arkansas, a bastion of white supremacy for many years, undertook a thorough reexamination of its ideals and priorities. No longer would it consider a candidate like James D. Johnson as a nominee to run for political office. The successful Democratic candidate in 1970, Dale Bumpers, was the first in a line of Democrat governors of Arkansas—including Bill Clinton, who later became president of the United States—to embrace new racially enlightened ideals and to make open and active efforts to court the black vote.[92]

Another consequence of a rising number of black registered voters was the number of black elected officials across Arkansas, which rose from just sixteen in 1967 to ninety-nine in 1972, a figure that represented the second-highest number in any southern state. ACHR board member Dr. William Townsend became one of three blacks elected to the Arkansas House of Representatives. By 1976, 94 percent of Arkansas's voting-age blacks were registered, the highest proportion of any state in the South.[93]

At the end of the 1960s, ACHR executive director Elijah Coleman declared that "The thrust of civil rights in the [19]70's will be to bring to fruition the long struggle against segregation and discrimination by substantially improving the day to day life conditions of the poor and the black in this country."[94] By that point, however, the civil rights movement in the form that it had existed in the 1950s and 1960s was coming to an end. The 1964 Civil Rights Act and the 1965 Voting Rights Act assisted in securing two of the movement's central goals: the abolition of segregation in public accommodations and facilities and unhindered black voting at the polls with the proactive help of the federal government. After the passage of this legislation the movement pursued what proved to be far more contentious and much less precisely defined goals such as ending *de facto* segregation, racial discrimination, and tackling black (and white) poverty. The rise of the Black Power movement in the mid-1960s and its embrace of black nationalism, black separatism, and black armed self-defense brought further movement controversy and division. This new stance alienated many whites who had previously supported the movement and further bolstered the popularity of more conservative politicians, culminating in Republican Richard M. Nixon's victory in the 1968 presidential election. The assassination of Martin Luther King Jr. in April 1968, who was viewed by many blacks and whites alike as the embodiment of the movement in the 1950s and 1960s, dramatically signaled the end of an era.[95]

Coleman's 1973 annual report presented a gloomy outlook for the ACHR, which read not only like an obituary for that organization, but for the civil rights movement as a whole. Coleman noted that there was

(1) A declining interest on the part of the general public for human relations and human rights activities . . . (2) An unwillingness on the part of the local business community to contribute financially to any kind of organization that has as its primary goal Social and Economic Change . . . (3) A new kind of attitude on the part of blacks that makes their association with whites less desirable . . . (4) New interests, concerns and commitments on the part of heretofore civil rights-oriented whites causing some defection from human relations organizations . . . (5) Large and small foundations that supported human relations and civil rights activities during the fifties and sixties do so now with extreme reluctance. In fact, human relations activities claim a very low priority with most funding sources.[96]

Due to these factors and an accompanying sharp decline in membership, by 1974 the ACHR executive board faced a stark choice: to disband, to find additional funds, or to merge with the Greater Little Rock Urban League, so that the two organizations could consolidate their activities. The executive board voted to merge with the local Urban League and the ACHR ceased to exist.[97]

The history of the ACHR suggests that the role of white activists in the civil rights struggle may be more important than their understated presence in the literature currently indicates. It also suggests that one way to effectively explore the history of white southern activism is through the local- and state-based approach that has proved so effective in transforming our understanding of black activism. Even a cursory examination of the ACHR reveals its interaction with other white activist groups such as the American Friends Service Committee and Fellowship of Reconciliation. Once historians begin to explore white southern activism more systematically, they will likely discover a small, tight-knit, but influential group of people who worked through different organizations with overlapping and often interlocking interests. To begin to tug at one strand of white activism, such as the ACHR and the other Human Relations Councils, quickly leads to, and begins to untangle, a much wider network of connections.

Rethinking the history of white southern activism will also force a rethinking of other aspects of the civil rights struggle. Currently, the literature tends to privilege those organizations that used direct-action, both nonviolently and, as more recently documented, through armed self-defense. While these were important tactics, Martin Luther King Jr. and many other black activists understood that their ultimate aim was to prompt recalcitrant whites to effect change. Organizations that could facilitate such negotiations and provide infrastructural support for direct action groups had a much less glamorous and much less visible role to play but, as Aldon Morris has suggested, were no less important for playing that role.

To mistake the absence of white southern activist organizations from the cutting edge of protest and demonstrations as stemming from timidity, as sometimes appears to be the case, is misguided. Many of the white activists in those organizations understood precisely the role that they could most usefully fulfill. They also understood the need for black activists to take control of their own struggle for liberation, long before SNCC's insistence on that point and the emergence of Black Power. Ironically, it was when white activists began to assume more prominent roles in direct action protests and civil rights organizing through SNCC—which previous generations of white activists were subsequently criticized for not doing—that schisms began to emerge, and the possibilities of a biracial movement began to collapse, heralding the end of organizations such as the Human Relations Councils.

Uncovering the history of white southern activism and the organizations through which it worked will force historians to think further about the contributions made by different groups within the civil rights movement, and how those differences strengthened the movement and contributed to its overall successes.

8

City Planning and the
Civil Rights Struggle

"A Study in Second-Class Citizenship":
Race, Urban Development, and Little Rock's
Gillam Park, 1934–2004

The historiography of the civil rights struggle has changed dramatically over the past quarter of a century. Early histories that appeared prior to the 1980s concentrated primarily on Martin Luther King Jr. and the familiar "Montgomery-to-Memphis" narrative of his life.[1] Since the 1980s, a number of studies examining the civil rights movement at local and state levels have questioned the usefulness and accuracy of the King-centric Montgomery-to-Memphis narrative as the sole way of understanding the civil rights movement. These studies have made it clear that civil rights struggles already existed in many of the communities where King and the organization he was president of, the Southern Christian Leadership Conference (SCLC), ran civil rights campaigns in the 1960s. Moreover, those struggles continued long after King and the SCLC had left those communities. Civil rights activism also thrived in many places that King and the SCLC never visited.[2]

As a result of these local and state studies, historians have increasingly framed the civil rights movement within the context of a much longer, ongoing struggle for black freedom and equality unfolding throughout the twentieth century at local, state, and national levels. This in turn has helped to broaden the range of issues that historians have explored in relation to the civil rights struggle, which have, for example, variously included the role of women's activism, the role of violence and armed-self defense, and international dimensions of the struggle.[3]

A different approach by urban historians has offered an important challenge to the way we conceptualize the civil rights movement. Studies by Thomas J. Sugrue, Arnold R. Hirsch, and others, have explored the role of race and urban development in cities across the United States.[4] In doing so, they have shifted the focus of historians from the short-term battles for desegregation and voting rights to the long-term structural issues of urban planning and neighborhood development. This shift in emphasis has in turn forced attention both on the areas in which the civil rights movement failed to have a decisive impact and to the relatively neglected episodes within the civil rights canon. These include, for example, Martin Luther King and the SCLC's 1965–66 Chicago campaign, which failed in its bid to win "open housing" for blacks in that northern city, and the failure of the 1966 civil rights bill that contained fair housing proposals.[5] Studies by urban historians suggest that to understand the wider implications of the civil rights struggle we need to broaden our focus beyond what have been traditionally perceived as the key issues and to pay more attention to those areas the movement failed to address.

The history of Gillam Park in Little Rock, Arkansas, is particularly instructive for understanding the link between race and urban development in that city and the nature of the ongoing struggle for black freedom and equality there. Gillam Park is made up of about 375 acres located in the southeast corner of Little Rock in the Granite Mountain area. Although at first glance it appears to be a marginal tract of land, distant from the main body of urban affairs, it has, in fact, often been at the heart of the debate over race and city planning. In the 1930s, the city purchased the property as a site for Little Rock's first "separate but equal" park. In the 1940s, the site became central to a campaign by black activists for a more comprehensive plan to develop black recreation facilities but also illustrated the growing divide between blacks pressing for equalization within the Jim Crow system and those urging the abolition of segregation and the integration of white facilities. In the 1950s, Gillam Park was the cornerstone of a multimillion dollar slum clearance and urban redevelopment plan that had a profound impact on the future of race, residence, and community resources in the city. Even in the twenty-first century, Gillam

Park remains part of the wider debate over race and urban development. Thus, the history of Gillam Park provides a unique opportunity to gain insight into race and city planning policy in its myriad phases of evolution over the past seventy years.

Mayor Horace A. Knowlton and the Little Rock City Council, with the approval and support of Little Rock Chamber of Commerce president Joshua K. Shepherd, authorized the purchase of Gillam Park at a meeting on November 22, 1934. The purchase addressed two problems. The first was the growing transient population in the city, made up of jobless and homeless victims of the Depression who were being fed and sheltered by the Federal Emergency Relief Administration. Complaints from Little Rock residents prompted the council to seek a site beyond the city limits to which the transients could be relocated.[6]

The presence of the transients intersected with a second problem: the lack of recreation facilities for Little Rock's black population. Although the city maintained six parks for the exclusive use of whites, it provided no recreation facilities at all for blacks. Those that did exist were privately, and not publicly, funded. These included Crump Park at Thirty-third and State streets, which hosted black baseball games; a vacant lot at Twenty-eighth and Spring streets where black boxing and tennis matches took place; and a ten-acre tract on the outskirts of Little Rock that provided a site for church picnics.[7] Because so many blacks lived in cramped and squalid conditions, recreation facilities were a pressing issue. The perennial problem of black children drowning in unsupervised water-filled holes on abandoned lots, which were used as makeshift swimming areas, increased the sense of urgency.[8] Moreover, the city had a legal obligation to provide such facilities for the black population. Under the "separate but equal" doctrine established by the U.S. Supreme Court in *Plessy v. Ferguson* (1896), segregated facilities were permitted, provided that they were of an equal standard for whites and blacks. In practice, the mandate of equal facilities for the races was rarely enforced. In some cases, as with black recreation in Little Rock, facilities were not provided at all.

In purchasing the land near Granite Mountain, the mayor and council hoped to win federal funds for relocating and temporarily housing its transient population and for the longer-term development of a segregated black park. Influential figures from Little Rock's black elite, including Dr. John G. Thornton, Dr. George William Stanley Ish, and Dr. Isaac T. Gillam II, were consulted on the purchase and gave their approval.[9] In April 1935, the city council suggested securing help from a New Deal agency, the Civilian Conservation Corps (CCC), to develop the site. It proposed that the city apply for funds to create a camp made up of black recruits to work on what had been named "John E. Bush Park" after one of the city's prominent black Republicans and a fraternal leader.[10] After that proposal failed, the city council at the end of 1935 proposed a bond issue of fifteen thousand dollars "to purchase, improve and to cover the city's contribution for the development of the colored park." The park bond issue was bundled with two other bond issues, one for $468,000 to construct and equip a municipal auditorium and another for $25,000 to build an addition to the city library.[11] Since both facilities were primarily for the use of the white population, the bond issue for the black park was added "as sop" to win black support for the white projects and to encourage white voters to support the black park project. All three of the bond issue proposals passed in January 1937.[12]

Transients were subsequently relocated to the site, but there was little progress in developing a black park other than a long and drawn-out process of fund appropriation.[13] By September 1938, with the black population growing impatient, Dr. Isaac T. Gillam II, a Howard- and Yale-educated school principal and the son of Little Rock black Reconstruction politician Isaac T. Gillam Sr., petitioned the council for the immediate development of a black park.[14] In February 1940, a delegation of other black leaders put forward another plan. They asked the city to accept an offer made by Little Rock's black Philander Smith College to donate a fifteen-acre tract of land southwest of the city for development as a black park.[15] However, the council instead applied for Works Progress Administration (WPA) money to develop the land on the Granite Mountain site. It agreed to put up $16,059 for the work if the federal government paid the remaining $49,933. The application proposed the construction of a log pavilion, 12 barbecue pits, a baseball diamond, picnic grounds, tables, benches, 1,500 feet of footpaths, a lake, and a swimming pool. The council estimated that the improvements would take 160 men six months to complete. After securing the funds, the park was renamed the "Isaac T. Gillam Sr., Memorial Park" and work began.[16]

By June 1941, the Little Rock City Council was already beginning to have second thoughts. Mayor J. V. Satterfield instructed members

of the Parks Committee to investigate whether the city should continue
with the Gillam Park project. Work that had already been done on the
site counted in its favor. Seventy WPA workers had taken three months
to construct a road through the woods to the park, clear a tract for a
baseball diamond, and build part of a rock and log pavilion. Around
ten thousand dollars in federal and city money had been spent, and
abandoning the site might mean forfeiting the WPA grant. However,
the mayor and council feared that continuing with the project would
be throwing good money after bad. The park was difficult to reach,
being four and a half miles from Broadway and Roosevelt streets, the
closest area of black residence. Nine-tenths of that distance was over
a gravel road, and three-tenths of that road was virtually impassable
by car. The distance of the park from existing city facilities also meant
that a further seven thousand dollars would have to be found to pipe
in drinking water. Black advocates of the park, led by Dr. Isaac T.
Gillam II, fought against the abandonment of the project, but WPA
work stopped. In an article headlined "Abandoning Negro Park
Would Climax Series of Blunders," the *Arkansas Gazette* feared that
Gillam Park might simply turn out to be an expensive "primeval rock
pile."[17]

Responding to the halt of WPA work, the complaints from black
citizens, and criticism from the *Arkansas Gazette,* members of the Parks
Committee toured the Gillam Park site. An *Arkansas Gazette* reporter
who accompanied them observed that many committee members
"quickly became discouraged with the Granite Mountain location."
Several expressed "amazement that it had been bought by the city for
a park," and one even suggested that the site was "more suitable for a
concentration camp." R. A. Boyce, the acting city engineer, advised
Parks Committee members that the project should be suspended until
it could be determined whether the county could supply the site with
water and build an adequate access road. In the wake of the visit,
Alderman Franklin E. Loy suggested trying to transfer the WPA program to a twenty-one-acre site on the Arkansas River, in the southeast
corner of the city. The site, Loy pointed out, was level, located within
two blocks of the East Ninth Street streetcar line in a predominantly
black neighborhood, and already partly owned by the city. Subsequent
protests from the black population over abandoning the Gillam Park
site were met with an assurance that it was only the site, and not the
idea of providing a black park, the city council was considering.[18]

In the meantime, the city council came under pressure from other groups sympathetic to black demands for recreation facilities. The interracial Greater Little Rock Urban League, which was an affiliate of the New York-based National Urban League, an organization dedicated to improving the conditions of black city dwellers, sent a petition asking "that if it is not found feasible to continue the development of the Granite Mountain site that an adequate site be developed immediately." The Greater Little Rock Council of Church Women presented a similar petition.[19] The *Arkansas Gazette* complained of "Much Bungling in Matter of Negroes Park." It pointed out that four mayoral administrations had failed to make any significant advance on the project. Moreover, the *Gazette* claimed that the whole affair had involved a string of improprieties from the start. It alleged that the council had paid far in excess of what the land was worth, that the bond issue had been drawn up in a way that placed an undue burden on taxpayers, and that the whole venture had been financed through the mayor's office by "unusual procedures." Precious little progress was evident. The removal of the roof from the WPA-built pavilion at Gillam Park to place on the hay barn at the white Litttle Rock Zoo, apparently with the approval of several city aldermen, was indicative of the farcical state of affairs. Glenn D. Douglas, a field engineer for the WPA, issued a formal complaint and demanded the return of the roof. The request was ignored. As a result, the Gillam Park pavilion rotted and had to be torn down.[20]

The project languished, with the city council even exploring the possibility of leasing Gillam Park for bauxite mining.[21] Only in December 1946 did discussion return to the issue of developing a black park. The Parks Committee put forward a motion "recommending to the Council that Gillam (Negro) Park be sold as soon as possible and that the proceeds thereof be placed in a special fund to be applied on the purchase and development of a new Negro Park site." Early the following year, the council voted "in principle" to "accept and maintain a public park for Negroes." The council approved a new site for the park of approximately forty acres bounded by West Sixteenth, West Twenty-first, Washington and Monroe streets. However, just a couple of months later a "protest petition signed by several hundred [white] residents of the city against the use of said property as a park for colored people" put an end to the idea.[22]

While the council continued to equivocate on building black recreation facilities, it faced a growing challenge from a more determined and organized Little Rock black population. World War II proved a watershed for black activism in the United States. Hundreds of thousands of blacks enlisted with the firm intention of winning what the *Pittsburgh Courier* termed the "double V": victory for democracy and equality at home as well as abroad. The leading civil rights organization of the time, the National Association for the Advancement of Colored People (NAACP), experienced a tenfold growth in membership, and a new civil rights organization, the Congress of Racial Equality (CORE), was founded in Chicago and began to experiment with nonviolent direct-action tactics to challenge white supremacy. As wartime industries received massive federal subsidies for expansion, blacks fought hard for their share of new job opportunities.[23]

In Arkansas, Pine Bluff attorney William Harold Flowers and his Committee on Negro Organizations (CNO) spearheaded voter registration drives in an attempt to build a mass black political voice in the state. In Little Rock, Sue Morris, a black Dunbar High School teacher, with the help and assistance of the NAACP, filed a class-action lawsuit on behalf of the city's black teachers for pay equal to white teachers. Lucious Christopher (L. C.) Bates and his wife, Daisy Bates, owners of a crusading new newspaper, the *Arkansas State Press,* successfully campaigned for the appointment of the first black police officers in twentieth-century Little Rock. This came after the paper reported black community's outrage at the downtown shooting of a black army sergeant from nearby Camp Robinson by a white city police officer. Dr. J. M. Robinson, president of the Arkansas Negro Democratic Association, pressured the Democratic Party of Arkansas to abandon its policy of racial exclusion in its primary elections.[24]

In the postwar years a number of younger black leaders, many of them war veterans, looked to build upon the political activism of figures such as Robison and Flowers and press for better conditions in Little Rock. Charles Bussey led a band of ex-servicemen to form the Veterans Good Government Association. Jeffrey Hawkins formed the East End Civic League to represent the interests of the black population there. I. S. McClinton formed a Young Negro Democrats organization, which later became the Arkansas Democratic Voters Association. William Harry Bass also emerged as an influential community spokesperson through his position as chief executive officer of the Greater Little Rock Urban League.[25]

Although all of the new black leaders and organizations shared the goal of black advancement, they often differed over the best way to achieve that end. Many viewed the equalization of facilities within the segregated order as the most realistic and achievable goal in the face of white hostility to more fundamental changes in race relations. Others, most notably L. C. and Daisy Bates at the *Arkansas State Press,* believed that only the integration of facilities would solve the problems the black community faced. They believed that equalization of facilities left the prospects of black advancement too much at the discretion of whites who could stall promised improvements whenever they wanted to or, indeed, simply abandon them altogether. Without political power or the force of the law to back their demands, the Bateses believed that any gains won by the black community through concessions alone would be of little enduring benefit.[26]

These different approaches to black advancement crystallized in the struggle for black recreational facilties. The *Arkansas State Press* insisted upon the desegregation of existing city parks rather than the building of new segregated parks for blacks. In 1947, *Arkansas State Press* columnist A. M. Judge stormed, "Every so often somebody out of nowhere comes up with a lot of 'Negro Park' bunk, and keeps the newspapers full of hot air for a few weeks, and then the whole thing dies down to where it started." Why, he asked, was the city straining its finances "to build and keep up another park" when it "already had several [perfectly good but segregated] parks." Judge asserted that the city "has no business trying to support a dual system for segregational purposes."[27] The city council responded to the criticism by renewing its efforts at Gillam Park. Preparations were made to run a road from state Highway 65 to the site, and $1,535 was spent on repairing the rotted main pavilion.[28] *Arkansas State Press* editor L. C. Bates remained unimpressed. "White people will go to no end to prove they are right when they know they are wrong," he wrote. "Look at all the time and money being spent (or make believe) on the so called Gillam Park for Negroes . . . if and when Gillam Park is developed, we still ain't got a damn thing."[29]

When the city council continued to stall on park development, two new black leaders put forward their own equalization plan. William Harry Bass and I. S. McClinton demanded a city bond issue of $359,000 to pay for the development of black recreation facilities. They threatened court action if their plan was turned down.[30] The *Arkansas Gazette* urged the city council and the city's white population to accept the proposal, pointing out that "Anybody who knows how things have been going in recent years in the matter of Negro civil rights should be sufficiently warned by that knowledge." It added, "it would be a reproach to Little Rock for the Negro Park matter to reach that stage. It is enough reproach for Little Rock that after 15 years groping and fumbling the city has not yet met the need for Negro recreation facilities."[31] This editorial policy was in line with the views of the *Arkansas Gazette*'s new executive editor, Harry S. Ashmore, a white war veteran and an advocate of southern social and racial reform, who supported the equalization of black facilities.[32]

After much discussion, the city council finally endorsed the bond issue proposal, even though an *Arkansas Gazette* reporter watching proceedings thought that it was "apparent several Aldermen doubt[ed] the large issue [would] be approved by the voters."[33] The most important thing for the council, however, was the hope that a vote would appease the black population and stave off court action. The vote would also allow the council to gauge the amount of support among white voters for the equalization of facilities now that some blacks were demanding complete integration. The city council therefore announced that a special city election would be held for a bond issue "for the purchase, development and improvement of public parks located either within or without the corporate" limits of Little Rock "and for the development and improvement of Gillam Park."[34]

The bond issue went to the voters on February 1, 1949. Then, as the *Arkansas State Press* described it, "the unexpected happened—the bond issue passed and has made the city the acme of deception and the laughing stock of the entire south." What had started, the *Arkansas State Press* claimed, as "a smart political scheme to garner Negro votes," had backfired. "$359,000 . . . is entirely too much money to be spent upon Negro recreation in Little Rock!" it declared, with the prediction that "it is not going to be spent any time in the near future if there is any way for the present administration to stop it." The paper's conclusion echoed the Bateses' sentiments that any advancement or improvement for the black community "will have to be gained through the courts or the ballots and not through BEGGING."[35]

The bond issue had passed by a narrow margin (2,936 to 2,812), with a turnout of just 19 percent of voters. Whether the absence of the majority of white voters from the polls indicated complacency about what they thought would be its inevitable defeat, or whether that absence represented a lack of outright opposition and therefore a silent acquiescence to the equalization of facilities was unclear. The increasing ability of new black politicians to bring out enough black voters to make a difference in close-run city elections was readily apparent.[36] Yet, as the Bateses and the *Arkansas State Press* had predicted, even with the passage of the bond issue, there was still no progress on the development of a black park. In May, the *Arkansas Democrat,* which had opposed the bond issue on the grounds of its cost, noted that the "Rush For Negro Park Now Limps." The bond issue "decision couldn't wait for the regular election," the *Arkansas Democrat* told readers, and yet "with summer at hand" the powers that be were "floundering in division, uncertainty and confusion, rehashing old delaying arguments." The paper demanded, "Let's get started on something. You're on the spot Mr. Mayor and members of the Council—a spot you picked for yourselves."[37]

At a Little Rock City Council session, William Nash, chair of the Planning Commission, reported that the city would hire the services of an architect and an engineer to assess the project before deciding how the bond money would be spent.[38] After the surveys had been completed, the Planning Commission recommended that a South End site located at Crump Field should be developed as a playground and athletic field; that one square block of Philander Smith College property at West Twentieth and Washington streets should be acquired and developed as a neighborhood park; and that the city should acquire land around Calhoun, Townsend, Seventh and Eighth streets, thereby expanding existing school grounds and building a playground for public use.

The Planning Commission recommendation apparently met with the approval of a large portion of the black population. Despite the *Arkansas State Press*'s opposition to Jim Crow facilities, Arkansas Negro Democratic Association president Dr. J. M. Robinson reported that 90 percent of blacks in the city supported the development of the South End site. A petition bearing 497 signatures was presented supporting Robinson's stand and specifically requesting a swimming pool within the city limits, instead of at the remote Gillam Park site. As one petitioner asked, "What man wants to send his child into the woods [to swim]?" A dissenting voice came from Dr. Isaac T. Gillam II, who had a vested interest in the development of the Gillam Park site since it would preserve his father's memory. Gillam claimed that all "responsible negroes favor the development of [Gillam] park." After listening

to the various representations, the Planning Commission sided with
the majority and approved the development of the South End site.[39]

Just as a consensus seemed to have been reached, a new development disrupted existing plans. The U.S. Congress passed the landmark
Housing Act of 1949, and it quickly became apparent that the law
would allow white city officials to use the black park bond issue not to
improve the condition of black facilities but, instead, to embark upon
an aggressive plan to create a more geographically segregated city.

Embodying lofty socially progressive ideals for a postwar generation, the Housing Act of 1949 declared that every American deserved
a "decent home and a suitable living environment." Three principle
policies were advanced to achieve that goal: a program of federally
funded slum clearance and urban redevelopment; a boosting of Federal
Housing Administration mortgage insurance; and a federal commitment to build 810,000 new public housing units within six years.
Although it shaped federal policy and aspirations for much of the rest
of the twentieth century, the act had a mixed legacy. The most contro-
versial aspect was the rapid racialization of urban redevelopment programs. "Slum clearance" quickly translated into "Negro clearance,"
just as its successor, "urban renewal," later became known as "Negro
removal." As historian Arnold R. Hirsch explains, northern cities used
the federal legislation to consolidate and extend their long-established
tradition of segregated neighborhoods. In southern towns and cities,
local officials often used the housing act to replace what had been the
close proximity of black and white areas of residence and even racially
mixed neighborhoods with segregated housing. Hard figures demonstrated just how racialized housing policy became. By January 1952,
the fifty-three earmarked slum clearance projects nationwide involved
the removal of 41,630 families, 85 percent of them black. The 266
slum sites proposed for redevelopment as public housing projects
involved the displacement of 55,778 families, 74 percent of them
black. Ultimately, more public housing units were torn down than
built under the act. The ambitious target of 810,000 new public housing units, which constituted only an estimated 10 percent of the
required stock, took not six but twenty years to build.[40]

The city council was quick to spot the potential for bringing federal money to Little Rock through the act. Equally, black and white
supporters of a black park, eyeing developments nationally and region-
ally, became increasingly worried about how that money would be

spent. Dr. J. M. Robinson wrote a letter to Mayor Sam Wassell telling him that "under no circumstances will it be satisfactory to dove-tail th[e] swimming pool and community center into any housing project wherein we will be compelled to wait an indefinite period of time for our project to develop." Joshua K. Shepherd, the former president of the Little Rock Chamber of Commerce who had played a pivotal role in purchasing Gillam Park, likewise advocated the establishment of a black park "divorcing it from the slum clearance and housing issue."[41] Nevertheless, the city council rescinded its approval of the carefully considered and professionally planned South End site and instead looked to Gillam Park for the location of all black recreation facilities.[42] In doing so, it directed the bond issue money for the park to be used as part of the matching funds required to lure federal money for a far more comprehensive program of slum clearance and urban redevelopment. A special election held in January 1950 ratified the city's slum clearance and urban redevelopment plans, and the black park bond issue was successfully used to help secure a federal grant of $9,641,000.[43]

Although the long-term implications of the 1949 Housing Act were unclear in 1950, the allocation of substantial federal funds to the city did lead to immediate developments at Gillam Park.[44] By August 1950, a swimming pool had been built, and an opening ceremony was held that featured speeches from many of those closely involved with the project over the years. The *Arkansas State Press* confessed its bewilderment. "We are a little puzzled over the dedication of a new pool exclusively for Negroes," ran its editorial. "We believe it came about twenty odd years too late for us to shout joy. In this day and time when the entire country is planning programs to stamp out segregation, it seems a little ironical that Little Rock Negroes should be dedicating the outmoded principles."[45] But most local black organizations continued to press for the development of Gillam Park to make it truly equal with white recreation facilities.[46] Less than a year after opening, the Gillam Park swimming pool was reported to be leaking.[47] The following year, it began losing money. The *Arkansas State Press* observed, "That is no more than natural. People do not support the things they do not want. [Blacks] did not want a swimming pool built out of the city in an insect infested mountain."[48] Events came to a head in July 1954, just two months after the U.S. Supreme Court's *Brown v. Board of Education* decision finally sounded the death knell for the "separate but equal" doctrine. Tommy Grigsby, a black boy, drowned in the Gillam Park swimming pool. At the time, the pool was undermanned with lifeguards, it lacked a respirator that might have saved the boy's life, and its remote location meant that a doctor and rescue squad could not reach Grigsby in time to resuscitate him. Grigsby was a member of the South End Boys Club, the *Arkansas State Press* noted, and the South End was where the majority of the black population had wanted the pool built in the first place. The *Arkansas State Press* lamented, "the whole affair was a study in second class citizenship."[49]

Tommy Grigsby's death would prove to be just one incident triggered by the passage of the 1949 Housing Act that would fit into a much larger story of second-class citizenship in Little Rock. On the surface, the city's slum clearance and urban redevelopment plans held out the promise of eradicating poor housing and replacing it with new public housing units. Black political leaders in the city enthusiastically supported the plans, believing that they would deliver significantly better conditions for the black population, and mobilized the black vote to make sure that the city's slum clearance and urban redevelopment plan passed at a special election in May 1950.[50] Yet white city planners had different ideas about slum clearance and urban redevelopment. Their focus was less on improving the conditions of the black community and more on using funds to perpetuate and extend segregation in the city. B. Finley Vinson, head of the Little Rock Housing Authority (LRHA) and its slum clearance and urban redevelopment director, admitted that "the city of Little Rock through its various agencies, including the housing authority, systematically worked to continue segregation" through its slum clearance and public housing projects.[51] At a meeting in 1964, Little Rock housing director Dowell Naylor was asked outright "Is development in housing in Little Rock drawing racial groups together or silently drawing them apart?" Naylor answered, "Drawing them apart."[52]

The intent of city planners to use federal housing policy as an instrument for achieving residential segregation became evident when black areas of residence were targeted for redevelopment apparently as much for their proximity to white neighborhoods as their slum status. The first part of the city designated as a "blighted area" for demolition and clearance was the square ten-block section bordered by High, Izard and West Fifteenth streets and Wright Avenue, which was at the heart of the downtown Little Rock black community.[53] Blacks viewed the area, as one resident, Lola S. Doutherd, put it, as "the choicest area of the Negro residential section. . . It contains many churches, schools, completely modern homes, paved paid out streets, and it is within easy walking distance to the business section of the city." Doutherd further alleged that the housing authority used "coercion and intimidation" to force black residents to sell their properties in the area. The authority "threatened the owners by telling them if they did not sell at the appraised price, they would be ordered in court and given less, or evicted from their homes," she claimed. When residents did sell under duress, they often found themselves with no alternative accommodation and too little money to buy elsewhere in the city. A group of local residents, led by R. O. Burgess, a locomotive machinist, launched an unsuccessful lawsuit to save their homes.[54] The Dunbar School Project, as it became known, was just one example of many similar stories of urban redevelopment in Little Rock.[55]

As the Little Rock Housing Authority evicted black residents downtown it built black public housing units on the edge of the city, as far away from white neighborhoods as possible. Appropriately enough, Gillam Park, the long-time site of a prospective Jim Crow park, became the initial focus of this relocation of the black population eastward. The first public housing projects built after the 1949 federal housing act were the four hundred units of the Joseph A. Booker Homes, which were adjacent to Gillam Park at Granite Mountain and named after a former president of Little Rock's black Arkansas Baptist College.[56] Subsequent housing projects would follow the pattern established with the Booker Homes. By 1990, the major public housing projects of the 1950s had 99 percent black occupancy and 41 percent of public housing units were located in predominantly black areas of east Little Rock. By contrast, predominantly white areas had only 5 percent of the city's public housing units. There were none at all in the far west of the city.[57]

The location of the Joseph A. Booker Homes demonstrated not only the intent of the housing authority to construct a more residentially segregated city but also the underlying rationale for doing so. Clearly defining certain parts of the city as "black" or "white" paved the way for the *de facto* segregation of numerous other associated facilities—particularly, with the looming prospect of a desegregation ruling by the U.S. Supreme Court in the early 1950s, schools. The construction in 1952 of Booker High School next to the Booker Homes

offers a prime example of this. By a stroke of convenient racial gerry-
mandering, Gillam Park, the Booker Homes, and Booker High School
all fell within the city limits and thus qualified for federal slum clearance and urban redevelopment funds, but the Little Rock School
District ended just short of the school. It fell instead within the jurisdiction and funding of the Pulaski County Special (Rural) School
District. When the school opened in September 1952, there was not
enough room to accommodate all of the children of the black families
resident at the Booker Homes. Over a hundred black students were
left stranded without provision for their education. The city refused to
take responsibility for them, with acting superintendent of Little Rock
schools Dr. Ed McCuiston suggesting that they pay a private tuition
fee of $12.50 a year to attend city schools. This was a sum beyond
those black families whose low income qualified them for public housing in the first place.[58] Such was the outrage among black and some
white sectors of the population in Little Rock that the Arkansas
General Assembly rushed through the "Booker Bill" which required
Booker High School to be incorporated into the Little Rock School
District. The Little Rock school board, which remained bitterly opposed
to incorporating Booker High School and lambasted the actions of
state legislators for compelling it to do so, appointed Virgil T. Blossom
as a new superintendent of schools.[59] Blossom would be the architect
of a new strategy that initiated a school building program that worked
hand-in-hand with city planners to see that segregated schools followed the pattern of segregated housing, ensuring that racial separation would continue in education.[60]

The business and professional elite's plans for slum clearance and
urban redevelopment shaped city school policy through the late 1950s
and 1960s.[61] Prominent Little Rock white liberal Adolphine Fletcher
Terry, a cofounder of the Women's Emergency Committee to Open
Our Schools in 1958, was particularly critical of the role played by
William F. Rector, a leading insurance and real estate man. In 1970,
she wrote: "Our school board has become more and more [Rector's]
creation; he is proud of the fact and he boasts of it. When new people
come to town, and are looking for homes, his agents take them to
additions in the far west and assure them 'there will never be a nigger
in the schools your children will attend.'"[62] New resident Albert Porter
had first-hand experience of this practice from a black perspective
when he moved to Little Rock in 1966 to take up a post as a business

manager at Philander Smith College. When he looked to purchase a new home, Porter was directed to Granite Heights, a new private housing development located near Gillam Park. When Porter asked to see housing in another part of the city, he was told, "this is where blacks live."[63]

Terry also accused city real estate agents of engaging in "block-busting" in the 1960s in downtown areas that were becoming absorbed into the growing black east end as Little Rock's white population moved relentlessly westward. Block-busting involved purposefully moving a black person or family into a white residential area to encourage whites to move out. As white residents deserted the area, often selling their homes cheaply, those houses were then sold to blacks at inflated prices that many black buyers had to accept, given the ongoing shortage of adequate private housing stock available to them. Meanwhile, new homes were built in the expanding affluent white suburbs of west Little Rock that were sold to those whites who wanted to escape interracial downtown neighborhoods and who could afford to do so.[64] In 1971, when legal action threatened to circumvent the purpose of residential segregation by forcing cross-city busing of students to ensure integrated schools, Rector announced the construction of the private Pulaski Academy for those who "don't like busing."[65] Between the public plans of the Little Rock Housing Authority and the private practices of Little Rock businesses and real estate agents, Little Rock became increasingly segregated by race, with the black population concentrated in the eastern and downtown areas and the white population concentrated in the west.

Of course, not all whites could afford to move. Although public housing projects like the Booker Homes at Gillam Park separated the black poor from the white poor, in the overlapping fringes of downtown areas black and white working-class families still competed over facilities. A number of historians have noted that class tensions fed into the racial conflict over school desegregation during the 1957 Little Rock school crisis.[66] As one white downtown resident complained to Little Rock Chamber of Commerce president E. Grainger Williams in 1959, "You of the Chamber of Commerce are financially able to send your children to private schools, you are able to live in a secluded housing project. You have no worries about integration, because you can evade every iota of it."[67]

A study conducted by Little Rock's Racial and Cultural Diversity Task Force in 1992 demonstrated the impact of the city's race-driven urban redevelopment plans since the 1950s. In 1941, a study sponsored by the Greater Little Rock Urban League noted, "While Negroes predominate in certain sections . . . in Little Rock, there are . . . no widespread . . . 'Negro sections' [of residence]."[68] Taking the city's census tracts as its benchmark, the 1992 study found that ten tracts in the east of the city were 90 percent black and housed 46 percent of the city's black population. Only 2 percent of Little Rock's white population lived in those neighborhoods. Nineteen tracts to the west housed 76 percent of the city's white population. A buffer zone between the two areas, containing fourteen census tracts, was notionally "integrated" with 54 percent white and 46 percent black residency. Citywide, however, the study concluded that 70 percent of Little Rock residents lived "in either an area of white or black isolation." The movement of people across the city to create these racially separate neighborhoods was evident. In the 1960s and 1970s, 41,000 whites moved from east to west Little Rock, while 17,000 blacks moved—or were moved—in the opposite direction. Black neighborhoods in the east were worse off in every way. Black families were poorer, with 64 percent earning less than $25,000 a year, while 60 percent of white families in the city earned over that amount. Overall, there was a 60 percent per capita income difference between blacks and whites. Of those families in the city below the poverty line, 68 percent were black. The unemployment rate for blacks was 153 percent higher than for whites. Crime was a far greater problem in black than in white neighborhoods. Although blacks made up approximately one-third of the city population, black people accounted for over 50 percent of those arrested by the Little Rock Police Department, and 97 percent of suspects of violent crime and 80 percent of the victims of violent crime were black. The most conspicuous development in the schools was the number of white students in the racially isolated census tracts of west Little Rock whose parents chose to opt them out of the public schools system altogether. Four out of every ten students in those areas attended private schools.[69]

Just as urban studies have challenged historians to rethink civil rights struggles in other localities, the history of Gillam Park and the slum clearance and urban redevelopment plans that it pioneered suggest the need to reevaluate postwar race relations in Little Rock. The defining event of the city's civil rights history has undoubtedly been seen as the 1957 Little Rock crisis. Yet, from an urban history perspective, it might well be argued that the city's most decisive response to

Brown v. Board of Education was the preemptive strategy of slum clearance and urban redevelopment in the early 1950s rather than the more dramatically staged massive resistance to school desegregation of the later 1950s. Without doubt, city planning policy shaped race relations more fundamentally over the long-term than the short-term effects of the school crisis. Indeed, the events of the school crisis unfolded within this already changing urban context. Slum clearance and urban redevelopment plans in part help explain why only nine black children ended up integrating Central High, which had almost two thousand white children in September 1957. Two new segregated schools, Horace Mann High in the east of the city for blacks and Hall High in the suburbs of the west for affluent whites, were built after the *Brown* decision had been handed down. This significantly limited the amount of desegregation that took place at Central High School. The need to construct these schools to serve that objective explains why school desegregation in Little Rock was delayed until 1957, over three years after *Brown*. Moreover, the targeting of Central High School as the focus for school desegregation explains the class tensions that played such an important role in the school crisis. Central High was located, as its name suggests, in a central, close-to-downtown neighborhood of working-class whites and blacks. Shifting patterns of race and residence that had already been set in motion by the city's slum clearance and urban redevelopment plans only served to intensify the struggle for control over downtown areas and facilities, which was an intrinsic part of the battle over desegregation. By keeping the events of the 1957 crisis at the forefront of Little Rock's civil rights history, we are in danger of missing the larger context within which that event unfolded.

An examination of Little Rock's slum clearance and urban redevelopment plans suggests that, even as civil rights activists battled to end segregation in the 1960s, their efforts were already being comprehensively undermined. What prompted segregation laws from the 1890s onward was the amount of interracial mixing that was actually taking place in rapidly expanding towns and cities. Segregation looked to counteract this race mixing by instituting laws that imposed a clear distinction between the races that might otherwise have been blurred by the extent of day-to-day contact.[70] With the city embarking upon a policy of residential racial separation from the 1950s onward, the need for segregation laws gradually eroded. If blacks and whites resided in different parts of the city and interracial contact radically lessened as a consequence, then there was no longer any need for laws to formally separate the races. Geographical separation replaced segregation as an instrument of racial discrimination by ensuring that many city facilities would remain race-specific by virtue of their location close to black or white areas of residence.

Changes in Little Rock's city government in the 1950s also conveniently coincided with changing urban demographics. In 1957, a mayor-alderman ward-based form of city government was replaced by a new manager-commissioner citywide government.[71] This meant that the potential for translating the growing concentration of the city's black population in certain areas into corresponding black political strength and representation was diluted by new "at-large" city elections that instead reflected the political strength of a white majority electorate. Like urban redevelopment in Little Rock, such structural changes in the 1950s would undermine the racial progress in other areas that would take place in the following decades.

Recent events warrant a postscript. In 2004, Gillam Park was again at the center of a struggle over city planning and community resources. A white businessman, Haskell Dickinson II, vice president of the Pine Bluff-based company McGeorge Equipment Rental, wanted to expand the granite excavation site at Gillam Park owned by subsidiary Granite Mountain Quarries. He initially offered to swap the city land his family owned in the affluent western suburbs of Little Rock that could be developed into a park for the Gillam Park land. When the proposal failed, he offered to swap land he had purchased elsewhere in the Gillam Park area. Dickinson's proposal dovetailed with the plans of a conservation group, Audubon Arkansas, which in 2003 had leased sixty-eight acres of Gillam Park land from the city. This land was the former site of Booker Homes, the pioneering housing project that did much to initiate the relocation of the black population to east Little Rock, and which had been demolished in the 1990s because of drug and crime problems.

Ken Smith, director of Audubon Arkansas, described the site as the "crown jewel" of Little Rock's park system and "one of the most significant tracts of undeveloped land in Arkansas." His organization proposed to construct a conservation area there and the land Dickinson was offering afforded better access to the site. Long-time black residents at Granite Heights vehemently objected to the land swap, which would bring the existing granite excavation site six hundred feet closer to their homes. Physician Worthie Springer Jr. led a chorus of dissent, complaining that the area, together with much of the predominantly black east end of Little Rock, "has been forever neglected." At a decisive vote on April 22, 2004, the Little Rock Parks and Recreation Commission tied four to four over the land swap. "The vote effectively kills [the] proposal," wrote *Arkansas Democrat-Gazette* reporter Andrew DeMillo, while cautiously adding the caveat: "for now."[72]

Once again the battle over Gillam Park was indicative of larger developments taking place in Little Rock. After decades of white westward expansion, in the late twentieth- and early twenty-first century white business interests began to turn back to downtown, central, and east Little Rock. In 1996, the River Market District development turned "a string of decaying warehouses into a viable neighborhood of trendy loft apartments, art galleries, bars and restaurants." The charity foundation Heifer International's headquarters are nearby, as is the William Jefferson Clinton Presidential Library. Developers are eyeing downtown riverfront land encroaching into the black east end of the city to turn into a multimillion dollar marina and condominiums.[73]

Exactly what this means for the city's race relations is unclear. Potentially, it holds out the prospect of reunifying white and black areas of residence and bringing them back together again. Equally, it may represent an advance of the white western suburbs that threatens to steamroller what remains of the most integrated parts of the city and again push blacks further out into the marginalized fringes of the east. As black east end resident Estella Watson points out, "If you are going to build condos along the river front, who can afford to live there? They're pushing blacks out. They're not giving us anything." Meanwhile, a change back to a ward-based system of city government in the early 1990s may well give blacks a greater political voice in unfolding city affairs. Whichever way the new struggle over Little Rock's downtown goes, it promises to shape the future of the city and its race relations well into the twenty-first century just as fundamentally as the last surge of urban redevelopment did in the mid-twentieth century.[74]

Notes

Chapter 1: The 1957 Little Rock Crisis

1. Overviews of the crisis include: Corrine Silverman, *The Little Rock Story* (Tuscaloosa: University of Alabama Press, 1958); Dewey Grantham, *The Regional Imagination: The South and Recent American History* (Nashville: Vanderbilt University Press, 1979), 185–97; Tony Freyer, *The Little Rock Crisis: A Constitutional Interpretation* (Westport, CT: Greenwood Press, 1984); Juan Williams, *Eyes on the Prize: America's Civil Rights Years, 1954–1965* (New York: Penguin Books, 1987), 91–119; John A. Kirk, *Redefining the Color Line: Black Activism in Little Rock, Arkansas, 1940–1970* (Gainesville: University Press of Florida, 2002), 106–38.

2. Michael J. Dabrishus, "The Documentary Heritage of the Central High Crisis: A Bibliographical Essay," in *Understanding the Little Rock Crisis: An Exercise in Remembrance and Reconciliation* eds. Elizabeth Jacoway and C. Fred Williams (Fayetteville: University of Arkansas Press, 1999), 153–61. See also "Little Rock School Integration, 1957," Special Collections, University of Arkansas Libraries, Fayetteville, http://libinfo.uark.edu/specialcollections/manuscripts/integration1957.asp.

3. Wilson Record and June Cassels Record, eds., *Little Rock, U.S.A.* (San Francisco: Chandler Publishing Co., 1960); "Fighting Back (1957–1962)," episode 2 in *Eyes on the Prize: America's Civil Rights Years, 1954–1965*, directed by Henry Hampton. Boston: Blackside, Inc., 1987; Clayborne Carson, David J. Garrow, Gerald Gill, Vincent Harding, and Darlene Clark Hine, eds. *The Eyes on the Prize Civil Rights Reader: Documents, Speeches, and Firsthand Accounts from the Black Freedom Struggle, 1954–1990,* (New York: Viking Penguin, 1991), 61–106; Henry Hampton and Steve Fayer, eds. *Voices of Freedom: An Oral History of the Civil Rights Movement from the 1950s through the 1980s* (New York: Vintage, 1994), 35–52; "Little Rock, Arkansas," episodes 11–15 in *Will The Circle Be Unbroken? An Audio History of the Civil Rights Movement in Five Southern Communities and the Music of Those Times,* George King, with Vertamae Grosvenor (Atlanta: Southern Regional Council, 1997) http://www.unbrokencircle.org/.

4. David Chappell, *Inside Agitators: White Southerners in the Civil Rights Movement* (Baltimore, Md.: Johns Hopkins University Press, 1994); David L. Chappell, "Diversity Within a Racial Group: White People in Little Rock, 1957–1959," *Arkansas Historical Quarterly* (Winter 1995): 444–56; C. Fred Williams, "Class: The Central Issue in the 1957 Little Rock School Crisis," *Arkansas Historical Quarterly* 56 (Autumn 1997): 341–44; Pete Daniel, *Lost Revolutions: The South in the 1950s* (Chapel Hill: University of North Carolina Press, 2000), 251–83; Karen Anderson, "The Little Rock School Desegregation Crisis: Moderation and Social Conflict," *Journal of Southern History* 70 (August 2004): 603–36.

5. John F. Wells, *Time Bomb: The Faubus Revolt* (Little Rock: General Publishing Co., 1962); Robert Sherrill, *Gothic Politics in the Deep South* (New York: Grossman Books, 1968), 79–124; John F. Wells, *Time Bomb: The Faubus Revolt: A Documentary: 1977 Addendum* (Little Rock: General Publishing Co., 1977); David Edwin Wallace, "The Little Rock Central Desegregation Crisis of 1957" (Ph.D. diss., University of Missouri, Columbia, 1977); David E. Wallace, "Orval Faubus: The Central Figure at Little Rock Central High School," *Arkansas Historical Quarterly* 39 (Winter 1980): 314–29.

6. Thomas F. Pettigrew and Ernest Q. Campbell, "Faubus and Segregation: An Analysis of Arkansas Voting," *The Public Opinion Quarterly* 24:3 (Autumn 1960): 436–47; Roy Reed, "Orval E. Faubus: Out of Socialism into Realism," *Arkansas Historical Quarterly* 54 (Spring 1995): 13–29; Roy Reed, *Faubus: The Life and Times of an American Prodigal* (Fayetteville: University of Arkansas Press, 1997); Roy Reed, "The Contest for the Soul of Orval Faubus," in *Understanding the Little Rock Crisis* eds. Jacoway and Williams, 99–105.

7. Orval E. Faubus, *In This Faraway Land: A Personal Journey of Infantry Combat in World War II* (Conway, AR: River Road Press, 1971); Orval E. Faubus, *Down From the Hills* (Little Rock: Pioneer Press, 1980); Orval E. Faubus, *Down From the Hills II* (Little Rock: Democrat Printing and Lithographing Company, 1986); Orval E. Faubus, *Man's Best Friend: The Little Australian, and Others* (Little Rock: Democrat Printing and Lithographing Company, 1991); Orval E. Faubus, *The Faubus Years: January 11, 1955, to January 10, 1967* (S.l.: s.n., 1991); Orval E. Faubus, interview with the author, December 3, 1992, Conway, Arkansas, Pryor Center for Oral and Visual Culture, University of Arkansas, Fayetteville.

8. Virgil T. Blossom, *It Has Happened Here* (New York: Harper, 1959); Numan V. Bartley, "Looking Back at Little Rock," *Arkansas Historical Quarterly* 25 (Summer 1966): 101–16; Numan V. Bartley, *The Rise of Massive Resistance: Race and Politics in the South during the 1950s* (Baton Rouge: Louisiana State University Press, 1969), 251–69 (quotation page 252); John A. Kirk, "'Massive Resistance and Minimum Compliance: The Origins of the 1957 Little Rock School Crisis and the Failure of School Desegregation in the South," in *Massive Resistance: Southern Opposition to the Second Reconstruction* ed. Clive Webb (New York: Oxford University Press, 2005), 76–98; Elizabeth Jacoway, "Richard C. Butler and the Little Rock School Board: The Quest to Maintain 'Educational Quality,'" *Arkansas Historical Quarterly* 65:1 (Spring 2006): 24–38.

9. Brooks L. Hays, *A Southern Moderate Speaks* (Chapel Hill: University of North Carolina Press, 1959), 130–94; Dale Alford and L'Moore Alford, *The Case of the Sleeping People (Finally Awakened by Little Rock School Frustrations)* (Little Rock: Pioneer Press, 1959); Sherman Adams, *First Hand Report: The Inside Story of the Eisenhower Administration* (New York: Harper, 1961), 253–78; Brooks L. Hays, *Politics Is My Parish, An Autobiography* (Baton Rouge: Louisiana State University Press, 1981),

179–98; D. Nathan Coulter, "A Political Martyr for Racial Progress in the South: Brooks Hays and the Electoral Consequences of the Little Rock Crisis" (B.A. thesis, Harvard University, 1982); John Kyle Day, "The Fall of a Southern Moderate: The Defeat of Brooks Hays in the 1958 Congressional Election for the Fifth District of Arkansas" (M.A. thesis, University of Arkansas, Fayetteville, 1999); John Kyle Day, "The Fall of a Southern Moderate: Congressman Brooks Hays and the Election of 1958," *Arkansas Historical Quarterly* 59 (Autumn 2000): 241–64; Terry D. Goddard, "Southern Social Justice: Brooks Hays and the Little Rock School Crisis," *Baptist History and Heritage* 38 (Spring 2003): 68–86.

10. Randall Bennett Woods, *Fulbright: A Biography* (Cambridge: Cambridge University Press, 1995); Brett J. Aucoin, "The Southern Manifesto and Southern Opposition to Desegregation," *Arkansas Historical Quarterly* 55 (Summer 1996): 173–93; Tony Badger, "'The Forerunner of Our Opposition': Arkansas and the Southern Manifesto," *Arkansas Historical Quarterly* 56 (Autumn 1997): 353–60; Tony Badger, "The White Reaction to *Brown*: Arkansas, the Southern Manifesto, and Massive Resistance," in *Understanding the Little Rock Crisis* eds. Jacoway and Williams, 83–97; John A. Kirk, "Arkansas, the *Brown* Decision, and the 1957 Little Rock School Crisis: A Local Perspective," in *Understanding the Little Rock Crisis* eds. Jacoway and Williams, 67–82; Tony Badger, "Southerners Who Refused to Sign the Southern Manifesto," *The Historical Journal* 42 (June 1999): 517–34.

11. Robert R. Brown, *Bigger Than Little Rock* (Greenwich, CT: Seabury Press, 1958); Ernest Q. Campbell and Thomas F. Pettigrew, *Christians in Racial Crisis: A Study of Little Rock's Ministry* (Washington, DC: Public Affairs Press, 1959); Ernest Q. Campell and Thomas F. Pettigrew, "Racial and Moral Crisis: The Role of Little Rock Ministers," *American Journal of Sociology* 64:5 (March 1959): 509–16; Mark Newman, "The Arkansas Baptist State Convention and Desegregation, 1954–1968," *Arkansas Historical Quarterly* 56 (Autumn 1997): 294–313; Carolyn Gray LeMaster, "Civil and Social Rights Efforts of Arkansas Jewry," in *The Quiet Voices: Southern Rabbis and Black Civil Rights, 1880s-1990s* eds. Mark Bauman and Berkley Kalin (Tuscaloosa: University of Alabama Press, 1997), 95–120; Clive Webb, *Fight Against Fear: Southern Jews and Black Civil Rights* (Athens: University of Georgia Press, 2001); Colbert Cartwright, "Walking My Lonesome Valley," unpublished manuscript; Dunbar H. Ogden III, "My Father Said 'Yes'," unpublished manuscript, both in private possession of family members.

12. David L. Chappell, "Religious Ideas of the Segregationists," *Journal of American Studies* 32 (August 1998): 237–62; David L. Chappell, *A Stone of Hope: Prophetic Religion and the Death of Jim Crow* (Chapel Hill: University of North Carolina Press, 2004); Jane Dailey, "Sex, Segregation, and the Sacred After *Brown*," *Journal of American History* 91:1 (June 2004): 119–44; David Chappell, "Disunity and Religious Institutions in the White South," in *Massive Resistance* ed. Webb, 136–50; Jane Dailey, "The Theology of Massive

Resistance: Sex, Segregation, and the Sacred After *Brown*," in *Massive Resistance* ed. Webb, 151–80.

13. Elizabeth Jacoway, "Taken By Surprise: Little Rock Business Leaders and Desegregation" in *Southern Businessmen and Desegregation* eds. Elizabeth Jacoway and David R. Colburn (Baton Rouge: Louisiana State University Press, 1982), 12–41; Tony Badger, "Segregation and the Southern Business Elite," *Journal of American Studies* 18:1 (1984): 105–9 (quoted page 108).

14. Harry S. Ashmore, *The Negro and The Schools* (Chapel Hill: University of North Carolina Press, 1954); *Arkansas Gazette, The Editorial Position of the Arkansas Gazette in the Little Rock Crisis* (Little Rock: Arkansas Gazette, 1957); Harry S. Ashmore, *An Epitaph For Dixie* (New York: W. W. Norton, 1958); Karr Shannon, *Integration Decision is Unconstitutional* (Little Rock: Democrat Print and Lithographing Co., 1958); *Arkansas Gazette, Crisis in the South: The Little Rock Story* (Little Rock: Arkansas Gazette, 1959); Harry S. Ashmore, *Hearts and Minds: The Anatomy of Racism from Roosevelt to Reagan* (New York: McGraw-Hill, 1982); Harry S. Ashmore, *Civil Rights and Wrongs: A Memoir of Race and Politics, 1944–1996* (Columbia: University of South Carolina Press, 1994); Griffin Smith, ed. *Little Rock, 1957: Pages from History of the Central High Crisis* (Little Rock: WEHCO Publishing, 1997); Nathania K. Sawyer, "Harry S. Ashmore: On the Way to Everywhere" (M.A. thesis, University of Arkansas at Little Rock, 2001).

15. Alford and Alford, *The Case of the Sleeping People;* Bartley, "Looking Back at Little Rock"; Bartley, *Rise of Massive Resistance;* Neil R. McMillen, "The White Citizens Council and Resistance to School Desegregation in Arkansas," *Arkansas Historical Quarterly* 30 (Summer 1971): 95–122; Neil R. McMillen, *The Citizens' Council: Organized Resistance to the Second Reconstruction, 1955–1964* (Urbana: University of Illinois Press, 1971); Michael R. Belknap, *Federal Law and Southern Order: Racial Violence and Constitutional Conflict in the Post-Brown South* (Athens: University of Georgia Press, 1987); Graeme Cope, "'A Thorn in the Side'?: The Mothers' League of Central High School and the Little Rock Desegregation Crisis of 1957," *Arkansas Historical Quarterly* 57 (Summer 1998): 160–90; Elizabeth Jacoway, "Jim Johnson of Arkansas: Segregationist Prototype," in *The Role of Ideas in the Civil Rights South* ed. Ted Ownby (Jackson: University of Mississippi Press, 2002), 137–55; Graeme Cope, "Honest White People of the Middle and Lower Classes? A Profile of the Capital Citizens' Council During the Little Rock Crisis of 1957," *Arkansas Historical Quarterly* 61 (Spring 2002): 36–58; Graeme Cope, "'Marginal Youngsters' and 'Hoodlums of Both Sexes'?: Student Segregationists During the Little Rock School Crisis," *Arkansas Historical Quarterly* 63 (Winter 2004): 380–403; Frances Lisa Baer, "Race over Rights: The Resistance to Public School Desegregation in Little Rock, Arkansas, and Beyond, 1959–1960" (Ph.D. diss., University of Alabama, 2004); Karen S. Anderson, "Violence and Southern Social Relations: The Little Rock, Arkansas, School Integration Crisis, 1954–1960," in *Massive Resistance* ed. Webb, 203–15.

16. George Lewis, *The White South and the Red Menace: Segregationists, Anitcommunism and Massive Resistance, 1945–1965* (Gainesville: University Press of Florida, 2004); Jeff Woods, *Black Struggle, Red Scare: Segregation and Anti-Communism in the South, 1948–1968* (Baton Rouge: Louisiana State University Press, 2004).

17. Jeff Woods, "'Designed to Harass': The Act 10 Controversy in Arkansas," *Arkansas Historical Quarterly* 56 (Winter 1997): 443–60.

18. Joseph Peter Kamp, *The Lowdown on Little Rock and the Plot to Sovietize the South* (New York: Headlines, 1957); James E. Jackson, *U.S. Negroes in Battle: From Little Rock to Watts: A Diary of Events, 1957–1965* (Moscow: Progress Publishers, 1967).

19. Robert W. Coakley, *Operation Arkansas* (Washington, DC: Histories Division, Office of the Chief of Military History, Department of the Army, 1967); Elizabeth Huckaby, *Crisis at Central High, Little Rock, 1957–58* (Baton Rouge: Louisiana State University Press, 1980); Lamont Johnson, dir., *Crisis at Central High* (CBS Entertainment Productions, 1981); Phoebe Christina Godfrey, "Sweet Little Girls?: Miscegenation, Desegregation and the Defense of Whiteness at Little Rock's Central High, 1957–1959" (Ph.D. diss., State University of New York at Binghamton, 2001); Phoebe Godfrey, "Bayonets, Brainwashing and Bathrooms: The Discourse of Race, Gender, and Sexuality in the Desegregation of Little Rock Central High," *Arkansas Historical Quarterly* 62 (Spring 2003): 42–67.

20. Sondra Hercher Gordy, "Teachers of the Lost Year, 1958–1959: Little Rock School District" (Ed.D. thesis, University of Arkansas at Little Rock, 1996); Sondra Gordy, "Empty Classrooms, Empty Hearts: Little Rock Secondary Teachers, 1958–1959," *Arkansas Historical Quarterly* 56 (Winter 1997): 427–42; Beth Roy, *Bitters in the Honey: Tales of Hope and Disappointment Across Divides of Race and Time* (Fayetteville: University of Arkansas Press, 1999); "The Lost Year Project" http://www.thelostyear.com/.

21. Gary Fullerton, "New Factories a Thing of Past in Little Rock," *Nashville Tennessean*, May 31, 1959; Michael Joseph Bercik, "The Little Rock School Crisis of 1957 and its Impact on the Economy of Arkansas" (Ph.D. diss., University of Pittsburgh, 1999); James C. Cobb, "The Lesson of Little Rock: Stability, Growth and Change in the American South," in *Understanding the Little Rock Crisis* eds. Jacoway and Williams, 107–22.

22. Michelle Leslie Davidson, "Vivion Brewer and the 1957 Little Rock Central High Crisis" (M.A. thesis, University of Arkansas, Fayetteville, 1994); Lorraine Gates, "Power from the Pedestal: The Women's Emergency Committee and the Little Rock School Crisis," *Arkansas Historical Quarterly* 55 (Spring 1996): 26–57; Sara Alderman Murphy, *Breaking the Silence: Little Rock's Women's Emergency Committee to Open Our Schools, 1958–1963* (Fayetteville: University of Arkansas Press, 1997); Elizabeth Jacoway, "Down from the Pedestal: Gender and Regional Culture in a Ladylike Assault on the Southern Way of Life," *Arkansas Historical Quarterly* 56 (Autumn 1997): 345–52; Sandra Hubbard, dir., *Women's Emergency Committee to Open Our Schools, 1958–1959* (Little Rock: Morning Star Studio, 1998); Vivion Lenon

Brewer, *The Embattled Ladies of Little Rock, 1958–1963: The Struggle to Save Public Education at Central High* (Fort Bragg, CA: Lost Coast Press, 1999); Laura A. Miller, *Fearless: Irene Gaston Samuel and the Life of a Southern Liberal* (Little Rock: Center for Arkansas Studies, 2002); Laura A. Miller, "Challenging the Segregationist Power Structure in Little Rock: The Women's Emergency Committee to Open Our Schools," in *Throwing Off the Cloak of Privilege: White Southern Women Activists in the Civil Rights Era* ed. Gail S. Murray (Gainesville: University Press of Florida, 2004), 153–80; Adolphine Terry, "Life is My Song, Also," unpublished manuscript, box 2, Fletcher-Terry Papers, RG A-13, Special Collections, University of Arkansas at Little Rock Libraries.

23. Henry M. Alexander, *The Little Rock Recall Election* (New York: McGraw Hill, 1960); Jacoway, "Taken By Surprise"; Kimberly M. Bess, "Good Men Doing Nothing: Desegregation in Little Rock Public Schools" (M.A. thesis, University of Arkansas, Fayetteville, 2005).

24. Woodrow Wilson Mann, "The Truth About Little Rock," *New York Herald Tribune,* January 19–31, 1958; Georg. C. Iggers, "An Arkansas Professor: The NAACP and the Grass Roots," in Record and Record, eds., *Little Rock, U.S.A,* 283–91; Thomas R. Wagy, "Governor LeRoy Collins of Florida and the Little Rock Crisis of 1957," *Arkansas Historical Quarterly* 38 (Summer 1979): 99–115; Tom Wagy, *Governor LeRoy Collins of Florida: Spokesman of the New South* (Tuscaloosa: University of Alabama Press, 1985), 84–103; Osro Cobb and Carol Griffee, *Osro Cobb of Arkansas: Memoirs of Historical Significance* (Little Rock: Rose Publishing Co., 1989); Tony Freyer, "Objectivity and Involvement: Georg C. Iggers and Writing the History of the Little Rock Crisis," in *Crossing Boundaries: The Exclusion and Inclusion of Minorities in Germany and the United States* ed. Larry Eugene Jones (New York: Berghahn Books, 2001), 172–92; Tony Freyer, "Crossing Borders in American Civil Rights Historiography," in *Crossing Boundaries* ed. Jones, 213–32; Nat Griswold, "The Second Reconstruction in Little Rock," unpublished manuscript, series 2: subject files, box 11, folder 8, Sara Alderman Murphy Papers, Special Collections, University of Arkansas Libraries, Fayetteville.

25. Daisy Bates, *The Long Shadow of Little Rock: A Memoir* (New York: David McKay Company, Inc., 1962); Jacqueline Trescott, "Daisy Bates: Before and After Little Rock," *Crisis,* June 1981, 232–35; Anne Standley, "The Role of Black Women in the Civil Rights Movement," in *Women in the Civil Rights Movement: Trailblazers and Torchbearers* eds. Vicki L. Crawford, Jacqueline Anne Rouse and Barbara Woods (Brooklyn, NY: Carlson Publishing, 1990), 183–202; Carolyn Calloway-Thomas and Thurman Gardner, "Daisy Bates and the Little Rock School Crisis: Forging the Way," *Journal of Black Studies* 26 (May 1996): 616–28; John A. Kirk, "Daisy Bates, the National Association for the Advancement of Colored People, and the 1957 Little Rock School Crisis: A Gendered Perspective," in *Gender in the Civil Rights Movement* eds. Peter J. Ling, and Sharon Monteith, (New York: Garland Publishing, 1999),

17–40; Linda Reed, "The Legacy of Daisy Bates," *Arkansas Historical Quarterly* 59 (Spring 2000): 76–83; Amy Polakow, *Daisy Bates: Civil Rights Crusader* (North Haven, CT: Linnet Books, 2003); John Adams, "'Arkansas Needs Leadership': Daisy Bates, Black Arkansas, and the NAACP" (M.A. thesis, University of Wisconsin, 2003); Grif Stockley, *Daisy Bates: Civil Rights Crusader from Arkansas* (Jackson: University Press of Mississippi, 2005); Sharon La Cruise, dir. "In the Shadow of Little Rock: The Life of Daisy Bates," (Sakkara Films, 2007).

26. Brynda Pappas, "L. C. Bates: Champion of Freedom," *Arkansas Gazette,* October 19, 1980; C. Calvin Smith, "From 'Separate but Equal to Desegregation': The Changing Philosophy of L. C. Bates," *Arkansas Historical Quarterly* 42 (Autumn 1983): 254–70; Irene Wassell, "L. C. Bates, Editor of the Arkansas State Press" (M.A. thesis, University of Arkansas, Little Rock, 1983).

27. Ted Poston, "Nine Kids Who Dared," *New York Post,* October 23–31, 1957; Clarence Laws, "Nine Courageous Students," *Crisis,* May 1958, 267–318; Moses J. Newson, "The Little Rock Nine," *Crisis,* November 1987, 40–44; Elizabeth Eckford, "The First Day," *Southern Exposure* 21 (Spring-Summer 1993): 1–27; Eric Laneuville, dir., *The Ernest Green Story* (Hollywood, CA: Buena Vista Video, 1993); Melba Pattillo Beals, *Warriors Don't Cry: A Searing Memoir of the Battle To Integrate Little Rock's Central High* (New York: Pocket Books, 1994); Melba Pattillo Beals, *White is a State of Mind: A Memoir* (New York: G. P. Putnam's Sons, 1999); Elizabeth Jacoway, "Not Anger But Sorrow: Minnijean Brown Trickey Remembers the Little Rock School Crisis," *Arkansas Historical Quarterly* 64 (Spring 2005): 1–26.

28. Iggers, "An Arkansas Professor"; Tilman Cothran and William Phillips, Jr., "Negro Leadership in a Crisis Situation," *Phylon* 22 (Spring 1961): 107–18; Wiley A. Branton "Little Rock Revisited: Desegregation to Resegregation." *Journal of Negro Education* 52:3 (Summer 1983): 250–69; Brian James Daugherity, "'With All Deliberate Speed': The NAACP and the Implementation of *Brown v. Board of Education* at a Local Level, Little Rock, Arkansas" (M.A. thesis, University of Montana, 1997); Kirk, *Redefining the Color Line;* Judith Kilpatrick, "Wiley Austin Branton and *Cooper v. Aaron:* America Fulfils Its Promise," *Arkansas Historical Quarterly* 65 (Spring 2006): 7–21.

29. Tony A. Freyer, "Politics and Law in the Little Rock Crisis, 1954–1957," *Arkansas Historical Quarterly* 40 (Autumn 1981): 195–219; Daniel A. Farber, "The Supreme Court and the Rule of Law: *Cooper v. Aaron* Revisited," *University of Illinois Law Review* (1982): 387–412; Freyer, *The Little Rock Crisis;* Jack Greenberg, *Crusaders in the Courts: How a Dedicated Band of Lawyers Fought for the Civil Rights Revolution* (New York: Basic Books, 1994), 225–43; Tony Freyer, "The Little Rock Crisis Reconsidered," *Arkansas Historical Quarterly* 56 (Autumn 1997): 361–370; David Kirp, "Retreat into Legalism: The Little Rock School Desegregation Case in Historic Perspective," *PS: Political Science and Politics* 30 (September 1997): 443–47;

Kermit L. Hall, "The Constitutional Lessons of the Little Rock Crisis," in *Understanding the Little Rock Crisis* eds. Jacoway and Williams, 123–140; Tony Freyer, "The Past as Future: The Little Rock Crisis and the Constitution," in *Understanding the Little Rock Crisis* eds. Jacoway and Williams, 141–151; Tony Freyer, "*Cooper v. Aaron*: Incident and Consequence," *Arkansas Historical Quarterly* 65 (Spring 2006): 1–6; Jacoway, "Richard C. Butler and the Little Rock School Board"; Kilpatrick, "Wiley Austin Branton"; Tony Freyer, *Rights Defied: America's Civil Rights Struggle, Little Rock, and Cooper v. Aaron (1958)* (Lawrence: University Press of Kansas, 2007).

30. Jack W. Peltason, *Fifty-Eight Lonely Men: Southern Federal Judges and School Desegregation* (Urbana: University of Illinois Press, 1971); J. Harvie Wilkinson III., *From Brown to Bakke: The Supreme Court and School Integration: 1954–1978* (New York: Oxford University Press, 1979); Jack Bass, *Unlikely Heroes: The Dramatic Story of the Southern Judges of the Fifth Circuit who Translated the Supreme Court's Brown Decision into a Revolution for Equality* (New York: Simon and Schuster, 1981); Michael J. Klarman, *From Jim Crow to Civil Rights: The Supreme Court and the Struggle for Racial Equality* (New York: Oxford University Press, 2004).

31. Adam Fairclough, "The Little Rock Crisis: Success or Failure for the NAACP?" *Arkansas Historical Quarterly* 56 (Autumn 1997): 371–75; Michael J. Klarman, "How *Brown* Changed Race Relations: The Backlash Thesis," *Journal of American History* 81:1 (June 1994): 81–118; Michael J. Klarman, *From Jim Crow to Civil Rights,* 344–442.

32. Dwight D. Eisenhower, *The White House Years: Waging Peace, 1956–1961* (Garden City, NY: Doubleday and Company, 1965); Philip Norton, *Eisenhower and Little Rock: A Case Study of Presidential Decision Making* (Hull U.K.: University of Hull, 1979); Ouseph Varkey, "Crisis Situations and Federal Systems: A Comparative Study of America and India," *Indian Journal of American Studies* 9:1 (1979): 65–79; James C. Durham, *A Moderate Amongst Extremists: Dwight D. Eisenhower and the School Desegregation Crisis* (Chicago: Nelson-Hall, 1981); Robert F. Burk, *The Eisenhower Administration and Black Civil Rights* (Knoxville: University of Tennessee Press, 1984); Michael S. Mayer, "With Much Deliberation and Some Speed: Eisenhower and the *Brown* Decision," *Journal of Southern History* 52 (February 1986): 43–76; Mark Stern, "Eisenhower and Kennedy: A Comparison of Confrontations at Little Rock and Ole Miss," *Policy Studies Journal* 21:3 (1993): 575–88; Steven R. Goldwitz and George Dionisopoulos, "Crisis at Little Rock: Eisenhower, History and Mediated Political Realities," in *Eisenhower's War of Words: Rhetoric and Leadership* ed. Martin J. Medhurst (East Lansing: Michigan State University Press, 1994); Paul Greenberg, "Eisenhower Draws the Racial Battle Lines with Orval Faubus," *Journal of Blacks in Higher Education* 18 (Winter 1997–98): 120–21.

33. John W. Anderson, *Eisenhower, Brownell, and the Congress: The Tangled Origins of the Civil Rights Bill of 1956–1957* (Tuscaloosa: University of Alabama Press, 1964); Michael R. Belknap, *Justice Department Civil Rights*

Policies Prior to 1960: Crucial Documents from the Files of Arthur Brann Caldwell (New York: Garland, 1991); Herbert Brownell, "Eisenhower's Civil Rights Program: A Personal Assessment," *Presidential Studies Quarterly* 21:2 (1991): 235–42; Herbert Brownell, with John P. Burke, *Advising Ike: The Memoirs of Attorney General Herbert Brownell* (Lawrence: University Press of Kansas, 1993).

34. Hoyt H. Purvis, "Little Rock and the Press" (M.A. thesis, University of Texas, 1963); Allison Graham, "Remapping Dogpatch: The Northern Media on the Southern Circuit," *Arkansas Historical Quarterly* 56 (Autumn 1997): 334–40; I. Wilmer Counts, *A Life is More Than a Moment: The Desegregation of Little Rock's Central High* (Bloomington: Indiana University Press, 1999).

35. Hannah Arendt, "Reflections on Little Rock," *Dissent* 6:1 (Winter 1959): 45–56; Gwendolyn Brooks, "The *Chicago Defender* Sends a Man to Little Rock," in *The Bean Eaters* (New York: Harper and Bros., 1960); Sue S. Park, "A Study in Tension: Gwendolyn Brooks's 'The *Chicago Defender* Sends a Man to Little Rock,'" *Black American Literature Forum* 11:1 (Spring 1977): 32–34; Richard H. King, "American Dilemmas, European Experiences," *Arkansas Historical Quarterly* 56 (Autumn 1997): 314–33; Hank Kilbanoff, "L. Alex Wilson," *Media Studies Journal* 14 (Summer 2000): 60–68; Richard H. King, *Race, Culture and the Intellectuals, 1940–1970* (Baltimore, MD.: Johns Hopkins University Press, 2004), 96–119; Vicky Lebeau, "The Unwelcome Child: Elizabeth Eckford and Hannah Arendt," *Journal of Visual Culture* 3:1 (2004) 52–62.

36. Charles Mingus, "Fables of Faubus," on *Mingus Ah Um* (Columbia, 1959); Charles Mingus, "Original Faubus Fables," on *Charles Mingus Presents Charles Mingus* (Candid, 1960); Brain Preistley, *Mingus: A Critical Biography* (London: Quartet Books, 1982), 86–87; The Normand Guilbeault Ensemble, "Fable of (George Dubya) Faubus," on *Mingus Erectus* (Ambiances Magnetiques, 2005).

37. Penny M. Von Eschen, *Race Against Empire: Black Americans and Anti-Colonialism, 1937–1957* (Ithaca: Cornell University Press, 1997), 179–80.

38. Harold R. Isaacs, "World Affairs and U.S. Race Relations: A Note on Little Rock," *The Public Opinion Quarterly* 22:3 (Autumn 1958): 364–370; Mary L. Dudziak, "The Little Rock Crisis and Foreign Affairs: Race, Resistance, and the Image of American Democracy," *Southern California Law Review* (September 1997): 1641–1716; Azza Salama Layton, "International Pressure and the US Government's Response to Little Rock," *Arkansas Historical Quarterly* 56 (Autumn 1997): 257–72; Melinda M. Schwenk, "Reforming the Negative Through History: The U. S. Information Agency and the 1957 Little Rock Integration Crisis," *Journal of Communication Inquiry* 23:3 (1999): 288–306; Mary Dudziak, *Cold War Civil Rights: Race and the Image of American Democracy,* (Princeton, N.J.: Princeton University Press, 2000), 115–151; Azza Salama Layton, *International Politics and Civil Rights Policies in the United States, 1941–1960,* (Cambridge: Cambridge University

Press, 2000), 107–39; Cary Fraser, "Crossing the Color Line in Little Rock: The Eisenhower Administration and the Dilemma of Race for US Foreign Policy," *Diplomatic History* 24 (Spring 2000): 233–64.

39. "The Revolution Since Little Rock," *Life,* September 29, 1967, 92–112; Paul Fair, "Little Rock: Then and Now," *Theory into Practice* 17:1 (February 1978): 39–42; Sybil Stevenson, "Reflections on Little Rock," *Theory into Practice* 17:2 (April 1978): 179–182; Branton "Little Rock Revisited"; Henry Woods and Beth Deere, "Reflections on the Little Rock School Case," *Arkansas Law Review* 44:4 (1991): 972–1006; Mary Caroline Proctor, "A History and Analysis of Federal Court Decisions in School Desegregation Cases: Implications for Arkansas" (Ph.D. diss., University of Mississippi, 1992); Robert L. Brown, "The Second Crisis of Little Rock: A Report on Desegregation Within the Little Rock Public Schools" (A Public Policy Project of the Winthrop Rockefeller Foundation, June 1998); Robert L. Brown, "The Third Little Rock Crisis," *Arkansas Historical Quarterly* 65:1 (Spring 2006): 39–44.

40. In addition to works cited above, see James W. Vander Zanden, "The Impact of Little Rock," *Journal of Educational Sociology* 35:8 (April 1962): 381–384; David Terrell, "Little Rock Story," *American Preservation* 1:1 (1977): 62–72; Chris Mayfield, "Little Rock, 1957–1960: 'The Middle Ground Turns to Quicksand," *Southern Exposure* 7:2 (1979): 40–44; John Egerton, "Little Rock, 1976: 'Going Back Would Be Unthinkable'," *Southern Exposure* 7:2 (1979): 45–46; Mike Masterson, "Little Rock, 1979: 'There Have Been Changes,'" *Southern Exposure* 7:2 (1979): 46–47; and Harry S. Ashmore, "The Lesson of Little Rock," *Media Studies Journal* 11 (Spring 1997): 6–15.

41. D. LaRouth S. Perry, "The 1957 Desegregation Crisis of Little Rock, Arkansas: A Meeting of Histories" (Ph.D. diss., Bowling Green State University, 1998); Damon W. Freeman, "Reexamining Central High: American Memory and Social Reality," *Organization of American Historians Newsletter* 28:1 (2000): 1, 3, 6; Cathy J. Collins, "Forgetting and Remembering: The Desegregation of Central High School in Little Rock, Arkansas: Race, Community Struggle, and Collective Memory" (Ph.D. diss., Fielding Graduate Institute, California, 2004).

42. Townsend Davis, *Weary Feet, Rested Souls: A Guided History of the Civil Rights Movement* (New York: W. W. Norton, 1998), 133–38; Johanna Miller Lewis, "Build a Museum and They Will Come: The Creation of the Central High Museum and Visitors Center," *The Public Historian* 22 (Fall 2000): 29–45.

43. Karen Anderson, *Little Rock* (Princeton, NJ: Princeton University Press, 2007); Freyer, *Rights Defied;* Elizabeth Jacoway, *Turn Away Thy Son: Little Rock, the Crisis That Shocked the Nation* (New York: Free Press, 2007); La Cruise, dir., "In the Shadow of Little Rock."

Chapter 2: The New Deal and the Civil Rights Struggle

1. On blacks and the New Deal see Allen Kiefer, "The Negro Under the New Deal," (Ph.D. diss., University of Wisconsin, 1961); Barton J. Bernstein, "The New Deal: The Conservative Achievements of Liberal Reform," in ed. Baton J. Bernstein *Towards a New Past: Dissenting Essays in American History* (New York: Pantheon Books, 1968), 263–88 (quoted page 279); Bernard Sternsher, ed., *The Negro in Depression and War: Prelude to Revolution, 1930–1945* (Chicago: Quadrangle Books, 1969); Raymond Wolters, *Negroes and the Great Depression: The Problem of Economic Recovery* (Westport, CT: Greenwood, 1970); Christopher G. Wye, "The New Deal and the Negro Community: Toward a Broader Conceptualization," *Journal of American History* (December 1972): 621–39; Ralph J. Bunche, *The Political Status of the Negro in the Age of FDR* (Chicago, IL: University of Chicago Press, 1973); Harvard Sitkoff, *A New Deal for Blacks: The Mergence of Civil Rights as a National Issue: Volume 1: The Depression Decade* (New York: Oxford University Press, 1978); John B. Kirby, *Black Americans in the Roosevelt Era: Liberalism and Race* (Knoxville: Tennessee University Press, 1980); Nancy J. Weiss, *Farewell to the Party of Lincoln: Black Politics in the Age of FDR* (Princeton, NJ: Princeton University Press, 1983); Patricia Sullivan, *Days of Hope: Race and Democracy in the New Deal Era* (Chapel Hill: University of North Carolina Press, 1996); and Kevin J. McMahon, *Reconsidering Roosevelt on Race: How the Presidency Paved the Road to Brown* (Chicago, IL: University of Chicago Press, 2003).

2. Anthony J. Badger, *The New Deal: The Depression Years, 1933–1940* (London: Macmillan Education, 1989), quoted 195–96, 252–53; Roger Biles, *The South and the New Deal* (Lexington: University of Kentucky Press, 1994), chap. 6.

3. Bernstein, "The New Deal," 279.

4. Aldon D. Morris, *The Origins of the Civil Rights Struggle: Black Communities Organizing for Change* (New York: Free Press, 1984), 78–80; Douglas L. Smith, *The New Deal and the Urban South* (Baton Rouge: Louisiana State University Press, 1988), chap. 12.

5. Weiss, *Farewell to the Party of Lincoln*, 211.

6. Sitkoff, *A New Deal for Blacks*, 334–5.

7. John A. Salmond, *The Civilian Conservation Corps, 1933–1942: A New Deal Case Study* (Durham, NC: Duke University Press, 1967); Leslie Alexander Lacy, *The Soil Soldiers: The Civilian Conservation Corps in the Great Depression* (Radnor, PA: Chilton Book Company, 1976); Stan Cohen, *The Tree Army: A Pictorial History of the Civilian Conservation Corps, 1933–1942* (Missoula, MT: Pictorial Histories Publishing Company, 1980); Perry H. Merrill, *Roosevelt's Forest Army: A History of the Civilian Conservation Corps, 1933–1942* (Montpelier, VT: P. H. Merrill, 1981); Robert Allen Ermentrout, *Forgotten Men: The Civilian Conservation Corps* (Smithtown, NY: Exposition Press, 1982); Edwin G. Hill, *In the Shadow of*

the Mountain: The Spirit of the Civilian Conservation Corps (Pullman, WA: Washington State University Press, 1990); M. Chester Nolte, ed., *The Civilian Conservation Corps: The Way We Remember It, 1933–1942* (Paducah, KY: Turner Publishing Company, 1990); Alfred E. Cornebise, *The CCC Chronicles: Camp Newspapers of the Civilian Conservation Corp, 1933–1942* (Jefferson, NC: McFarland, 2004).

   8. Salmond, *The Civilian Conservation Corps*, chap. 5; John A. Salmond, "The Civilian Conservation Corps and the Negro," *Journal of American History* 52:1 (June 1965): 75–88; Calvin W. Gower, "The Civilian Conservation Corps and American Education: Threat to Local Control?" *History of Education Quarterly* 7:1 (Spring 1967): 58–70; Charles Johnson, "The Army, the Negro and the Civilian Conservation Corps," *Military Affairs* 36:3 (October 1972): 82–88; Calvin W. Gower, "The Struggle of Blacks for Leadership Positions in the Civilian Conservation Corps: 1933–1942," *Journal of Negro History* 61:2 (April 1976): 123–35.

   9. Christine E. Savage, *New Deal Adobe: The Civilian Conservation Corps and the Reconstruction of Mission La Purisima, 1934–1942* (Santa Barbara: Fithian Press, 1999); Olen Cole, Jr., *The African American Experience in the Civilian Conservation Corps* (Gainesville: University Press of Florida, 1999); Richard Melzer, *Coming of Age in the Great Depression: The Civilian Conservation Corps in New Mexico, 1933–1942* (Las Cruces, NM: Yucca Tree Press, 2000); Annick Hivert Carthew, *Proud to Work: A Pictorial History of Michigan's Civilian Conservation Corps Camps* (Manchester, MI: Wilderness Adventure Books, 2006); Renee Corona Kolvet and Victoria Ford, *The Civilian Conservation Corps in Nevada: From Boys to Men* (Reno: University of Nevada Press, 2006); Robert J. Moore, *The Civilian Conservation Corps in Arizona's Rim Country: Working in the Woods* (Reno: University of Nevada Press, 2006); Joseph M. Speakman, *At Work in Pennsylvania's Woods: The Civilian Conservation Corps in Pennsylvania* (Philadelphia: Penn State Press, 2006).

   10. Weiss, *Farewell to the Party of Lincoln*, 55; Salmond, The *Civilian Conservation Corps*, 94.

   11. Biles, *The South and the New Deal*, 112; Kirby, *Black Americans in the Roosevelt Era*, 49.

   12. The best existing overview of the work of the CCC in Arkansas, which also includes some discussion of the black experience, is Joey McCarty, "Civilian Conservation Corps Camps in Arkansas" (M.A. thesis, University of Arkansas, Fayetteville, 1977). See also Sandra Taylor Smith, *The Civilian Conservation Corps in Arkansas, 1933–1942* (Little Rock: Arkansas Historic Preservation Program, n.d.).

   13. Johnson, "The Army, the Negro and the CCC," 82.

   14. Salmond, *The Civilian Conservation Corps*, 88–91.

   15. Salmond, *The Civilian Conservation Corps*, 90–91.

   16. On the Elaine riots see Richard C. Cortner, *A Mob Intent on Death: The NAACP and the Arkansas Riot Cases* (Middletown, CT: Wesleyan University Press, 1988); *Arkansas Historical Quarterly* 58 (Autumn 1999);

Grif Stockley, *Blood in their Eyes: The Elaine Race Massacres of 1919* (Fayetteville: University of Arkansas Press, 2001); *Arkansas Review: A Journal of Delta Studies* 32 (August 2001); Grif Stockley and Jeannie M. Whayne, "Federal Troops and the Elaine Massacres: A Colloquy," *Arkansas Historical Quarterly* 61 (Autumn 2002): 272–83.

17. Nan Elizabeth Woodruff, *American Congo: The American Freedom Struggle in the Delta* (Cambridge, MA: Harvard University Press, 2003), 1–2. On the Arkansas Delta see also Margaret Jones Bolsterli, *Born in the Delta: Reflections on the Making of a Southern White Sensibility* (Knoxville: University of Tennessee Press, 1991); Jennie M. Whayne and Willard B. Gatewood, eds., *The Arkansas Delta: Land of Paradox* (Fayetteville: University of Arkansas Press, 1993); Jeannie M. Whayne, ed. *Shadows Over Sunnyside: An Arkansas Plantation in Transition, 1830–1945* (Fayetteville: University of Arkansas, 1993); Fon Louise Gordon, *Caste and Class: The Black Experience in Arkansas, 1880–1920* (Athens: University of Georgia Press, 1995); and Jeannie M. Whayne, *A New Plantation South: Land, Labor, and Federal Favor in Twentieth-Century Arkansas* (Charlottesville: University Press of Virginia, 1996).

18. Salmond, *The Civilian Conservation Corps*, 94–96; Johnson, "The Army, the Negro and the CCC," 82.

19. "Arkansas's Negro CCC Camp," *Arkansas Gazette*, February 15, 1934.

20. Anonymous report, September 4, 1935, "Selected Documents Relating to the Work of the Civilian Conservation Corps in Arkansas: 1934–1942," Microfilm, Record Group 35, Records of the Civilian Conservation Corps, National Archives of America, Washington DC [hereafter cited as CCC Microfilm (Washington, DC)].

21. Salmond, *The Civilian Conservation Corps*, 92–98.

22. Telegram from Warren Residents to Oren Harris, August 6. 1941, box 1209, in "Civilian Conservation Corps, 1941–44" folder, Oren Harris Papers, Special Collections, University of Arkansas, Fayetteville (hereafter cited as Harris Papers).

23. Telegram from Homer Adkins to Hattie Carraway, August 10, 1941, box 1209, in "Civilian Conservation Corps, 1941–44," folder, Harris Papers.

24. Telegram from Oren Harris to Duval L. Purkins, August 16, 1941, box 1209, in "Civilian Conservation Corps, 1941–44," folder, Harris Papers.

25. Telegram from F. E. Hul, Brig. Gen. US Army, 7th Corps, Omaha, Nebraska, to Oren Harris, August 11, 1941, box 1209, in "Civilian Conservation Corps, 1941–44," folder, Harris Papers.

26. Carneal Warfield to Oren Harris, October 19, 1941, box 1209, in "Civilian Conservation Corps, 1941–44," folder, Harris Papers.

27. Oren Harris to James J. McEntee, October 18, 1941, box 1209, in "Civilian Conservation Corps, 1941–44," folder, Harris Papers.

28. Charles H. Taylor to Oren Harris, October 23, 1941, box 1209, in "Civilian Conservation Corps, 1941–44," folder, Harris Papers.

29. Johnson, "The Army, the Negro and the CCC," 83; Salmond, *The Civilian Conservation Corps*, 98–99.

30. Weiss, *Farewell to the Party of Lincoln,* 53.

31. Average white enrolment was about ten months, for blacks almost fifteen. Salmond, *The Civilian Conservation Corps,* 101.

32. Walter Davenport, "The Drought and Other Blessings," *Collier's Weekly,* July 11, 1931, 10–11, 50–51; Floyd Sharp, *Traveling Recovery Road: The Story of Relief, Work-Relief and Rehabilitation in Arkansas* (Little Rock: Emergency Relief Administration, 1936); Gail S. Murray, "Forty Years Ago: The Great Depression Comes to Arkansas," *Arkansas Historical Quarterly* 29 (Winter 1970): 291–312; Pete Daniel, *Deep'n as it Come: The 1927 Mississippi River Flood* (New York: Oxford University Press, 1977).

33. Howard W. Oxley, "The Civilian Conservation Corps and the Education of the Negro," *Journal of Negro Education* 7:3 (July 1938): 375–82; Calvin W. Gower, "The Struggle of Blacks for Leadership Positions in the Civilian Conservation Corps: 1933–1942," *Journal of Negro History* 61:2 (April 1976): 123–35; Marion Thompson Wright, "Negro Youth and the Federal Emergency Programs: CCC and NYA," *Journal of Negro Education* 9:3 (July 1940): 397–407.

34. Oxley, "The Civilian Conservation Corps," 376; Sitkoff, *A New Deal for Blacks,* 74.

35. Ralph W. Adams, Education Adviser, Charlotte CCC Camp Educational Reports, November 18, 1938; January 21, 1941; February 24, 1942; Harvey V. McDaniel, Jr., Education Adviser, Forrest City CCC Camp Educational Reports, July 21, 1939; March 26, 1940; William W. Willoughby, Education Adviser, Strong CCC Camp Educational Reports, May 1, 1935; September 4, 1935; Herbert Smith, Education Adviser, Rosston CCC Camp Educational Report, September 15, 1938, CCC Microfilm (Washington, DC). On the importance of radio in the civil rights struggle see Brian Ward, *Radio and the Struggle for Civil Rights in the South* (Gainesville: University Press of Florida, 2004).

36. Clipping from *Commercial Dispatch,* (Columbus, Mississippi) n.d., Billups Family, Local History Files, Billups-Garth Archives, Columbus-Lowndes Public Library, Mississippi. I am grateful to archives and manuscript librarian Benjamin Petersen for helping to locate this information.

37. J. S. Billups to Charles H. Kenlan, July 12, 1938; Statement of Bill White, CCC Microfilm (Washington, DC).

38. J. S. Billups to Charles H. Kenlan, July 12, 1938; Statements from Elsbery Broadnax, Maxie Vance, and Jesse Johnson, CCC Microfilm (Washington, DC).

39. Statements of Elmer Kennedy and Bill White, CCC Microfilm (Washington, DC).

40. Statement of Jess Weatherford, CCC Microfilm (Washington, DC).

41. Statements of Bill White, Elmer Kennedy, and Maxie Vance, CCC Microfilm (Washington, DC).

42. Statements of Capt. F. T. McQueen and Colonel Neal M. Snyder, CCC Microfilm (Washington, DC).

43. Statements of S. R. Bradley, Capt. F. T. McQueen, Henry Smith, Robert

Cotton, James Heorld, Plato Trimen, David Kelly, Nesley Ferguson, Julius Matlock, Willie Daniel, Jacob Ashmore, Martin O'Donell, Jesse Walker, and Sammie Lee Wilson, CCC Microfilm (Washington, DC).

44. Western Union Telegram, Henry Smith to Robert Fechner, July 8, 1938, CCC Microfilm (Washington, DC).

45. J. S. Billups to Charles H. Kenlan, July 12, 1938, CCC Microfilm (Washington, DC).

46. Statements of S. R. Bradley and Charles C. Derden, CCC Microfilm (Washington, DC).

47. Statements of S. R. Bradley, Lt. Carlos Emmanuelli, Lt. W. A. Regnier, and additional statement of Lt. W. A. Regnier, CCC Microfilm (Washington, DC).

48. Statements of S. R. Bradley and Charles C. Derden; J. J. McEntee, Acting Director, CCC, to US Attorney General, July 26, 1938, CCC Microfilm (Washington, DC).

49. Statement of Samuel T. Miller, CCC Microfilm (Washington, DC).

50. Statements of Samuel T. Miller, Henry Smith, Luther P. Brown, and Alford Anderson, CCC Microfilm (Washington, DC).

51. Statement of Earl Morris, CCC Microfilm (Washington, DC).

52. Statement of Harvey McDonald, CCC Microfilm (Washington, DC).

53. Statement of Cornelius Sommerville, CCC Microfilm (Washington, DC).

54. J. S. Billups to Charles H. Kenlan, July 12, 1938, CCC Microfilm (Washington, DC).

55. J. S. Billups, "A Confidential Report to be Held in the Washington Office," n.d., CCC Microfilm (Washington, DC).

56. Board of Inquiry, Forrest City, August 8, 1938; Maj. G. C. Graham to Adjutant General, August 25, 1938, CCC Microfilm (Washington, DC).

57. Western Union Telegram, Gov. Carl E. Bailey to Robert Fechner, August 27, 1938, CCC Microfilm (Washington, DC).

58. Western Union Telegram, J. J. McEntee to Gov. Carl E. Bailey, August 30, 1938, CCC Microfilm (Washington, DC).

59. Fred A. Isgrig, US Attorney, to US Attorney General, August 4, 1938, September 21, 1938, October 13, 1938, CCC Microfilm (Washington, DC).

60. Biles, *The South and the New Deal*, 103, 123.

Chapter 3: Politics and the Early Civil Rights Struggle

1. Quote from Nancy J. Weiss, *Farewell to the Party of Lincoln: Black Politics in the Age of FDR* (Princeton, NJ: Princeton University Press), xiii. The literature on the impact of the New Deal on American politics and the "solid South" is vast and beyond summation in a single footnote. Useful starting points include: James T. Patterson, *Congressional Conservatism and the New Deal: The Growth of a Conservative Coalition in Congress, 1933–1939* (Lexington: University of Kentucky Press, 1967); Dewey W. Grantham, *The Life and Death of the Solid South: A Political History* (Lexington: University

Press of Kentucky, 1988); Steve Fraser and Gary Gerstle, eds., *The Rise and Fall of the New Deal Order, 1930–1980* (Princeton, NJ: Princeton University Press, 1989); Numan V. Bartley, *The New South, 1945–1980* (Baton Rouge: Louisiana State University Press, 1995); Kari A. Frederickson, *The Dixiecrat Revolt and the End of the Solid South, 1932–1968* (Chapel Hill: University of North Carolina Press, 2001); and William Chafe, ed., *The Achievement of American Liberalism: The New Deal and Its Legacies* (New York: Columbia University Press, 2003).

2. Harvard Sitkoff, *A New Deal for Blacks: The Emergence of Civil Rights as a National Issue: Volume 1: The Depression Decade* (New York: Oxford University Press, 1978); Weiss, *Farewell to the Party of Lincoln.*

3. See, for example, Jack M. Bloom, *Race, Class and the Civil Rights Movement* (Bloomington: Indiana University Press, 1987).

4. Weiss, *Farewell to the Party of Lincoln*, 3–5.

5. Weiss, *Farewell to the Party of Lincoln*, 5–6.

6. Weiss, *Farewell to the Party of Lincoln*, 6–11. On Smith, Hoover, and the 1928 election, see Allan Lichtman, *Prejudice and Old Politics: The Presidential Election of 1928* (Chapel Hill: University of North Carolina Press, 1979); Donn C. Neal, *The World Beyond the Hudson: Alfred E. Smith and National Politics, 1918–1928* (New York: Garland, 1983); Donald J. Liso, *Hoover, Blacks, and Lily-Whites: A Study in Southern Strategies* (Chapel Hill: University of North Carolina, 1985); Kenneth Allen, *Components of Electoral Evolution: Realignment in the United States, 1912–1940* (New York: Garland, 1988); Robert A. Slayton, *Empire Statesman: The Rise and Redemption of Alfred E. Smith* (New York: Free Press, 2001); Chris M. Finan, *Alfred E. Smith: The Happy Warrior* (New York: Hill and Wang, 2002). On Senator Joseph T. Robinson, see Cecil Edeard Weller, *Joe T. Robinson: Always a Loyal Democrat* (Fayetteville: University of Arkansas Press, 1998).

7. Tom Dillard, "'To the Back of the Elephant': Racial Conflict in the Arkansas Republican Party," *Arkansas Historical Quarterly* 33 (Spring 1974): 3–15. A more detailed account can be found in Todd E. Lewis, "Race Relations in Arkansas, 1910–1929" (Ph.D. diss., University of Arkansas, Fayetteville, 1995). I am grateful to Dr. Lewis for making his thesis available to me.

8. Tom Dillard, "Scipio Jones," *Arkansas Historical Quarterly* 31 (Autumn 1972): 201–19.

9. V. O. Key, Jr., *Southern Politics in State and Nation* (New York: Alfred A. Knopf, 1949), 183–204.

10. Dillard, "To the Back of the Elephant"; Willard B. Gatewood, "Negro Legislators in Arkansas 1891: A Document," *Arkansas Historical Quarterly* 30 (Autumn 1972): 220–33; Blake Wintory, "William Hines Furbush: African-American Carpetbagger, Republican, Fusionist, and Democrat," *Arkansas Historical Quarterly* 63:2 (Summer 2004): 107–65.

11. *Arkansas Gazette*, July 21, 1970; Tom Dillard, "Perseverance: Black History in Pulaski County, Arkansas: An Excerpt," *Pulaski County Historical Review* 31 (Winter 1983): 61–73; Dale Lya Pierson, "John Robinson, M.D.,

1879–1970," *Pulaski County Historical Review* 41 (Winter 1993): 91–93; Lewis, "Race Relations in Arkansas," 432.

12. *Arkansas Gazette,* September 17, 1944; Lewis, "Race Relations in Arkansas," 432–33.

13. Lewis, "Race Relations in Arkansas," 433–34.

14. "Special Investigation of the John Carter Lynching, Little Rock, Ark.," group I, series C, container 349, in folder "Sub-File-Lynching-Little Rock, Ark. 1918–1927," NAACP Papers Library of Congress, Washington, DC [hereafter cited as NAACP Papers (Washington, DC)]; *Arkansas Gazette,* May 4, 5, 6, 7, 1927.

15. Elizabeth Jacoway, "An Introduction: Civil Rights in a Changing South," in *Southern Businessmen and Desegregation* eds. Elizabeth Jacoway and David Colburn (Baton Rouge: Louisiana State University Press, 1982), 2–14; Todd E. Lewis, "Mob Justice in the 'American Congo': 'Judge Lynch' in Arkansas during the Decade after World War I," *Arkansas Historical Quarterly* 52 (Summer 1993): 156–84.

16. *Arkansas Gazette,* May 4, 5, 6, 7, 1927.

17. *Survey of Negroes in Little Rock and North Little Rock, Compiled by the Writers' Program of the Work Projects Administration in the State of Arkansas* (Little Rock: Urban League of Greater Little Rock, 1941), 95.

18. Lewis, "Race Relations in Arkansas," 434–35. Lewis's evidence moves back ANDA's founding three months earlier than my previous accounts.

19. "Constitution and By-Laws and Order of Incorporation of the Arkansas Negro Democratic Association of Arkansas," box 26, file 296, in folder "Black Matters," Governor Sid McMath Papers, Arkansas History Commission, Little Rock, Arkansas.

20. Lewis, "Race Relations in Arkansas," 436.

21. Lewis, "Race Relations in Arkansas," 436–41.

22. Dr. J. M. Robinson to J. F. McClerkin, August 6, 1928, Dr. John Marshall Robinson Papers, Little Rock, Arkansas (hereafter cited as Robinson Papers). These are held in the private possession of Robinson's great-grandson Terry Pierson, to whom I am grateful for granting me access. See also John A. Hibbler to William T. Andrews, September 27, 1929, group I, series D, container 44, in folder "Cases Supported—Arkansas Primary Case 1928–1929," NAACP Papers (Washington, DC); and Darlene Clark Hine, *Black Victory: The Rise and Fall of the White Primary in Texas* (Millwood, NY: KTO Press, 1979), 72–85.

23. John A. Hibbler to William T. Andrews, September 27, 1929; William T. Andrews to John A. Hibbler, June 12, 1930, both in group I, series D, container 44, in folder "Cases Supported—Arkansas Primary Case 1928–1929," NAACP Papers (Washington, DC).

24. Walter White to Arthur Spingarn, November 7, 1929, miscellaneous correspondence, 1917–25, 1928–32, NAACP Papers, Microfilm, Special Collections, University of Arkansas Libraries, Fayetteville, [hereafter cited as NAACP Microfilm (Fayetteville)].

25. *Arkansas Gazette,* November 27, 1928.

26. *Arkansas Gazette,* March 26, 1930.

27. William T. Andrews to John A. Hibbler, July 19, 1930, group I, series D, container 44, in folder "Cases Supported—Arkansas Primary Case 1928–1929," NAACP Papers (Washington, DC); Hine, *Black Victory,* 115.

28. On blacks and World War II, see Richard M. Dalfumie, "The 'Forgotten Years' of the Negro Revolution," *Journal of American History* 55 (June 1968): 90–106; Richard M. Dalfumie, *Desegregation of the U.S. Armed Forces: Fighting on Two Fronts, 1939–1953* (Columbia: University of Missouri Press, 1969); Harvard Sitkoff, "Racial Militancy and Interracial Violence in the Second World War," *Journal of American History* 58 (June 1971): 661–81; Lee Finkle, *Forum for Protest: The Black Press during World War II* (Cranbury, NJ: Associated University Presses, 1975); John Morton Blum, *V Was for Victory: Politics and American Culture during World War II* (New York: Harcourt Brace Jovanovich, 1976); Neil A. Wynn, *The Afro-American and the Second World War* (London: Paul Elek, 1976); James Albert Burran, III, "Racial Violence in the South during World War II" (Ph.D. diss., University of Virginia, 1977); and Merle E. Reed, *Seedtime for the Modern Civil Rights Movement: The President's Committee on Fair Employment Practice, 1941–1946* (Baton Rouge: Louisiana State University Press, 1991).

29. *Brinkley Argus* (Brinkley, Arkansas), May 2, 1935, clipping in Floyd Sharp Scrapbooks 1933–1943, No. 11 "Civilian Conservation Corps (CCC) 1933–1935," Arkansas History Commission, Little Rock.

30. For a fuller account of Flowers and the CNO, see chap. 4.

31. *Arkansas Gazette,* December 8, 1940.

32. Hine, *Black Victory,* 202–7.

33. Hine, *Black Victory,* 202–7.

34. *Arkansas Gazette,* April 12, 1942.

35. *Arkansas Gazette,* July 22, 23, 1942.

36. *Arkansas Gazette,* July 24, 25, 27, 1942.

37. *Arkansas Gazette,* July 29, 1942.

38. Text of speech delivered by Dr. J. M. Robinson to the National Voters League, Birmingham, Alabama, April 4, 1945, Robinson Papers; *Arkansas Gazette,* August 4, 1942.

39. Text of speech delivered by Dr. J. M. Robinson to the National Voters League, Birmingham, Alabama, April 4, 1945, Robinson Papers; Hine, *Black Victory,* 212–229.

40. *Arkansas Gazette,* April 4, 1944.

41. *Arkansas Gazette,* April 11, 1944.

42. *Arkansas Gazette,* April 22, 1944.

43. Text of speech delivered by Dr. J. M. Robinson to the National Voters League, Birmingham, Alabama, April 4, 1945, Robinson Papers; *Arkansas Gazette,* May 17, 1944.

44. *Arkansas Gazette,* May 18, 1944.

45. Dr. J. M. Robinson to Sam Rorex, July 18, 1944, group II, series B, container 210, in folder "Voting, Arkansas, 1943–47," NAACP Papers (Washington, DC); *Arkansas Gazette,* June 4, 1944.

46. Text of speech delivered by Dr. J. M. Robinson to the National Voters League, Birmingham, Alabama, April 4, 1945, Robinson Papers; C. Calvin Smith, "The Politics of Evasion: Arkansas's Reaction to *Smith* v. *Allwright,* 1944," *Journal of Negro History* 67 (Spring 1982): 47.

47. *Arkansas Gazette,* July 20, 1944.

48. Text of speech delivered by Dr. J. M. Robinson to the National Voters League, Birmingham, Alabama, April 4, 1945, Robinson Papers; J. R. Booker to Thurgood Marshall, March 21, 1945; Thurgood Marshall to J. R. Booker, March 27, 1945; Thurgood Marshall to Dr. E. A. Dennard, April 23, 1945, all in group II, series B, container 210, in folder "Voting, Arkansas, 1943–1947," NAACP Papers (Washington, DC); *Arkansas Gazette,* July 26, 1944; Henry M. Alexander, "The Double Primary" *Arkansas Historical Quarterly* 3:3 (Autumn 1944), 217–268; Smith, "The Politics of Evasion," 48–49.

49. *Arkansas Gazette,* September 17, 1944.

50. *Arkansas Gazette,* September 23, 1944.

51. *Arkansas State Press,* November 17, 1944.

52. Charles Bussey, interview with the author, December 4, 1992, Little Rock, Arkansas, Pryor Center for Oral and Visual Culture; Jeffery Hawkins, interview with author, September 30, 1992, Little Rock, Arkansas, Pryor Center for Oral and Visual Culture.

53. Bussey and Hawkins interviews; Perlesta A. Hollingsworth, interview with author, April 13, 1993, Little Rock, Arkansas, Pryor Center for Oral and Visual Culture; Mrs. I. S. McClinton, interview with author, October 9, 1992, Little Rock, Arkansas, Pryor Center for Oral and Visual Culture; William "Sonny" Walker, telephone interview with the author, August 31, 1993, Atlanta, Georgia.

54. Bussey, Hawkins, and McClinton interviews.

55. *Arkansas Gazette,* May 5, 1950.

56. *Arkansas State Press,* December 29, 1950.

57. *Arkansas State Press,* November 30, 1951; Daisy Bates, interview with the author, August 14, 1992, Little Rock, Arkansas, Pryor Center for Oral and Visual Culture.

58. *Arkansas State Press,* September 17, 1948.

59. *Arkansas State Press,* June 4, 1950.

60. *Arkansas State Press,* June 4, 1950.

61. *Arkansas State Press,* June 7, 1950; *Arkansas Gazette,* June 8, 1950.

62. *Arkansas Democrat,* June 13, 1950.

63. *Arkansas Democrat,* June 15, 1950.

64. *Arkansas Democrat,* June 16, 1950.

65. *Arkansas Democrat,* July 6, 1950.

66. *Arkansas State Press,* September 1, 1950.

67. Sidney S. McMath, interview with the author, December 8, 1992, Little Rock, Arkansas, Pryor Center for Oral and Visual Culture. On the "GI revolt" and southern liberalism, see Tony Badger, "Fatalism, not Gradualism: Race and the Crisis of Southern Liberalism, 1945–1965," in eds. Brain Ward and Tony Badger *The Making of Martin Luther King and the Civil Rights Movement* (London: Macmillan, 1996), 67–95. On the McMath administration, see Jim Lester, *A Man For Arkansas: Sid McMath and the Southern*

Reform Tradition (Little Rock: Rose Publishing Co., 1976) and Sidney S. McMath, *Promises Kept: A Memoir* (Fayetteville: University of Arkansas Press, 2003). On Guthridge's later career, see Neil R. McMillen, "The White Citizens Council and Resistance to School Desegregation in Arkansas," *Arkansas Historical Quarterly* 30 (Summer 1971): 95–122.

    68. *Arkansas Gazette,* August 21, 1952.

    69. *Arkansas State Press,* August 29, 1952.

    70. *Arkansas Gazette,* August 30, 1952.

Chapter 4: Mass Mobilization and the Early Civil Rights Struggle

    1. William H. Chafe, *Civilities and Civil Rights: Greensboro, North Carolina and the Black Struggle For Freedom* (New York: Oxford University Press, 1980); David R. Colburn, *Racial Change and Community Crisis: St. Augustine, Florida, 1877–1980* (New York: Columbia University Press, 1985); Robert J. Norrell, *Reaping the Whirlwind: The Civil Rights Movement in Tuskegee* (New York: Alfred A. Knopf, 1985); George C. Wright, *Life Behind a Veil: Blacks in Louisville, Kentucky, 1865–1930* (Baton Rouge: Louisiana State University Press, 1985); Neil McMillen, *Dark Journey: Black Mississippians in the Age of Jim Crow* (Urbana: University of Illinois Press, 1989); John Dittmer, *Local People: The Struggle For Civil Rights in Mississippi* (Urbana: University of Illinois Press, 1994); Adam Fairclough, *Race and Democracy: The Civil Rights Struggle in Louisiana, 1915–1972* (Athens: University of Georgia Press, 1995); Charles M. Payne, *I've Got the Light of Freedom: The Organizing Tradition and the Mississippi Freedom Struggle* (Berkeley: University of California Press, 1995); Glenn T. Eskew, *But For Birmingham: The Local and National Movements in the Civil Rights Struggle* (Chapel Hill: University of North Carolina Press, 1997); Abel A. Bartley, *Keeping the Faith: Race, Politics and Social Development in Jacksonville, Florida, 1940–1970* (Westport, CT: Greenwood Press, 2000); Stephen G. N. Tuck, *Beyond Atlanta: The Struggle for Racial Equality in Georgia, 1940–1980* (Athens: University of Georgia Press, 2001); John A. Kirk, *Redefining the Color Line: Black Activism in Little Rock, Arkansas, 1940–1970* (Gainesville: University Press of Florida, 2002); Andrew M. Manis, *Macon Black and White: An Unutterable Separation in the American Century* (Macon: Mercer University Press and the Tubman African American Museum, 2004); J. Todd Moye, *Let the People Decide: Black Freedom and White Resistance Movements in Sunflower County, Mississippi, 1945–1986* (Chapel Hill: University of North Carolina Press, 2004); Bobby L. Lovett, *The Civil Rights Movement in Tennessee: A Narrative History* (Knoxville: University of Tennessee Press, 2005); Peter F. Lau, *Democracy Rising: South Carolina and the Fight for Black Equality since 1865* (Lexington: University Press of Kentucky, 2006).

    2. On the concept of an "organization of organizations" see Aldon D. Moris, *The Origins of the Civil Rights Movement: Black Communities Organizing for Change* (New York: Free Press, 1984), 100.

    3. Press release, (n.d.) W. H. Flowers Papers, Pine Bluff, Arkansas (here-

after cited as Flowers Papers). The collection is held in the private possession of Flowers's daughter Stephanie Flowers, to whom I am grateful for granting me access.

4. Maya Angelou, *I Know Why the Caged Bird Sings* (New York: Random House, 1969), 47.

5. *Arkansas Gazette,* July 31, 1988.

6. W. H. Flowers to Walter White, October 31, 1938, Flowers Papers.

7. Charles Houston to W. H. Flowers, November 22, 1938; Thurgood Marshall to W. H. Flowers, April 14, 1939, Flowers Papers.

8. "Application for Charter and Official Authorization," reel 4, frames 0785–0787, NAACP Papers, Microfilm, Special Collections, University of Arkansas Libraries, Little Rock [hereafter cited as NAACP Microfilm (Little Rock)].

9. August Meier to John H. Bracey Jr. "The NAACP as a Reform Movement, 1909–1965: 'To Reach the Conscience of America,'" *Journal of Southern History* 59:1 (February 1993): 3–30. See also Richard C. Cortner, *A Mob Intent on Death: The NAACP and the Arkansas Riot Cases* (Middletown, CT, 1988).

10. W. A. Springfield to William Pickens, January 5, 1925, NAACP Microfilm (Little Rock).

11. Mrs. H. L. Porter to Roy Wilkins, November 2, 1934, NAACP Microfilm (Little Rock).

12. A. E. Bush and P. L. Dorman, *History of the Mosaic Templars of America* (Little Rock: Central Printing Company, 1924).

13. Walter White to Arthur Spingarn, November 7, 1929, "miscellaneous correspondence, 1917–25, 1928–32," NAACP Papers, Microfilm, University of Arkansas, Fayetteville, Special Collections [hereafter cited as NAACP Microfilm (Fayetteville)].

14. William Pickens to W. H. Flowers, May 10, 1940, group II, series C, container 10, in folder "Pine Bluff, Ark., 1940–1947," NAACP Papers, Library of Congress, Washington, DC [hereafter cited as NAACP Papers (Washington, DC)].

15. The *CNO Spectator,* July 1, 1940, Flowers Papers.

16. V. O. Key, Jr., *Southern Politics in State and Nation* (New York: Alfred A. Knopf, 1949), 183.

17. For details on Robinson, ANDA, and early black political struggles, see chap. 3.

18. The *CNO Spectator*, July 1, 1940, Flowers Papers.

19. The *CNO Spectator*, July 1, 1940, Flowers Papers

20. Press release, October 12, 1940, Flowers Papers. Accounts appeared in various black newspapers nationally; see Flowers to William H. Nunn, October 5, 1940, Flowers Papers.

21. "Partial text of keynote address of W. Harold Flowers, delivered Friday evening, September 27, 1940 at the opening of the 'First Conference on Negro Organization,' held at Lakeview, Arkansas," September 27, 1940, Flowers Papers.

22. Press release, January 1, 1941, Flowers Papers.

23. Press release, September 4, 1941, Flowers Papers; *Arkansas State Press*, September 19, 1941.

24. *Arkansas State Press*, September 19, 1941.

25. Press release, September 11, 1941, Flowers Papers.

26. *Arkansas State Press*, May 15, 1942.

27. *Arkansas State Press*, March 6, 1942.

28. Thomas E. Patterson, *History of the Arkansas State Teachers Association* (Washington, DC: National Education Association, 1981), 89–91.

29. The *CNO Spectator*, July 15, 1940.

30. Mrs. H. L. Porter to William Pickens, June 9, 1940, group II, series C, container 9, in folder "Little Rock, Arkansas, 1940–1947," NAACP Papers (Washington, DC)

31. W. H. Flowers to Ella Baker, August 18, 1945, group II, series C, container 11, in folder "Arkansas State Conference, April 1945-December 1948," NAACP Papers (Washington, DC).

32. C. Calvin Smith, "The Politics of Evasion: Arkansas' Reaction to *Smith v. Allwright*, 1944," *Journal of Negro History* 67:1 (Spring 1982): 40–51.

33. Steven Lawson, *Running for Freedom: Civil Rights and Black Politics in America since 1941* (New York: MacGraw-Hill, 1991), 85.

34. *Arkansas Gazette,* July 31, 1988.

35. Guerdon D. Nichols, "Breaking The Color Barrier at the University of Arkansas," *Arkansas Historical Quarterly* 27 (Spring 1968): 3–21.

36. *Arkansas State Press,* July 15, 1949.

37. Rev. W. Marcus Taylor to Ella Baker, December 4, 1945, group II, series C, container 9, in folder "Little Rock, Arkansas, 1940–1970," NAACP Papers (Washington, DC).

38. Gloster B. Current to Thurgood Marshall, (n.d.), group II, series C, container 11, in folder "Arkansas State Conference, April 1945-December 1948," NAACP Papers (Washington, DC).

39. Lucille Black to W. H. Flowers, January 15, 1948, group II, series C, container 10, in folder "Pine Bluff, Ark., 1948–1955," NAACP Papers (Washington, DC).

40. Donald Jones to Gloster B. Current, (n.d.), group II, series C, container 11, in folder "Arkansas State Conference, April 1945-December 1948," NAACP Papers (Washington, DC).

41. Mrs. L. C. Bates to Miss Mary W. Ovington, December 9, 1948, group II, series C, container 10, in folder "Little Rock, Ark., 1948–1955," NAACP Papers (Washington, DC).

42. Gloster B. Current to Mrs. L. C. Bates, January 19, 1949, group II, series C, container 10, in folder "Little Rock, Ark., 1948–1955," NAACP Papers (Washington, DC).

43. Donald Jones to Gloster B. Current, February 24, 1949, group II, series C, container 11, in folder "Arkansas State Conference 1949–1950," NAACP Papers (Washington, DC).

44. "Resolution," September 3, 1949, group II, series C, container 10, in folder "Pine Bluff, Ark, 1948–1955," NAACP Papers (Washington, DC).

45. Walter White to Pine Bluff NAACP, February 25, 1949; Roy Wilkins to Arkansas Branches of the NAACP, May 10, 1949, both group II, series C, container 10, in folder "Pine Bluff, Ark, 1948–1955," NAACP Papers (Washington, DC).

46. Lulu B. White to Gloster B. Current, November 1, 1950, group II, series C, container 11, in folder "Arkansas State Conference 1949–1950," NAACP Papers (Washington, DC).

47. Memorandum, Gloster B. Current to the Staff, Branches and Regional Offices August 7, 1951, group II, series C, container 11, in folder "Arkansas State Conference 1951–1952," NAACP Papers (Washington, DC).

48. Gloster B. Current to U. Simpson Tate, August 20, 1952, group II, series C, branch files 1940–1955, container 11, in folder "Arkansas State Conference 1951–1952," NAACP Papers (Washington, DC).

49. Georg Iggers, "An Arkansas Professor: The NAACP and the Grassroots," in Wilson Record and Jane Cassells Record, *Little Rock, U.S.A.: Materials for Analysis* (San Francisco: Chandler, 1960), 283–91.

50. Daisy Bates, *The Long Shadow of Little Rock* (New York: David McKay, 1962).

Chapter 5: Gender and the Civil Rights Struggle

1. Vicki L. Crawford, Jacqueline Anne Rouse, and Barbara Woods, eds., *Women in the Civil Rights Movement: Trailblazers and Torchbearers, 1941–1965* (Brooklyn, NY: Carlson Publishing, 1990).

2. Anne Standley, "The Role of Black Women in the Civil Rights Movement," in ed. Crawford, *Women in the Civil Rights Movement*, 188–90. Since this article was first published in 1999 a number of works have appeared that answer the call for more on the life of Bates. These include: Linda Reed, "The Legacy of Daisy Bates," *Arkansas Historical Quarterly* 59 (Spring 2000): 76–83; Amy Polakow, *Daisy Bates: Civil Rights Crusader* (North Haven, CT: Linnet Books, 2003); John Adams, "'Arkansas Needs Leadership': Daisy Bates, Black Arkansas, and the NAACP" (M.A. thesis, University of Wisconsin, 2003); Grif Stockley, *Daisy Bates: Civil Rights Crusader from Arkansas* (Jackson: University of Mississippi Press, 2005); Sharon La Cruise, dir. "In the Shadow of Little Rock: The Life of Daisy Bates," (Sakkara Films, 2007).

3. Grace Jordan McFadden, "Septima P. Clark and the Struggle for Human Rights," and Alice G. Knotts, "Methodist Women Integrate Schools and Housing, 1952–1959," both in ed. Crawford, *Women in the Civil Rights Movement*.

4. Joan Hoff, "Introduction: An Overview of Women's History in the United States" in ed. Gayle V. Fischer *Journal of Women's History Guide to Periodical Literature* (Bloomington: Indiana University Press), 9–37.

5. Charles Payne, "Men Led, But Women Organized: Movement Participation of Women in the Mississippi Delta," in ed. Crawford, *Women in the Civil Rights Movement*.

6. Belinda Robnett, "African American Women in the Civil Rights Movement, 1954–1965: Gender, Leadership, and Micromobilization," *American Journal of Sociology* 101(May 1996): 1661–93.

7. See for example, Tony Freyer, *The Little Rock Crisis: A Constitutional Interpretation* (Westport, CT: Greenwood Press, 1984).

8. Daisy Bates, *The Long Shadow of Little Rock: A Memoir* (New York: David McKay Company, Inc., 1962); *Eyes on the Prize: America's Civil Rights Years, 1954–1965*, directed by Henry Hampton. Boston: Blackside, Inc. 1987; Daisy Bates Papers, Special Collections Division, University of Arkansas Libraries, Fayetteville; Daisy Bates Papers, State Historical Society of Wisconsin, Madison.

9. Register of the Daisy Bates Papers at the State Historical Society of Wisconsin, Madison, 1.

10. *Arkansas Gazette,* January 1, 1963; September 1, 1963.

11. Sara Evans, *Personal Politics: The Roots of Women's Liberation in the Civil Rights Movement and the New Left* (New York: Alfred A. Knopf, 1979).

12. Bates, *Long Shadow,* 6–31.

13. Bates, *Long Shadow,* 10–12.

14. Bates, *Long Shadow,* 8.

15. Bates, *Long Shadow,* 12.

16. Bates, *Long Shadow,* 14.

17. Bates, *Long Shadow,* 24.

18. Bates, *Long Shadow,* 28–29.

19. Bates, *Long Shadow,* 29–30.

20. Bates, *Long Shadow,* 29.

21. Bates, *Long Shadow,* 8–9.

22. Bates, *Long Shadow,* 9.

23. Bates, *Long Shadow,* 15.

24. Bates, *Long Shadow,* 17.

25. Bates, *Long Shadow,* 7–8.

26. Bates, *Long Shadow,* 14.

27. Bates, *Long Shadow,* 21–22.

28. Bates, *Long Shadow,* 25.

29. Bates, *Long Shadow,* 26

30. Bates, *Long Shadow,* 27.

31. Bates, *Long Shadow,* 28.

32. Aldon D. Morris, *The Origins of the Civil Rights Movement: Black Communities Organizing for Change* (New York: Free Press, 1984), 4–12; Payne, "Men Led, But Women Organized."

33. Bates, *Long Shadow,* 20–21.

34. Bates, *Long Shadow,* 13.

35. Bates, *Long Shadow,* 13.

36. Bates, *Long Shadow,* 24–25.

37. Bates, *Long Shadow,* 7–9.

38. Bates, *Long Shadow,* 9–20.

39. Bates, *Long Shadow,* 13–15.

40. Bates, *Long Shadow,* 12.

41. Bates, *Long Shadow,* 16

42. Bates, *Long Shadow,* 12.

43. Bates, *Long Shadow,* 15.

44. Bates, *Long Shadow,* 16.

45. Bates, *Long Shadow,* 17.

46. Bates, *Long Shadow,* 23.

47. Bates, *Long Shadow,* 17.

48. Bates, *Long Shadow,* 21.

49. Bates, *Long Shadow,* 18.

50. Bates, *Long Shadow,* 18.

51. Bates, *Long Shadow,* 19.

52. Bates, *Long Shadow,* 7, 9, 10, 13, 21, 25–26.

53. C. Calvin Smith, "'From Separate But Equal to Desegregation': The Changing Philosophy of L. C. Bates," *Arkansas Historical Quarterly* 62(Autumn 1983): 254–270; the Register of the Daisy Bates Papers at the State Historical Society of Wisconsin, Madison, gives Daisy Bates's year of birth as 1922; Smith gives L. C. Bates's year of birth as 1901.

54. Bates, *Long Shadow,* 33.

55. *Arkansas Gazette,* January 1, 1963; September 1, 1963.

56. For example, see Edwin E. Dunaway, interview with author, September 26, 1992, Little Rock, Arkansas, Pryor Center for Oral and Visual History.

57. Bates, *Long Shadow,* 33–34.

58. Bates, *Long Shadow,* 38–39.

59. Irene Wassell, "L. C. Bates, Editor of the *Arkansas State Press*" (M.A. thesis, University of Arkansas; Smith, 1983), "'From Separate But Equal to Desegregation.'"

60. *Arkansas State Press,* March 27, 1942; April 5, 1942.

61. *Arkansas State Press,* August 21, 1942.

62. *Arkansas State Press,* December 29, 1950.

63. *Arkansas State Press,* November 30, 1951.

64. *Arkansas State Press,* April 14, 1950.

65. *Arkansas State Press,* September 17, 1948.

66. *Arkansas State Press,* December 29, 1950.

67. Dunaway interview.

68. William Pickens to Carrie Sheppherdson, January 5, 1925, reel 4, frame 0897, NAACP Papers, Microfilm, Special Collections, University of Arkansas Libraries, Little Rock [hereafter cited as NAACP Microfilm (Little Rock)].

69. Mrs. H. L. Porter to Roy Wilkins, November 14, 1933, reel 4, frames 0039–0040, NAACP Microfilm (Little Rock).

70. Mark Tushnet, *The NAACP's Legal Strategy Against Segregated Education, 1925–1950* (Chapel Hill: University of North Carolina Press, 1987); Miss Solar M. Caretners to Melvin O. Austin, February 22, 1941, and Miss Solar B. Caretners to Walter White, February 22, 1941, group II, series B, container 174, in folder "Teachers Salaries, Arkansas, Little Rock, *Morris v.*

School Board (General) 1941–1943), NAACP Papers, Library of Congress, Washington, DC [hereafter cited as NAACP Papers (Washington, DC)].

71. Sue Morris, interview with the author, January 8, 1993, Little Rock, Arkansas, Pryor Center for Oral and Visual Culture; *Arkansas Gazette,* March 1, 1942.

72. *Arkansas Gazette,* January 6, 1944.

73. Tushnet, *NAACP's Legal Strategy,* 90.

74. Press release, June 21, 1945, group II, series B, container 174, in folder "Teachers Salaries, Arkansas, Little Rock, *Morris v. School Board* (General) 1941–1943)," NAACP Papers (Washington, DC).

75. Rev. Marcus Taylor to Ella Baker, December 4, 1945, group II, series C, container 9, in folder "Little Rock, Arkansas, 1940–1947," NAACP Papers (Washington, DC).

76. Gloster B. Current to Thurgood Marshall (memorandum, n.d.), group II, series C, container 11, in folder "Arkansas State Conference, April 1945-December 1948," NAACP Papers (Washington, DC).

77. Lucille Black to W. H. Flowers, January 15, 1948, group II, series C, container 10, in folder "Pine Bluff, Ark., 1948–1955," and Donald Jones to Gloster B. Current (memorandum, n. d.), group II, series C, container 11, in folder "Arkansas State Conference, April 1945-December 1948," NAACP Papers (Washington D. C.).

78. Wassell, "L. C. Bates," 36.

79. Daisy Bates, interview with the author, August 14, 1992, Little Rock, Arkansas, Pryor Center for Oral and Visual Culture.

80. Mrs. L. C. Bates to Miss Mary Ovington, December 9, 1948, group II, series C, container 10, in folder "Little Rock, Ark., 1948–1955, " NAACP Papers (Washington, DC).

81. Mr. Gloster B. Current to Mrs. L. C. Bates, January 19, 1949, group II, series C, container 10, in folder "Little Rock, Arkansas, 1948–1955," NAACP (Washington, DC).

82. Donald Jones to Gloster B. Current, February 24, 1949, group II, series C, container 10, in folder "Arkansas State Conference 1949–1950," NAACP Papers (Washington, DC).

83. Walter White to Pine Bluff NAACP, February 25, 1949; Roy Wilkins to Arkansas Branches of the NAACP, May 10, 1949, group II, series C, container 10, in folder "Pine Bluff, Ark., 1948–1955," NAACP Papers (Washington, DC).

84. Lulu B. White to Gloster B. Current, November 1, 1950, group II, series C, container 11, in folder "Arkansas State Conference 1949–1950," NAACP Papers (Washington, DC).

85. U. Simpson Tate to Gloster B. Current, August 20, 1952, group II, series C, container 11, folder "Arkansas State Conference 1951–1952," NAACP Papers (Washington, DC).

86. Bates, *Long Shadow,* 47–48.

87. Bates, *Long Shadow,* 32–69.

88. Tilman C. Cothran and William Phillips Jr., "Negro Leadership in a Crisis Situation," *Phylon* 22:2 (Spring 1961): 107–18.

89. Irving J. Spitzberg, *Racial Politics in Little Rock 1954–1964* (New York: Garland Pubishing, 1987), 129.

90. Bates, *Long Shadow,* 107–112.

91. *Arkansas State Press,* April 10, 1959.

92. Morris, *Origins of the Civil Rights Movement,* 192.

93. *Arkansas Gazette,* March 18, 1960.

94. *Arkansas Democrat,* March 13, 1960; Dunaway interview.

95. *Southern School News,* January 1960, 6.

96. C. D. Coleman, Director of Community Services, Southern Field Division, to M. T. Puryear, Southern Field Director, October 5, 1959, group II, series D, container 26, in folder "Little Rock, Arkansas," National Urban League Papers, Library of Congress, Washington, DC.

97. John Walker to Paul Rilling, November 17, 1959, reel 141, series IV, container 234, Southern Regional Council Papers, Microfilm, Library of Congress, Washington DC.

98. *Southern School News,* November 1959, 8.

99. *Arkansas Gazette,* November 10, 1959.

100. Nat Griswold, "The Second Reconstruction in Little Rock," unpublished manuscript, series 2, box 11, folder 8, Sara Alderman Murphy Papers, Special Collections, University of Arkansas Libraries, Fayetteville.

101. Griswold, "Second Reconstruction," 129.

102. Bates, *Long Shadow,* 161–170.

103. Griswold, "Second Reconstruction," 11–15.

104. *Arkansas Gazette,* September 15, 1963.

Chapter 6: White Opposition to the Civil Rights Struggle

1. Martin Luther King Jr., "Letter from Birmingham City Jail," in ed. James M. Washington *A Testament of Hope: The Essential Writings and Speeches of Martin Luther King Jr.* (San Francisco: HarperCollins, 1986), 295.

2. Martin Luther King Jr., *Where Do We Go From Here: Chaos or Community?* (New York: Harper and Row, 1967), 11.

3. See, for example, Dwight D.Eisenhower, *Waging Peace* (Garden City, NY: Doubleday, 1965); Brooks L. Hays, *A Southern Moderate Speaks* (Chapel Hill: University of North Carolina Press, 1959) and *Politics Is My Parish: An Autobiography* (Baton Rouge: Louisiana State University Press, 1981); Orval E. Faubus, *Down From the Hills* (Little Rock: Pioneer Press, 1980) and *Down From the Hills II* (Little Rock: Democrat Printing and Lithograph, 1986); Virgil T. Blossom, *It Has Happened Here* (New York: Harper, 1959); Roy Reed, *Faubus: The Life and Times of an American Prodigal* (Fayetteville: University of Arkansas Press, 1997); Numan V. Bartley, *The Rise of Massive Resistance: Race and Politics in the South during the 1950s* (Baton Rouge: Louisiana State University Press, 1969), chap. 14; Elizabeth Jacoway, "Taken By Surprise: Little Rock Business Leaders and Desegregation," in eds. Elizabeth Jacoway and David Colburn, *Southern Businessmen and Desegregation* (Baton Rouge: Louisiana State University Press, 1982); Tony Freyer, *The Little Rock Crisis: A*

Constitutional Interpretation (Westport, CT: Greenwood Press, 1984); and Corrine Silverman, *The Little Rock Story* (Tuscaloosa: University of Alabama Press, 1958).

4. On massive resistance, see Bartley, *Rise of Massive Resistance.* On Blossom's attitude to school desegregation, see Blossom, *It Has Happened Here,* 13–15.

5. Bartley, *Rise of Massive Resistance,* 252.

6. For examples of earlier, generally more upbeat assessments of southern liberals, see Thomas A. Krueger, *And Promises to Keep: The Southern Conference for Human Welfare, 1938-1948* (Nashville: Vanderbilt University Press, 1967); Morton Sosna, *In Search of the Silent South: Southern Liberals and the Race Issue* (Guildford, NY: Columbia University Press, 1971); Jacquelyn Dowd Hall, *Revolt Against Chivalry: Jessee Daniel Ames and the Women's Campaign Against Lynching* (Guildford, NY: Columbia University Press, 1979); Anthony P. Dunbar, *Against the Grain: Southern Radicals and Prophets, 1929-1959* (Charlottesville: University Press of Virginia, 1981); Charles Eagles, *Jonathan Daniels and Race Relations: The Evolution of a Southern Liberal* (Knoxville: University of Tennessee Press, 1982); Linda Reed, *Simple Decency and Common Sense: The Southern Conference Movement, 1938-1963* (Bloomington: Indiana University Press, 1991); Frank T. Adams, *James A. Dombrowski: An American Heretic, 1897-1984* (Knoxville: University of Tennessee Press, 1992); John Egerton, *Speak Now Against the Day: The Generation Before the Civil Rights Movement in the South* (New York: Alfred A. Knopf, 1994).

6. David Chappell, *Inside Agitators: White Southerners in the Civil Rights Movement* (Baltimore: John Hopkins University Press, 1994).

7. Blossom, *It Has Happened Here,* 11–13.

8. A. F. House to Arthur B. Caldwell, July 21, 1958, box 5, folder 7, Arthur Brann Caldwell Papers, Special Collections, University of Arkansas Libraries, Fayetteville.

9. Georg C. Iggers, "An Arkansas Professor: The NAACP and the Grass Roots," in eds. Wilson Record and Jane Cassels Record *Little Rock, U.S.A.* (San Francisco: Chandler Publishing Co., 1960), 286; Little Rock Board of Education to Legal Redress Committee NAACP, Arkansas, September 9, 1954, Virgil T. Blossom Papers, Special Collections, University of Arkansas Libraries, Fayetteville.

10. Iggers, "Arkansas Professor," 286–287.

11. "The Status of Desegregation in Arkansas—Some Measures of Progress," group II, series B, container 136, in folder "Schools, Arkansas, 1946–55," NAACP Papers, Library of Congress, Washington, DC [hereafter cited as NAACP Papers (Washington, DC)]; *Southern School News,* May 1955, 2.

12. *Southern School News,* March 1955, 2

13. *Southern School News,* April 1955, 7.

14. On *Brown II* and its aftermath, see J. Harvie Wilkinson III, *From Brown to Bakke: The Supreme Court and School Integration: 1954–1978* (New York: Oxford University Press, 1979) 61–95.

15. Wilkinson, *From Brown to Bakke*, 61–95; David R. Goldfield, *Black, White and Southern: Race Relations and Southern Culture, 1940 to the Present* (Baton Rouge: Louisiana State University Press, 1990), 81; Michael S. Mayer, "With Much Deliberation and Some Speed: Eisenhower and the *Brown* Decision," *Journal of Southern History* 52:1 (February 1986): 43–76.

16. *Southern School News*, July 1955, 3; Iggers, "Arkansas Professor," 287.

17. Iggers, "Arkansas Professor," 287.

18. Iggers, "Arkansas Professor," 287–88.

19. *Southern School News*, September 1955, 10; Wiley A. Branton to William G. Cooper, August 21, 1954, box 4, folder 10, Daisy Bates Papers, State Historical Society of Wisconsin, Madison [hereafter cited as Bates Papers (Madison)].

20. *Southern School News*, July 1955, 3; August 1955, 15; September 1955, 10.

21. Mildred L. Bond to Roy Wilkins, August 6, 1955, box 4, folder 10, Bates Papers (Madison).

22. *Southern School News*, August 1955, 15.

23. "A 'Morally Right' Decision," *Life*, July 25, 1955, 29–31.

24. "A 'Morally Right' Decision," *Life*, July 25, 1955, 29–31.

25. Cabell Phillips, "Integration: Battle of Hoxie, Arkansas," *New York Times Magazine*, September 25, 1955, 12, 68–76.

26. *Southern School News*, September 1955, 10.

27. Neil R. McMillen, "The White Citizens Council and Resistance to School Desegregation in Arkansas," *Arkansas Historical Quarterly* 30 (Summer 1971): 97–100; Jerry J. Vervack, "The Hoxie Imbroligo," *Arkansas Historical Quarterly* 48 (Spring 1989): 22.

28. Arthur Brann Caldwell, "The Hoxie Case—The Story of the First School in the Old South to Integrate in the Wake of the *Brown* Decisions," 6–20, supplied courtesy of William Penix (attorney for the Hoxie school board).

29. The best guide to the White Citizens' Councils is Neil R. McMillen, *The Citizens' Council: Organized Resistance to the Second Reconstruction, 1955–1964* (Urbana: University of Illinois Press, 1971). On the composition of the ACCA, see "Race Relations in Little Rock Before 1957," series 1, box 20, folder 197, Arkansas Council on Human Relations Papers 1954–1968, Special Collections, University of Arkansas Libraries, Fayetteville (hereinafter cited as ACHR Papers).

30. Dianne D. Blair, *Arkansas Politics and Government: Do The People Rule?* (Lincoln: University of Nebraska Press, 1988), 65.

31. Iggers, "Arkansas Professor," 288–289.

32. *Southern School News*, February 1956, 11.

33. *Southern School News*, March 1956, 4; Wiley A. Branton, "Little Rock Revisited: Desegregation to Resegregation," *Journal of Negro Education* 52 (Summer 1983): 253.

34. Iggers, "Arkansas Professor," 290.

35. Freyer, *Little Rock Crisis*, 52.

36. Branton, "Little Rock Revisited," 254; Freyer, *Little Rock Crisis*, 56–58.

37. "Our Reason for Appeal," Rev. J. C. Crenchaw, n.d., box 4, folder 10, Bates Papers (Madison); Branton, "Little Rock Revisited," 255–56.

38. *Southern School News*, May 1957, 2; Branton, "Little Rock Revisited," 255–56.

39. "Statement by Rev. J. C. Crenchaw," n.d., box 4, folder 10, Bates Papers (Madison); *Southern School News*, May 1957, 2.

40. Wiley A. Branton to A. F. House, July 10, 1957, Blossom Papers.

41. *Southern School News*, July 1957, 10.

42. "What is Happening in Desegregation in Arkansas," January 1957, series 1, box 29, folder 302, ACHR Papers.

43. Catherine Barnes, *Journey From Jim Crow: The Desegregation of Southern Transit* (Guildford, NY: Columbia University Press, 1983), 118–19; Ozell Sutton, interview with the author, August 7, 1993, Little Rock, Arkansas, Pryor Center for Oral and Visual Culture; Rev. Rufus King Young, interview with the author, February 16, 1993, Little Rock, Arkansas, Pryor Center for Oral and Visual Culture.

44. "What is Happening in Desegregation in Arkansas."

45. On the Montgomery bus boycott, see Adam Fairclough, *To Redeem the Soul of America: The Southern Christian Leadership Conference and Martin Luther King, Jr.* (Athens: University of Georgia Press, 1987), 11–35.

46. "Report of Conference Between Little Rock School Superintendent and NAACP Representatives, May 29, 1957," group II, series A, container 98, in folder "Desegregation of Schools, Arkansas, Little Rock, Central High, 1956–1957," NAACP Papers (Washington, DC).

47. "Report of Conference."

48. "Report of Conference."

49. "Report of Conference."

50. "Report of Conference."

51. Mrs. L. C. Bates to Mr. Robert L. Carter, August 2, 1957, group II, series A, container 98, in folder "Desegregation of Schools, Arkansas, Little Rock, Central High, 1956–1957," NAACP Papers (Washington, DC); Blossom, *It Has Happened Here*, 19–21.

52. Daisy Bates, *The Long Shadow of Little Rock: A Memoir* (New York: David McKay Company, Inc., 1962), 59.

53. *Southern School News*, September 1957, 6; Roy Reed, *Faubus*, 196–97; Robert Sherrill, *Gothic Politics in the Deep South* (New York: Grossman Books, 1968), 105–6.

54. On the Mothers' League, see Graeme Cope, "'A Thorn in the Side'?: The Mothers' League of Central High School and the Little Rock Desegregation Crisis of 1957," *Arkansas Historical Quarterly* 57 (Summer 1998), 160–90.

55. Warren Olney III, assistant U.S. attorney general for the Civil Rights Division of the Justice Department, to Arthur B. Caldwell, assistant to the assistant U.S. attorney general, September 13, 1957, box 5, folder 2, Caldwell

Papers; Reed, *Faubus,* 199; Silverman, *Little Rock Story,* 6–7.

56. Branton, "Little Rock Revisited," 259–260; Reed, *Faubus,* 199–200; Silverman, *The Little Rock Story,* 7.

57. Irving J. Spitzberg, *Racial Politics in Little Rock 1954–1964* (New York: Garland Publishing, 1987), 65.

58. "Telephone Report from assistant U.S. attorney James E. Gallman, Little Rock, Arkansas, on the integration situation, September 3, 1957," box 5, folder 2, Caldwell Papers; Reed, *Faubus,* 208.

59. "Telephone Report"; Branton, "Little Rock Revisited," 260.

60. John A Kirk, *Redefining the Color Line: Black Activism in Little Rock, Arkansas, 1940–1970* (Gainesville: University of Florida Press, 2002), chap. 5.

61. Bartley, *Rise of Massive Resistance,* chap. 14.

62. Jacoway, "Taken By Surprise."

63. Kirk, *Redefining the Color Line,* chap. 6.

64. Jacoway and Colburn, eds., *Southern Businessmen and Desegregation;* Tony Badger, "Segregation and the Southern Business Elite," *Journal of American Studies* 18 (April 1984): 105–9.

65. Orval E. Faubus, interview with the author, December 3, 1992, Conway, Arkansas, Pryor Center for Oral and Visual Culture. For a more detailed account of Faubus' upbringing and political career, see Reed, *Faubus.*

66. *Southern School News,* March 1955, 2. On the reactions of liberal southern politicians to *Brown,* see Tony Badger, "Fatalism, Not Gradualism: Race and the Crisis of Southern Liberalism, 1945–1965," in eds. Brian Ward and Tony Badger *The Making of Martin Luther King and the Civil Rights Movement* (London: Macmillan, 1996), 67–95.

67. Faubus interview.

68. *Southern School News,* August 1956, 3; Reed, *Faubus,* 178–79; Faubus interview.

69. *Southern School News,* September 1955, 10; McMillen, "The White Citizens' Council," 108.

70. *Arkansas Democrat,* August 3, 1957.

71. *Southern School News,* August 1957, 7.

72. *Southern School News,* July 1957, 10; August 1957, 7.

73. McMillen, "White Citizens' Council," 104; Reed, *Faubus,* 188.

74. Warren Olney III, assistant U.S. attorney general for the Civil Rights Division of the Justice Department, to Arthur B. Caldwell, assistant to the assistant U.S. attorney general, September 13, 1957, box 5, folder 2, Caldwell Papers; Faubus interview.

75. Kirk, *Redefining the Color Line,* chap. 5 and 6.

76. *Arkansas Gazette,* May 23, 1965; August 30, 1966; December 17, 30, 1967; University Task Force on the Little Rock School District, *Plain Talk: The Future of Little Rock's Public Schools* (Little Rock: University of Arkansas, 1997), 19; Staff Report of the U.S. Commission on Civil Rights, "School Desegregation in Little Rock, Arkansas," June 1977, Special Collections, University of Arkansas Libraries, Fayetteville, 4–5; Wilkinson, *From Brown to Bakke,* 104.

Chapter 7: White Support for the Civil Rights Struggle

1. An earlier version of this essay was delivered as a paper at a conference on "The Southern Regional Council," University of Florida, Gainesville, October 23–26, 2003. I am grateful to Brian Ward for his invitation to attend and to the University of Florida for providing financial assistance. The conference was composed of academics and movement activists who offered helpful and instructive comments on my work. I am particularly grateful to Luz Borrero, David Chalmers, David Chappell, Connie Curry, Jane Dailey, Jack Davis, Leslie Dunbar, Paul Gaston, Matthew Lassiter, Timothy Minchin, Kimberly Nichols, Robert J. Norrell, J. Douglas Smith, Morton Sosna, Steve Suitts, Timothy Tyson, and Brian Ward for sharing their thoughts with me.

2. Aldon D. Morris, *The Origins of the Civil Rights Movement: Black Communities Organizing for Change* (New York: Free Press, 1984).

3. See chap. 4, footnote 1.

4. Morris, *Origins of the Civil Rights Movement,* 139–73.

5. Morris, *Origins of the Civil Rights Movement,* 140–41.

6. *Arkansas Gazette,* June 1, 1964; Norma Huff to Annie Gillam, May 4, 1940, reel 64, series I, container 1987, Southern Regional Council Papers, Microfilm, Library of Congress, Washington, DC [hereafter cited as SRC Microfilm (Washington, DC)].

7. Leslie W. Dunbar, "The Southern Regional Council," *Annals of the American Academy of Political and Social Science* 357 (January 1965), 108–12.

8. Arkansas Council on Human Relations, Executive Board Meeting, May 18, 1974, box 1, folder 3, Frank N. Gordon Papers, Special Collections, University of Arkansas Libraries, Fayetteville (hereafter cited as Gordon Papers).

9. Arkansas Council on Human Relations (An Interpretation), May 30, 1955, box 16, folder 152, Arkansas Council on Human Relations (ACHR) Papers, Special Collections, University of Arkansas Libraries, Fayetteville (hereafter cited as ACHR Papers).

10. *Arkansas Gazette,* June 1, 1964.

11. Frank N. Gordon to Robert M. Denham, May 11, 1965, Gordon Papers.

12. Ernest Dumas, "Fred Darragh's Legacy," *Arkansas Times,* March 28, 2003; Nat Griswold to Friend, May 28, 1955, box 15, folder 149, ACHR Papers.

13. Griswold to Friend, May 28, 1955.

14. On Ashmore, see Harry S. Ashmore, *Hearts and Minds: The Anatomy of Racism from Roosevelt to Reagan* (New York: McGraw-Hill, 1982); and *Civil Rights and Wrongs: A Memoir of Race and Politics, 1944–1996* (Columbia: University of South Carolina Press, 1997).

15. Arkansas Council on Human Relations (An Interpretation).

16. Griswold to Christopher C. Mercer, April 9, 1955, box 15, folder 151, ACHR Papers.

17. On the desegregation of the law school see Kirk, *Redefining the Color Line,* 55–62.

18. Christopher C. Mercer, interview with author, April 19, 1993, Little Rock, Arkansas, Pryor Center for Oral and Visual Culture.

19. Frederick B. Routh to Fred K. Darragh, March 23, 1955; Fred K. Darragh to George S. Mitchell, March 25, 1955, both in box 15, folder 151, ACHR Papers.

20. *Arkansas Gazette,* June 1, 1964.

21. Minutes of the ACHR Executive Committee Hearing, July 11, 1955, reel 141, series IV, container 223, SRC Microfilm (Washington, DC).

22. Memorandum from Harry S. Ashmore to Phil Coombe, Phil Hamer and Harold Fleming, May 18, 1954, reel 39, series I, container 1333, SRC Microfilm (Washington, DC).

23. Griffin Smith Jr., "Localism and Segregation: Racial Patterns in Little Rock, Arkansas 1945–54" (M.A. thesis, Columbia University, New York, 1965), 52–53, 80, 94–95; Edwin E. Dunaway, interview with the author, September 26, 1992, Little Rock, Arkansas, Pryor Center for Oral and Visual Culture; Ozell Sutton, telephone interview with the author, August 7, 1993, Atlanta, Georgia.

24. On Arkansas's reaction to *Brown* see Kirk, *Redefining the Color Line,* chap. 4.

25. Mildred L. Bond to Roy Wilkins, August 6, 1955, box 4, folder 10, Daisy Bates Papers, State Historical Society of Wisconsin, Madison.

26. *Southern School News,* August 1955, 15.

27. Griswold to K. E. Vance, July 14, 1955, box 16, folder 160, ACHR Papers.

28. "A 'Morally Right' Decision," *Life,* July 25, 1955, 29–31; Arthur B. Caldwell, "The Hoxie Case—The Story of the First School in the Old South to Integrate in the Wake of the Brown Decisions," courtesy of William Penix, Jonesboro, Arkansas.

29. Nat R. Griswold, "The Second Reconstruction in Little Rock," book 2, chap. 4, 3, unpublished manuscript, series 2, box 11, folder 8, Sara Alderman Murphy Papers, Special Collections, University of Arkansas Libraries, Fayetteville.

30. "A 'Morally Right' Decision," *Life,* July 25, 1955, 29–31.

31. Cabell Phillips, "Integration: Battle of Hoxie, Arkansas," *New York Times Magazine,* September 25, 1955, 12, 68–76.

32. Griswold, "The Second Reconstruction," book 2, chap. 4, 4.

33. Griswold to Vance, August 9, 1955, box 16, folder 160, ACHR Papers.

34. Griswold, "The Second Reconstruction," book 2, chap. 4, 4.

35. *Southern School News,* September 1955, 10.

36. Neil R. McMillen, "The White Citizens Council and Resistance to School Desegregation in Arkansas," *Arkansas Historical Quarterly* 30 (Summer 1971): 97–100; Jerry J. Vervack, "The Hoxie Imbroligo," *Arkansas Historical Quarterly* 48 (Spring 1989): 22.

37. Arthur Brann Caldwell, "The Hoxie Case"; Griswold, "The Second Reconstruction," book 2, chap. 4, 4–6.

38. *Southern School News,* December 1956, 8.

39. On the Blossom Plan see John A. Kirk, "Massive Resistance and Minimum Compliance: The Origins of the 1957 Little Rock School Crisis," in ed. Clive Webb *Massive Resistance: Southern Opposition to the Second Reconstruction* (New York: Oxford University Press, 2005), also published as chap. 6 in this volume.

40. Griswold to George Mitchell, June 22, 1955, reel 141, series IV, container 220, SRC Microfilm (Washington, DC).

41. Griswold, "The Second Reconstruction," book 2, chap. 3, 2–3.

42. On the *Cooper* v. *Aaron* (1956) lawsuit see Kirk, *Redefining the Color Line,* chap. 4, and Tony Freyer, *The Little Rock Crisis: A Constitutional Interpretation* (Westport, CT: Greenwood Press, 1984), chap. 2.

43. "A Request to the Southern Regional Council," c. Sept. 1957, reel 141, series IV, container 219, SRC Microfilm (Washington, DC).

44. On the Little Rock crisis see Kirk, *Redefining the Color Line,* chap. 5.

45. Memorandum from Mike Yarrow to Ed Saunders, October 3, 1957, box 20, folder 200; Glenn Smiley, "Report on Little Rock," September 1957, box 6, folder 60, both in ACHR Papers.

46. C. H. Yarrow to Hugh Moore, October 15, 1957, box 8, folder 78, ACHR Papers.

47. C. H. Yarrow to Griswold, February 14, 1958, box 6, folder 60; *Arkansas Gazette* clipping, n.d., box 16, folder 152, both in ACHR Papers.

48. "Quaker Agency Tries to Ease Little Rock Tensions," newspaper clipping, n.d., box 6, folder 60, ACHR Papers.

49. Memorandum from Thelma How and Melvin Zuck to Carl and Shirley Dudley, July 13, 1958, and August 16, 1958, box 6, folder 60, ACHR Papers.

50. Memorandum from Thelma How and Melvin Zuck to Carl and Shirley Dudley, August 16, 1958, box 6, folder 60, ACHR Papers

51. ACHR Minutes of Executive Meeting, March 1960, reel 141, series IV, container 223, SRC Microfilm (Washington, DC).

52. On the economic impact of the school crisis see Gary Fullerton, "New Factories Thing of the Past in Little Rock," *Nashville Tennessean,* May 31, 1959.

53. Willard A. Hawkins to Members and Friends, November 14, 1961, box 19, folder 190, ACHR Papers; Griswold, "The Second Reconstruction," book 2, chap. 1, 16.

54. On the black community in Little Rock during the school crisis, see Kirk, *Redefining the Color Line,* chap. 5.

55. Memorandum from C. D. Coleman to M. T. Puryear, October 5, 1959, group II, series D, container 26, folder "Affiliates File, Little Rock, Arkansas," National Urban League Papers, Library of Congress, Washington, DC

56. John Walker to Paul Rilling, November 17, 1959, reel 141, series IV, container 234, SRC Microfilm (Washington, DC).

57. Griswold to Fred Routh, August 6, 1958, reel 141, series IV, container 220, SRC Microfilm (Washington, DC).

58. John Walker to Dr. William Phillips, June 24, 1960, box 22, folder 218, ACHR Papers.

59. Griswold to John Walker, November 29, 1960, box 8, folder 83, ACHR Papers.

60. J. H. Wheeler to Griswold, Jan 18, 1960; Griswold to J. H. Wheeler, Jan 19, 1960, both in box 2, folder 19, ACHR Papers; ACHR Minutes of the Executive Committee, February 5, 1960, box 22, folder 218, ACHR Papers.

61. Griswold to J. H. Wheeler, Jan 19, 1960, box 2, folder 19, ACHR Papers.

62. Griswold, "The Second Reconstruction," book 2, chap. 6, 9.

63. On the Little Rock sit-ins see Kirk, *Redefining the Color Line,* 141–46.

64. Memo from Little Rock ACHR to SRC, December 6, 1960, reel 141, series IV, container 218, SRC Microfilm (Washington, DC).

65. ACHR Minutes of the General Membership Meeting, October 8, 1960, box 22, folder 218, ACHR Papers.

66. Griswold to Worth Long, October 11, 1960, box 7, folder 77, ACHR Papers.

67. ACHR Minutes of the Executive Committee, November 30, 1960, box 22, folder 218, ACHR Papers.

68. Memo from Little Rock ACHR to SRC, December 6, 1960, reel 141, series IV, container 218, SRC Microfilm (Washington, DC).

69. Griswold to Gustave Faulk, February 21, 1961, box 8, folder 78, ACHR Papers.

70. ACHR Minutes of the Executive Committee, July 13, 1961, box 22, folder 219, ACHR Papers.

71. On the Freedom Rides in Little Rock see Kirk, *Redefining the Color Line,* 146–50.

72. Sutton interview; Dr. Maurice A. Jackson, interview with the author, February 10, 1993, Little Rock, Arkansas, Pryor Center for Oral and Visual Culture; Dr. W. H. Townsend, interview with the author, April 25, 1993, Little Rock, Arkansas, Pryor Center for Oral and Visual Culture.

73. ACHR minutes of the Executive Committee, February 8, 1962, box 22, folder 219, ACHR Papers.

74. Griswold to Paul Rilling, October 30, 1961, box 8, folder 78, ACHR Papers.

75. Ozell Sutton to Burke Marshall, February 21, 1962, box 8, folder 81, ACHR Papers.

76. *Arkansas Gazette,* March 9, 1962.

77. *Arkansas Gazette,* March 10, 1962.

78. Telegram from Dorothy Miller to Griswold, n.d., box 33, folder 335, ACHR Papers; Griswold, "The Second Reconstruction," book II, chap. VI, 15–16.

79. Report, May 30, 1962, box 8, folder 5, Student Nonviolent Coordinating Committee Arkansas Project Records, State Historical Society of Wisconsin, Madison.

80. Sutton interview.

81. "Public Accommodations and Downtown Employment, May, 1964," box 19, folder 190, ACHR Papers; Irving J. Spitzberg, *Racial Politics in Little Rock 1954–1964* (New York: Garland Publishing, 1987), 145–47.

82. On events in Birmingham, see Glenn T. Eskew, *But For Birmingham: The Local and National Movements in the Civil Rights Struggle* (Chapel Hill: University of North Carolina Press, 1997).

83. John Britton, "Image Makers Erasing 1957 from the City's Calendar," *Jet,* April 4, 1963, 14–19.

84. *Arkansas Gazette,* June 1, 1964.

85. For an indication of the circumstances in which the ACHR operated in the mid- to late-1960s see Kirk, *Redefining the Color Line,* chap. 7.

86. Elijah Coleman, interview with the author, May 5, 1993, Pine Bluff, Arkansas.

87. Elijah Coleman, "Arkansas Council on Human Relations 20th Annual Report," February 17, 1973, box 1, folder 4, Gordon Papers.

88. Wiley Branton to Ozell Sutton, June 29, 1966; "A Voter Registration Project proposed to the VEP, Atlanta, June 16, 1966"; Vernon Jordan to Elijah Coleman, September 22, 1966, all on reel 184, frames 1859–1862, 1863, 1890–1897, SRC Microfilm (Washington, DC); *Arkansas Gazette,* August 2, 1964 and December 12, 1966; David J. Garrow, *Bearing the Cross: Martin Luther King Jr. and the Southern Christian Leadership Conference* (New York: William Morrow, 1986), 161–64; Coleman and Sutton interviews.

89. Frank Lambright, interview with the author, May 7, 1993, Little Rock, Arkansas, Pryor Center for Oral and Visual Culture; Sara Alderman Murphy, interview with the author, April 29, 1993, Little Rock, Arkansas, Pryor Center for Oral and Visual Culture; Irene Samuel, interview with the author, October 9, 1992, Little Rock, Arkansas, Pryor Center for Oral and Visual Culture; John Ward, interview with the author, April 28, 1993, Conway, Arkansas, Pryor Center for Oral and Visual Culture.

90. *Arkansas Gazette,* December 11, 12, 1966; Ward interview.

91. Calvin R. Ledbetter Jr., "Arkansas Amendment for Voter Registration without Poll Tax Payment," *Arkansas Historical Quarterly,* 54 (Summer 1995): 134–62.

92. *Arkansas Gazette,* October 22, 1970; David R. Goldfield, *Black, White and Southern: Race Relations and Southern Culture, 1940 to the Present* (Baton Rouge: Louisiana State University Press, 1990), 196.

93. *Arkansas Gazette,* February 4, 1973; Steven F. Lawson, *Running For Freedom: Civil Rights and Black Politics Since 1941* (New York: McGraw-Hill, 1991), 85; Coleman interview; Leroy Brownlee, interview with the author, May 5, 1993, Little Rock, Arkansas, Pryor Center for Oral and Visual Culture; Perlesta A. Hollingworth, interview with the author, April 13, 1993, Little Rock, Arkansas, Pryor Center for Oral and Visual Culture.

94. Elijah Coleman, "Arkansas Council on Human Relations," (n.d.), box 1, folder 4, Gordon Papers.

95. John A. Kirk, *Martin Luther King, Jr.* (London: Pearson Longman, 2004), see chap. 5 and 6 and Conclusion. On the conservative insurgency of the 1960s see Dan T. Carter, *The Politics of Rage: George Wallace, the Origins of the New Conservatism, and the Transformation of American Politics* (New York: Simon and Schuster, 1995).

96. Elijah Coleman, "Arkansas Council on Human Relations 20th Annual

Report," February 17, 1973, box 1, folder 4, Gordon Papers.

97. ACHR Executive Board Annual Meeting, May 18, 1974, box 1, folder 3, Gordon Papers.

Chapter 8: City Planning and the Civil Rights Struggle

1. See, for example, Lawrence D. Reddick, *Crusader Without Violence: A Biography of Martin Luther King, Jr.* (New York: Harper & Bros., 1959); Lerone Bennett Jr., *What Manner of Man: A Biography of Martin Luther King, Jr.* (Chicago: Johnson Publishing, 1964); William Robert Miller, *Martin Luther King, Jr.: His Life, Martyrdom and Meaning for the World* (New York: Weybright and Talley, 1968); David L. Lewis, *King: A Critical Biography* (Urbana: University of Illinois Press, 1970); and Jim Bishop, *The Days of Martin Luther King* (New York: G. P. Putnam's Sons, 1971).

2. See chap. 4, footnote 1.

3. On women's activism in the movement see Vicki Crawford, Jacqueline Rouse, and Barbara Woods, eds., *Women in the Civil Rights Movement: Trailblazers and Torchbearers, 1941–1965,* (Brooklyn, NY: Carlson Publishing, 1990); Belinda Robnett, *How Long? How Long? African American Women in the Struggle for Civil Rights* (New York: Oxford University Press, 1997); Peter J. Ling and Sharon Monteith, eds., *Gender in the Civil Rights Movement* (New York: Garland Publishing, 1999 reprinted New Brunswick, NJ: Rutgers University Press, 2004); and Bettye Collier-Thomas and V. P. Franklin, eds., *Sisters in the Struggle: African American Women in the Civil Rights-Black Power Movement* (New York: New York University Press, 2001). On the role of violence and armed self-defense see, Timothy B. Tyson, *Radio Free Dixie: Robert F. Williams and the Roots of Black Power* (Chapel Hill: University of North Carolina Press, 1999) and Lance Hill, *The Deacons for Defense: Armed Resistance and the Civil Rights Movement* (Chapel Hill: University of North Carolina Press, 2004). On international dimensions see Michael L. Krenn, ed., *Race and U.S. Foreign Policy During the Cold War* (New York: Garland Publishing, 1998); Michael L. Krenn, *Black Diplomacy: African Americans and the State Department, 1945–1969* (Armoruk, NY: M. E. Sharpe, 1999); Mary L. Dudziak, *Cold War Civil Rights: Race and the Image of Democracy* (Princeton, NJ: Princeton University Press, 2000); Thomas Borstelmann, *The Cold War and the Color Line: American Race Relations in the Global Arena* (Cambridge, MA: Harvard University Press, 2002); and Carol Anderson, *Eyes Off the Prize: The United Nations and the African American Struggle for Human Rights, 1944–1955* (New York: Cambridge University Press, 2003).

4. Thomas J. Sugrue, *The Origins of the Urban Crisis: Race and Inequality in Postwar Detroit* (Princeton, NJ: Princeton University Press, 1996) and "Crabgrass-Roots Politics: Race, Rights and Reaction Against Liberalism in the Urban North, 1940–1964," *Journal of American History* 82:2 (September 1995): 551–578; Arnold R. Hirsch, *Making the Second Ghetto: Race and Housing in Chicago, 1940–1960* (Illinois: University of Chicago Press, 1983) and "Massive Resistance in the Urban North: Trumbull

Park, Chicago, 1953–1966," *Journal of American History* 82:2 (September 1995): 522–50. A number of other works have explored similar themes, notably most recently, Robert O. Self, *American Babylon: Race and the Struggle for Postwar Oakland* (Princeton, NJ: Princeton University Press, 2003).

5. Alan B. Anderson and George W. Pickering, *Confronting the Color Line: The Broken Promise of the Civil Rights Movement in Chicago* (Athens: University of Georgia Press, 1986) and James R. Ralph Jr., *Northern Protest: Martin Luther King, Jr., Chicago, and the Civil Rights Movement* (Cambridge, MA: Harvard University Press, 1993). On the 1966 civil rights bill see Stephen Grant Meyer, *As Long As They Don't Move Next Door: Segregation and Racial Conflict in American Neighborhoods* (Lanham, MD: Rowman and Littlefield, 2000).

6. *Arkansas Gazette,* November 23, 1934; *Arkansas Democrat,* November 23, 1934, clippings in Mayor Sam Wassell's Scrapbook, Arkansas History Commission, Little Rock.

7. *Survey of Negroes in Little Rock and North Little Rock, Compiled by the Writers' Program of the Work Projects Administration in the State of Arkansas* (Little Rock: Urban League of Greater Little Rock, 1941), 55–60.

8. *Survey of Negroes,* 61–65; Mrs. I. S. McClinton and Mrs. Mattie Davis, interview with the author, October 9, 1992, Little Rock, Pryor Center for Oral and Visual Culture.

9. *Arkansas Gazette,* November 23, 1934; *Arkansas Democrat,* November 23, 1934; City of Little Rock Council Record 1932–1936, Book X, November 26, December 12, 1934 and January 28, 1935, City Hall, Little Rock.

10. City of Little Rock Council Record 1932–1936, Book X, April 29, November 25, 1935; January 6, May 11, 1936. On John E. Bush, see A. E. Bush and P. L. Dorman, *History of the Mosaic Templars of America—Its Founders and Officials* (Little Rock: Central Printing Co., 1924); John William Graves, *Town and Country: Race Relations in an Urban/Rural Context, Arkansas, 1865–1905* (Fayetteville: University of Arkansas Press, 1990); Willard B. Gatewood, *Aristocrats of Color: The Black Elite, 1880–1920* (Bloomington: Indiana University Press, 1990); Fon Louise Gordon, *Caste and Class: The Black Experience in Arkansas, 1880–1920* (Athens: University of Georgia Press, 1995); Tom W. Dillard, "Perseverance: Black History in Pulaski County, Arkansas: An Excerpt," *Pulaski County Historical Review* 31 (Winter 1983): 62–73; and C. Calvin Smith, "John E. Bush of Arkansas, 1890–1910," *Ozark Historical Review* 2 (Spring 1973): 50–51

11. City of Little Rock Council Record 1936–1940, Book Y, December 10, 1936.

12. Irving J. Spitzberg, *Racial Politics in Little Rock, 1954–1964* (New York: Garland Publishing, 1987), 125; City of Little Rock Council Record 1936–1940, Book Y, December 11, 1936, January 28, 1937.

13. City of Little Rock Council Record 1936–1940, Book Y, October 29, 1937, January 10, 17, 31, February 7, July 28, 1938.

14. City of Little Rock Council Record 1936–1940, Book Y, September 26, 1938.

15. City of Little Rock Council Record 1936–1940, Book Y, February 19, 1940.

16. *Arkansas Gazette,* June 14, 1940; City of Little Rock Council Record 1936–1940, Book Z, February 26, June 24, July 22, 1940, January 24, 1941.

17. *Arkansas Gazette,* June 29, 1941.

18. *Arkansas Gazette,* July 1, 1941.

19. City of Little Rock Council Record 1936–1940, Book Z, July 7, 1941.

20. City of Little Rock Council Record 1936–1940, Book Z, December 16, 1940; City of Little Rock Council Record 1936–1940, Book A-1, October 19, 1942; *Arkansas Gazette,* August 19, 1945.

21. City of Little Rock Council Record 1936–1940, Book Z, July 7, 1941, March 9, 1942, August 30, October 4, 1943.

22. City of Little Rock Council Record, Book A-2, December 9, 1946, April 28, May 19, June 2, 1947.

23. On blacks and World War II, see Richard M. Dalfumie, "The 'Forgotten Years' of the Negro Revolution," *Journal of American History* 55 (June 1968): 90–106, and *Desegregation of the U.S. Armed Forces: Fighting on Two Fronts, 1939–1953* (Columbia: University of Missouri Press, 1969); Harvard Sitkoff, "Racial Militancy and Interracial Violence in the Second World War," *Journal of American History* 58 (June 1971): 661–81; Lee Finkle, *Forum for Protest: The Black Press during World War II* (Cranbury, NJ: Associated University Presses, 1975); John Morton Blum, *V Was for Victory: Politics and American Culture during World War II* (New York: Harcourt Brace Jovanovich, 1976); Neil A. Wynn, *The Afro-American and the Second World War* (London: Paul Elek, 1976); James Albert Burran III, "Racial Violence in the South during World War II," Ph.D. dissertation, University of Virginia, 1977; and Merle E. Reed, *Seedtime for the Modern Civil Rights Movement: The President's Committee on Fair Employment Practice, 1941–1946* (Baton Rougue: Louisiana State University Press, 1991).

24. C. Calvin Smith, *War and Wartime Changes: The Transformation of Arkansas, 1940–1945* (Fayetteville: University of Arkansas Press, 1986) contains a chapter specifically on developments affecting black Arkansans. On blacks in Little Rock and Arkansas in the war see also Kirk, *Redefining the Color Line,* chap. 2.

25. Charles Bussey, interview with the author, December 4, 1992, Little Rock, Pryor Center for Oral and Visual Culture; Jeffery Hawkins, interview with the author, September 30, 1992, Little Rock, Pryor Center for Oral and Visual Culture; Perlesta A. Hollingsworth, interview with the author, April 13, 1993, Little Rock, Pryor Center for Oral and Visual Culture; Mrs. I. S. McClinton, interview with the author, October 9, 1992, Little Rock, Pryor Center for Oral and Visual Culture; Sonny Walker, telephone interview with author, August 31, 1993.

26. For a discussion of L. C. Bates's views see C. Calvin. Smith, "From 'Separate but Equal to Desegregation': The Changing Philosophy of L. C.

Bates." *Arkansas Historical Quarterly* 42 (Autumn 1983): 254–270. For Daisy Bates's views see Daisy Bates, *The Long Shadow of Little Rock: A Memoir* (New York: David McKay Company, Inc., 1962).

27. *Arkansas State Press,* June 13, 1947.

28. City of Little Rock Council Record, Book A-2, April 26, June 21, March 3, 1948.

29. *Arkansas State Press,* June 25, 1948.

30. City of Little Rock Council Record, Book A-3, December 6, 1948; *Arkansas Gazette,* November 24, 1948 and December 3, 1948; *Arkansas Democrat,* November 24, 1948. For the full details of the proposal see Little Rock Parks and Recreation Commission, "Information Handbook on Negro Park and Recreation Bond Issue Proposal," Pamphlet Collection Item 5605, Special Collections Division, University of Arkansas Libraries, Little Rock.

31. *Arkansas Gazette,* December 4, 1948.

32. For Ashmore's views see Harry S. Ashmore, *The Negro and The Schools* (Chapel Hill: University of North Carolina Press, 1954); *An Epitaph For Dixie* (New York: W. W. Norton, 1958); *Hearts and Minds: The Anatomy of Racism from Roosevelt to Reagan* (New York: McGraw-Hill, 1982); and *Civil Rights and Wrongs: A Memoir of Race and Politics, 1944–1996* (Columbia: University of South Carolina Press, 1997).

33. *Arkansas Gazette,* December 16, 1948.

34. City of Little Rock Council Record, Book A-3, December 27, 1948.

35. *Arkansas State Press,* December 16, 1949.

36. *Arkansas Gazette* February 2, 1949; *Arkansas Democrat,* February 2, 1949.

37. *Arkansas Democrat,* May 11, 14, 1949.

38. City of Little Rock Council Record, Book A-3, May 16, 1948; *Arkansas Gazette,* May 13, 1949.

39. City of Little Rock Council Record, Book A-3, June 6, June 13, 1949; *Arkansas Gazette,* June 7, 14, 1949.

40. On the Housing Act of 1949 see the special issue of *Housing Policy Debate* 11 (Issue 2, 2000): 291–520 (published by the Fannie Mae Foundation and available online at http://www.fanniemaefoundation.org/programs/hpd/v11i2-index.shtml), particularly Robert E. Lang and Rebecca R. Sohmer, "Editors Introduction"; Alexander von Hoffman, "A Study in Contradictions: The Origins and Legacy of the Housing Act of 1949"; Arnold R. Hirsch, "Searching for 'Sound Negro Policy': A Racial Agenda for the Housing Acts of 1949 and 1954"; Jon C. Teaford, "Urban Renewal and Its Aftermath"; and Charles J. Orlebeke, "The Evolution of Low-Income Housing Policy, 1949 to 1999."

41. *Arkansas Democrat,* November 24; *Arkansas Gazette,* November 25, 1949.

42. *Arkansas Gazette,* December 20, 1949.

43. *Arkansas Gazette,* January 5, 1950.

44. *Arkansas Gazette,* February 5, 1950; *Arkansas Democrat,* February 5, 1950.

45. "Souvenir Program, Gillam Park Swimming Pool Opening, Sunday, August 20th," Mayor Sam Wassell Scrapbook; *Arkansas Gazette,* August 21, 1950; *Arkansas Democrat,* August 21, 1950; *Arkansas State Press,* 25 August, 1950; City of Little Rock Council Record, Book A-4, July 14, 1952.

46. *Arkansas Democrat,* April 10, 1951.

47. *Arkansas Gazette,* June 5, 1951.

48. *Arkansas State Press,* August 29, 1952.

49. *Arkansas State Press,* July 8, 1954.

50. *Arkansas Gazette,* May 10, 1950; *Arkansas Democrat,* May 10, 1950.

51. B. Finley Vinson, interview with the author, February 25, 1993, Little Rock, Pryor Center for Oral and Visual Culture.

52. Arkansas' Greater Little Rock Conference on Religion and Race, "Confronting the Little Rock Housing Problem," box 7, folder 76, Arkansas Council on Human Relations Papers, Special Collections, University of Arkansas Libraries, Fayetteville.

53. *Arkansas Gazette,* January 29, June 8, 1952.

54. *Arkansas Gazette,* June 8, August 29 (quotation), October 2, 1952. See also the materials on *R. O. Burgess et. al v. Little Rock Housing Authority et. al.* in Leffel and U. A. Gentry papers, box 1, folder 9, Special Collections, University of Arkansas Libraries, Little Rock.

55. See Nat Griswold, "The Second Reconstruction in Little Rock," unpublished manuscript, series 2, box 11, folder 8, Sara Alderman Murphy Papers, Special Collections, University of Arkansas Libraries, Fayetteville; Ben F. Johnson III, *Arkansas in Modern America, 1930–1999* (Fayetteville: University of Arkansas Press, 2000), 148–61; Martha Walters, "Little Rock Urban Renewal," *Pulaski County Historical Review* 24 (March 1976): 12–16; Margaret Arnold, "Little Rock's Vanishing Black Communities," *Arkansas Times* (June 1978): 36–43; and Stuart Eurman, "Consolidating Cities: An Urban Fiction," *Pulaski County Historical Review* 42 (Spring 1994): 19–22.

56. *Arkansas Gazette,* July 13, 1950; February 11, 1951.

57. "A Report of the Racial and Cultural Diversity Task Force," submitted to The Steering Committee of Future—Little Rock, December 31, 1992. Copy in author's possession.

58. *Arkansas Gazette,* February 15, 20, 21, 1953.

59. *Arkansas Gazette,* February 27, March 3, 4, 6, 1953.

60. *Arkansas Gazette,* March 6, 1953.

61. See Kirk, *Redefining the Color Line,* chap. 6 and 7.

62. Adolphine Fletcher Terry to Mr. William H. McClean, Commercial National Bank, Little Rock, Arkansas, March 9, 1970, Fletcher-Terry Papers, series I, box 3, folder 3, Special Collections, University of Arkansas Libraries, Little Rock.

63. Albert Porter, interview with the author, May 7, 1993, Little Rock, Pryor Center for Oral and Visual Culture.

64. Terry to McClean, March 9, 1970, Fletcher-Terry Papers.

65. *Arkansas Democrat-Gazette,* October 26, 2003.

66. See, for example, Numan V. Bartley, *The Rise of Massive Resistance:*

Race and Politics in the South during the 1950s (Baton Rouge: Louisiana State University Press, 1969), chap. 14; C. Fred Williams, "Class: The Central Issue in the 1957 Little Rock School Crisis," *Arkansas Historical Quarterly* 56 (Autumn 1997): 341–44; Pete Daniel, *Lost Revolutions: The South in the 1950s* (Chapel Hill: University of North Carolina Press, 2000), chap. 12; and Karen Anderson, "The Little Rock School Desegregation Crisis: Moderation and Social Conflict," *Journal of Southern History* 70:3 (August 2004): 603–36.

67. Unsigned letter to E. Grainger Williams, March 25, 1959, box 1, folder 1, E. Grainger Williams Papers, Special Collections, University of Arkansas Libraries, Little Rock.

68. *Survey of Negroes,* 61.

69. "Report of the Racial and Cultural Diversity Task Force."

70. Howard Rabinowitz, *Race Relations in the Urban South, 1865–1890* (New York: Oxford University Press, 1978) argues that segregation emerged as an alternative to separation and exclusion during that period. John William Graves, in *Town and Country: Race Relations in an Urban/Rural Context* and "Jim Crow in Arkansas: A Reconsideration of Urban Race Relations in the Post Reconstruction South," *Journal of Southern History* 55:3 (August 1989): 421–48, argues for a relatively more fluid and complex set of race relations emerging across Arkansas at the time.

71. Elizabeth Jacoway, "Taken By Surprise: Little Rock Business Leaders and Desegregation" in ed. Elizabeth Jacoway and David R. Colburn *Southern Businessmen and Desegregation* (Baton Rouge: Louisiana State University Press, 1982), 21.

72. *Arkansas Democrat-Gazette,* March 27, April 8, and July 29, 2000, March 15, 2003, March 9, 26, April 23, 2004.

73. *Arkansas Democrat-Gazette,* October 6, 2002.

74. *Arkansas Democrat-Gazette,* May 31, 2001.

Index

JOHN A. KIRK is professor of U.S. history at Royal Holloway,
University of London. He is the author of three books,
including *Redefining the Color Line: Black Activism
in Little Rock, Arkansas, 1940-1970*, which won the
J. G. Ragsdale Book Award for Arkansas history.